EUROPE ON TRIAL

EUROPE
ON TRIAL

*The Story of Collaboration, Resistance,
and Retribution During World War II*

István Deák

Columbia University

Foreword by
Norman M. Naimark

Stanford University

Routledge
Taylor & Francis Group
New York London

First published 2015 by Westview Press

Published 2018 by Routledge
711 Third Avenue, New York, NY 10017, USA
2 Park Square, Milton Park, Abingdon, Oxon OX14 4RN

Routledge is an imprint of the Taylor & Francis Group, an informa business

Every effort has been made to secure required permissions for all text, images, maps, and other art reprinted in this volume.

Some material in this book has been adapted with permission from the author's previously published work. Chapter 5, "Germany's Many Allies: A Blessing or a Curse?," includes excerpts from "The Worst of Friends: Germany and Its Allies in East Central Europe—Struggles for Local Dominance and Ethnic Cleansing, 1938–1945," in *Territorial Revisionism and the Allies of Germany in the Second World War: Goals, Expectations, Practices,* edited by Marina Cattaruzza, Stefan Dyroff, and Dieter Langewiesche (New York: Berghahn Books, 2013). Chapter 10, "Purging Hitler's Europe," includes excerpts from "Misjudgment at Nuremberg," published in the *New York Review of Books,* October 7, 1993.

Cover photo: German soldiers and Italian fascist militia line up passersby following the Communist partisan attack on German military policemen on the via Rasella in Rome, March 23, 1944. The attack led to the massacre, by the German SS, of 335 uninvolved Italians in the Ardeatine Cave. Source: Bundesarchiv, Bild 101I-312-0983-03 / Photo: Koch (cropped)

A CIP catalog record for this book is available from the Library of Congress.

ISBN 13: 978-0-8133-4789-9 (pbk)

In memory of Dr. Juris Béla Stollár (1917–1944)
and his then-fiancée, Éva Deák Veress (1922–2010)

CONTENTS

FOREWORD

The military battles and diplomatic wrangling of World War II in Europe reached a bittersweet conclusion for many Europeans: the defeat of Nazi Germany, to be sure, but also the advance of Soviet power on the continent. For many East Europeans, in particular, the Soviet postwar occupation remains a much more consequential part of their historical consciousness than the Nazi control of Europe that preceded it. For many West Europeans occupied by or allied with the Germans, the overwhelming image of Nazi evil conveniently blots out their own collaboration and connivance with German aims. Black-and-white evaluations of national virtue or immorality in World War II usually do not hold up under close scrutiny. True, Hitler and "the bad guys" lost; a new and much more civilized Europe eventually emerged from the rubble and ashes of the old. But along with the contests on the battlefield and the machinations of international politics, the process of victory contained within itself a whole series of unpredictable and ironic twists of fate. It is at this level of how the war was experienced by Europeans that István Deák excels and *Europe on Trial* is so important. This is not the war that most Europeans want to remember today, nor is it the war analyzed in grand military and diplomatic histories.

István Deák is Seth Low Professor Emeritus at Columbia University. He is the author of a number of prizewinning studies of the history of the late Habsburg monarchy.[1] But Deák has also exhibited an abiding interest in World War II as a test case of the societal and moral mettle of Europeans. He coedited and wrote a pioneering study of retributive justice in postwar Europe with Tony Judt and Jan Gross and authored a series of important review essays in the *New York Review of Books* and the *New Republic* that explored the most recent literature about such topics as the

Holocaust, collaboration, and resistance.[2] Many of these articles were published in his 2001 *Essays on Hitler's Europe*.[3] The culmination of this work and thinking is *Europe on Trial*. Deák's final verdict on how well the Europeans withstood the moral and ethical challenges of the war is not that of a judge, who determines the guilt or innocence of the accused. Yet the feeling the reader has when putting down the book is that the case for the prosecution is stronger, while that for the defense, which understandably dominates the national consciousness of the individual peoples of Europe today, is considerably weaker. Even the Germans have begun to talk about being victims, as well as perpetrators.

Behind Deák's work is a depth of moral passion that comes, perhaps, from his own youthful experiences in wartime Hungary, including a stint in a forced-labor battalion and being a witness to the siege of Budapest toward the end of the war.[4] But that passion never gets in the way of his deep respect for the actual circumstances that dictated historical choices. Constantly, he asks the reader: What would you do if you were in the position of a poor Polish peasant, begged by Jews to hide them, or of an unemployed Norwegian youth, urged by the Quisling government to join the Waffen SS, or of a Serb resistance fighter, caught between the terror of the German occupation and hostile threats of the Communist partisans? What would you do as a government official in orderly Holland under Nazi rule? Would you have efficiently and dutifully supplied the Nazis with a list of Jews, who would eventually be transported to Auschwitz and eliminated? He even asks us to put ourselves in the place of the German occupiers. What you would do if you were a Wehrmacht official in Italy (or France or Poland), faced daily with attacks and bombings that killed and maimed your soldiers and undermined your military efforts? Would you have ordered the execution of civilians or prisoners as reprisals? And if so, how many executions would have been justified?

In Deák's rendition of the war, the dilemmas that individuals faced reflect on an everyday level the egregious cynicism of high politics in war. Take the Nazi-Soviet Pact of August 1939, in which the Soviets precipitously abandoned their principled antifascism in order to reap the potential benefits of a German war in the West and to incorporate the eastern parts of Poland (western Belorussia and western Ukraine) into the Soviet Union. The Soviets waited until the Nazis had defeated the Poles and seized Warsaw before invading the East. During their occupation of eastern Poland, they murdered twenty-two thousand Polish officers and officials and deported an even larger number of their family members to camps in northern Kazakhstan. When asked by Polish officials what happened to their officers, Soviet officials initially responded that they must have left the country through central Asia. Later Soviet officials blamed the massacre on the Nazis and denied complicity until the very end of the Soviet Union. These cynical moves do not, of course, say anything about the brutal secret protocols of the pact that gave Stalin license to incorporate the Baltic states and Bessarabia (Moldova) into the Soviet Union.

Or think about the relations between Hungary and Romania during the war, both of which professed loyalty to their alliance with Nazi Germany while using every available opportunity, of which there were many, to attack and undermine the efforts of the other in the hopes of seizing territory that each believed was theirs. In fact, Deák tells us, one of the reasons the Nazis could advance their armies so swiftly from one end of the continent to the other was the unwillingness of potential opponents to give up their antagonisms toward each other in order to face the Nazi threat. In general, the Europeans would rather have allowed the Germans to have their way on the continent than give up their sometimes quite petty squabbles with their neighbors. This is as true in the Low Countries and Scandinavia as it was in Eastern Europe. The French, thought to be powerful militarily and ready to fight to the death for their sovereignty, did everything they could to keep their Nazi occupiers happy with them. Vichy France was a near-perfect government of collaborators, while occupied Paris too easily made the Germans feel welcome and at home.

The self-serving hypocrisy of states during this period captures only a part of the deeply ironic character of the instructive "war stories" told by Deák. The Austrians, for example, were among Hitler's most ardent supporters and, even more consequentially, served the Nazis in crucial military, political, and economic functions. Yet they were designated by the Allies as the first "victims" of the Nazis in the Moscow Declaration of October 1943. The peaceable and pragmatic Danes conspired with local Nazi officials to organize the dramatic sea rescue of the Danish Jews from certain destruction. Yet the Danes were an official ally of Nazi Germany and even joined the Anti-Comintern Pact in November 1941.

German officers and Nazi officials themselves sometimes behaved quite well, even nobly, in Western Europe, indeed even better than could be expected in the situation of occupation and war. At the same time, they pursued bestial policies in Poland, Russia, and Ukraine, killing, torturing, burning, and terrorizing their way through the region, sometimes enlisting Poles, Balts, Russians, Ukrainians, and others to help them with their dirty work, sometimes turning on their helpmates and destroying them and their families. Meanwhile, local peoples sometimes used the temporary favor of the Nazis to advance their own causes against their local ethnic rivals. The unpredictable behavior of the occupied peoples combined with the divergent goals of the Nazi occupiers leave us with a kaleidoscopic picture of European life during the war. No two situations were alike; variability was the rule.

This then brings us to the Holocaust, the Shoah, or to what the Nazis called the "Final Solution to the Jewish Question." The Third Reich's determination to murder all the Jews of Europe developed over time. Crucial was a series of murderous decisions made in conjunction with Operation Barbarossa, the invasion of the Soviet Union on June 22, 1941, and the escalating violence on the Eastern front. Generally, Deák does not dwell on the much-studied "road to genocide" and elimination of the Jews by mass executions or in death camps. Instead, he uses a wide-angle lens on his historical camera to capture disheartening scenes of Jewish persecution from across the continent. The common denominator was that very few Europeans came to the aid of their Jewish brethren. True, there was not much they could do. But it was also the case that the Holocaust could never have been accomplished with the efficiency and completeness that it was without the active participation of hundreds of thousands of non-German Europeans and the indifference of tens of millions of others.

As the scene shifts from Norway or Poland to Italy or Slovakia, the dynamics of Jewish persecution differed. Deák tells some familiar stories of "saving Jews" in Denmark and Bulgaria, as well as describes instances of individual and group heroism, including that of scattered pockets of Jewish resisters. But the overall picture is deeply depressing. Europeans routinely identified, seized, abused, transported, persecuted, guarded, and executed the Jews, often without any orders to do so, not to mention as a consequence of coercion on the part of the Germans. Some did it out of avarice and greed, some out of anti-Semitic hatred and nationalist resentments, some simply because the opportunity seemed to be there. Here, it should be clear: Europe and Europeans did not pass the test of the war.

It was—and remains—too easy to blame just Hitler and the Nazis. For survivors and their families, there are both bitterness and some satisfaction that nearly seventy years after the destruction, new museums go up all over the continent that remember and mourn the loss of a vibrant and unique European civilization that is gone forever.

The end of the war did not bring peace, nor did it curtail the radical consequences of the social and political change that characterized Nazi rule and resistance. Continuities between the wartime period and the postwar one are much more profound than between the prewar period and the war. In many countries—Poland, Latvia, France, Ukraine, and Italy among them—civil war erupted on the heels of the Nazi retreat and continued, in some East European cases, until the early 1950s. Hitler had unleashed an earthquake of anti-Semitism during the war that continued after war's end with aftershocks of pogroms and persecution in Poland, Hungary, and elsewhere. East Europeans—Czechs, Poles, Hungarians, Yugoslavs—seemed to have absorbed the lessons of Nazi ethnic cleansing by brutally expelling their German populations that had often lived in those localities for centuries. Sanctioned by Allied decisions at Potsdam in July and August 1945, the forced removal of some 13 million Germans—along with the elimination of the Jews—permanently altered the social and political, not to mention cultural, landscape of Eastern Europe.

Coursing throughout Deák's treatment of this history is a strong sense of the ultimate injustice of it all, even if many perpetrators faced some measure of punishment for their crimes after the war. The spontaneous retribution that took place in newly liberated Europe, whether in France, Belgium, Norway, or Yugoslavia, did not seem calibrated to the specific crimes committed by the actual collaborators and oppressors. Women who harmed no one by their actions had their hair shorn and were otherwise humiliated and brutalized, often because they had relationships with German soldiers, sometimes—though not always—simply to survive or keep their families fed and sheltered. Thousands of completely innocent Norwegian babies fathered by German soldiers were denied citizenship by the postwar Norwegian government. Yet major Nazi criminals escaped criminal justice by escaping to South America and even being recruited to Soviet, British, or American military establishments. The onset of the Cold War meant that countless fascists and Nazis became upstanding members of postwar police and civil administrations on both sides of the Iron Curtain.

The Nuremberg Tribunal, while setting an important precedent for trying war crimes and crimes against humanity, hypocritically, if understandably, omitted the crimes of the Allied victors, most notably the Soviet Union. There can be no question that this was "victors' justice." It is hard to imagine it could have been otherwise. Even at that, only a handful of Nazi perpetrators were convicted and hanged for some of the most vicious crimes of the century. On balance, Deák reminds us, there was some measure of justice achieved at Nuremberg and in the thousands of trials that took place across the continent. But just like the difficulty European citizens faced when dealing with moral issues during the conflict, it was hard to achieve the right pitch in prosecuting war criminals, while trying to rebuild societies and polities after the war. Imperfect as it often is, "history" itself may be the best means of all to seek justice. But the craft of history requires the readiness to accept ambiguity and the imperfectability of human behavior; it means understanding the challenges faced by victims, perpetrators, and those in between; and it demands respect for the facts as we know them. István Deák is a master craftsman. Every student of World War II should read this book.

NORMAN M. NAIMARK
Stanford University

NOTES

1. See, in particular, István Deák, *The Lawful Revolution: Louis Kossuth and the Hungarians, 1848–1849* (New York: Columbia University Press, 1979) and *Beyond Nationalism: A Social and Political History of the Habsburg Officer Corps, 1848–1918* (New York: Oxford University Press, 1990).

2. István Deák, Jan T. Gross, and Tony Judt, eds., *The Politics of Retribution in Europe: World War II and Its Aftermath* (Princeton, NJ: Princeton University Press, 2000).

3. István Deák, *Essays on Hitler's Europe* (Lincoln: University of Nebraska Press, 2001).

4. For biographical information, see Holly Case's interview with Deák, available online: http://ecommons.library.cornell.edu/handle/1813/34132.

PREFACE

The origins of this book lie in the death of a young Hungarian journalist, Béla Stollár, whom Hungarian fascist Arrow Cross militiamen killed in a gun battle toward the end of World War II, during which Hungary had been Nazi Germany's ally. It happened on Christmas Eve in 1944; Béla was my sister's fiancé. About six members of his larger group, made up mainly of military deserters and Jewish escapees from forced-labor companies, died with him. Because he had not been a member of the underground Communist Party—on the contrary, because he had never hidden his dislike of the Communists—later, under Communist rule, Béla Stollár was memorialized by a narrow little street in the heart of Budapest, named after him. And even this street, where he actually died, was eventually halved by a large new government building. Today, hardly anyone in Hungary remembers his name, even though the country's anti-Nazi resistance movement was a minuscule affair. Only in Jerusalem did the Yad Vashem Museum, in 2003, recognize him as one of the "Righteous Among the Nations," a distinction given to persons of non-Jewish origin who risked their lives to save Jewish lives. Béla Stollár was one of the few Europeans who actually gave their lives so that others may have lived.

What followed at that time was my sister's indescribable suffering, our family's worry about the loss of a protector, and my sadness over the disappearance of a "wise old" friend—he was twenty-seven and I eighteen at that time. The terrible historical problems hidden in this seemingly simple story of heroism and self-sacrifice dawned on me only many decades later and slowly convinced me to try to take up the themes. In fact, in Béla Stollár's tragedy, we find many of the contradictory features of wartime collaboration, resistance, and retribution. What did he and his companions die for? Was their goal worth the sacrifice? One of his group's purposes was to help those who were threatened by death simply for being Jews. But Stollár and friends also planned to seize a neighboring newspaper building, just before the arrival of the Soviet Red Army, which at that time was already besieging Budapest. There they would set up the liberated city's first free, democratic, but definitely non-Communist-oriented newspaper. Yet what were their chances of setting up anything while major armies were clashing in the streets? How long would the paper have lasted before falling under Communist control or being suppressed by the new Communist authorities?

Also, could we not say that members of the Arrow Cross militia against them were similar ideologues who risked their lives for a cause, even if it was an unworthy cause? In fact, the Arrow Cross men were mostly bandits who, rather than fighting for their cause by battling the Soviet Red Amy at the front, preferred to search out, rob, and kill Jews. But what about the "bystanders," the building superintendent and his wife whom the Arrow Cross accused of having sheltered the resistance group and who were shot dead on the spot? Or the uninvolved couple who happened to be visiting the superintendent at the time and were, too, shot? Or the more than a dozen Jewish civilians who happened to be hiding in the building and without this incident may have remained undiscovered and unharmed? (The Red Army would conquer the area in three weeks.) How many innocent bystanders constitute reasonable "collateral damage" for any resistance activity?

The problem of "duty" in connection with Béla Stollár's life and martyrdom has been a further inspiration for me. Who in this incident actually did his duty and a duty to whom: God, country, the government, justice, humanity? Stollár, a civilian, had been drafted into the military during the war and, as an excellent sports journalist and champion stenographer, was posted to the Ministry of Defense with the rank of sergeant. There he had access to documents and weapons that enabled him to provide persecuted Jews with false identity cards and to create his seemingly legal resistance group, which was then betrayed. According to law, he was a mutineer and a traitor, yet what he actually tried to do was save an important public building from destruction in the Hungarian capital whose military defense and total destruction helped, at most, the Germans but not the Hungarians.

There were nearly forty thousand Hungarian combat soldiers besieged in what Hitler called "Fortress Budapest." They had taken the same military oath as Stollár. Many of them went into hiding and put on civilian clothes; others did not dare leave their ranks for fear of execution, but, certainly, many officers and men were convinced that they were doing their duty by continuing to fight. Never mind the useless and definitely lost war.

Was the Hungarian government at that time entitled to expect obedience from any of its uniformed and nonuniformed citizens? On December 24, 1944, more than half of the country was already in Soviet hands, while the pro-Nazi government had fled the capital. German troops had been occupying Hungary since March 1944, but the old royal Hungarian army remained a staunch ally of Germany. Meanwhile, a provisional national assembly that the Soviet high command had helped to set up in an eastern Hungarian city formed a provisional antifascist coalition government, which, on December 23, sued for an armistice with the Soviet Union. The message was communicated by radio to besieged Budapest. Frankly, neither government was "legitimate," for one had been created by a German SS coup d'état in October and the other was being organized by the Soviet Red Army. Later, under Communist rule, only "determined enemies of fascism" were considered patriots; in today's nationalist, conservative, "Christian" Hungary, the public and the law are inclined in the opposite direction.

One aspect of Stollár's life and death inspires only negative thoughts in me: to the best of my knowledge, no one was investigated and none sentenced for what occurred during that event. Polite, modest, brilliantly intelligent, and cultivated, Béla Stollár did, then, have a great influence on my development and work, although, to be honest, I never showed an inclination to imitate his heroism and self-sacrifice.

———

By 1948, three years after the liberation of Hungary, the postwar democratic coalition government had been fatally undermined by its Communist members. I then successfully conspired to leave for France, sensing, correctly, that soon no one would be allowed to go anywhere. Paris was a young East European's dream, the city of Jean-Paul Sartre, of Albert Camus, and of "existentialism," which many in France interpreted, strangely, as meaning no need for cleanliness. In the hotel room I occupied for a monthly rent of five US dollars, cleanliness was a near impossibility in any case. In reality, French life at that time was dominated by government crises, the war *en Indochine,* seemingly dangerous Communist bids for power, and the memory of wartime collaboration and resistance, followed by "the purges." From conversations at the Sorbonne, where I attempted to restart my studies of medieval history and geography, it became clear to me that some people had "done it all" during the war. There had been many true heroes whom one idolized, but there were also those who had alternately worked with the German occupiers, opposed the Germans, fought against other French people, and, at war's end, helped to punish the guilty, often in order to turn attention away from their own guilt. Refugee life for me was similarly one of contradictions: utter poverty and near starvation, interrupted by unauthorized physical labor and by sudden, surprising assistance tendered by American relief organizations.

Part-time study at the Sorbonne was rewarding, even though most lectures consisted of famous old men reading aloud their notes, which, in a mimeographed form, were purchasable anyway in front of the lecture halls. Final exams were, however, most challenging, with their ruthless insistence on phenomenal factual knowledge and absolutely impeccable French. The names of those who had passed a test toward the *licence ès lettres* were posted on the wall, and that was it. The desperately hoped-for route to scholarly glory in France was closed to me in any case, a refugee bogged down by the mutually unobtainable work permit and the permit for a long-term stay in France. Nor could I hope, as foreign born, for a teaching position in a state high school—and there were scarce other types of high schools in the country.

Thanks to UN-arranged international agreements, travel and even temporary work abroad were available for us, passportless refugees, such as harvesting potatoes in surprisingly impoverished Great Britain. And thus, after some illegal journalistic activity at the newspaper *Combat* of World War II resistance fame, I applied for and received a position at Radio Free Europe (RFE) in Munich, at first as an archivist-librarian and later as an editor. This allowed me to take some courses at two Munich-based universities. It was again a very different life, marked by those of us RFE employees who had been hired from outside Germany, enjoying, in an awkward way, the considerable privileges of an officer of the American occupation forces. This US-sponsored and- funded Cold War institution enabled us to broadcast programs to Eastern Europe that, in the final analysis, must have done some good to people who at home were basically told nothing but lies. But because this employment brought great difficulties to my poor family at home, I used the occasion to emigrate, in 1956, to the first country that was willing to receive me permanently: the United States.

In Paris I had once been a great fan of Garry Davis, a World War II US bomber pilot, who around 1948 declared himself a world citizen and tried to turn in his passport at the US Embassy. Davis invited others to register for "world citizenship," which twenty thousand of us did with great enthusiasm but, of course, to no avail. The world was definitely not "one." I met with the real "one world," however, upon my arrival in New York, on a very warm night, in a small supermarket in Manhattan. No one in the store could put together a decent sentence in English, yet no one cared, and I have been at home here ever since.

Although no doubt hospitable, the United States too was a world of contradictions: at Columbia University, where I was accepted as a graduate student in history, based on my piles of semidiplomas from Budapest, Paris, and Munich, registration insisted that I state my race ("Caucasian") and my religion, although the latter soon became "facultative," and the stating of race was eventually forbidden. It was later reinstituted in the interest of "affirmative action."

The sense of absolute personal freedom has not left me since, in my undoubtedly privileged position, and I even came to terms, gradually, with the great anxiety and contradiction of my life: my "Semitic" ancestry and my strict Roman Catholic upbringing. I tried to forget both but never could because, fundamentally, what knowledge I have comes from my Cistercian monk-teachers in Budapest, and what I have been living with for many years now, as have many others, is the memory of the Holocaust. Once unknown as a term and nearly ignored as a problem, the Holocaust is today a universal theme.

In many ways, Columbia University has changed little during the past sixty-odd years—not the power structure, or really the teaching methods. The direction is clearly, however, toward the equality of genders and internationalization from which only a few domestic minorities have not been able to draw great benefits. I myself was pulled away by gentle pressure from medieval and Western European history toward modern Central and Eastern Europe. The world was tremendously interested in the goings on within the "Soviet bloc." I have been shifting my emphasis ever since among such themes as cultural politics in the Weimar Republic, the Hungarian national revolution of 1849–1849, the death of multinational empires, World Wars I and II, fascism, socialism, nationalism, and the officer corps of the Habsburg Austro-Hungarian army. The latter was made up of eleven nationalities, and I am convinced that the officers, also from eleven nationalities, did much better than generally supposed in enabling Central Europeans to live together and to thrive in the pre–World War I decades. Even generals from the North Atlantic Treaty Organization (NATO) wanted to hear from me about it, all in the interest of eventually building a Pan-European army. But, of course, nothing has come from it as yet.

Researching the thick dossiers of officers, full of unbelievably detailed and often intimate information in the Vienna and other military archives, was a great joy; I recommend such types of social historical analysis to all.

All this would have been impossible without my new American family, a university that has paid my salary and benefits unfailingly through economic crises and student revolts and always permits you to say anything you would like to the students. What luck!

For the rest of this preface, let me thank the individuals who have done the most to make this book possible. There is, first of all, Fritz Stern at Columbia University, who more than fifty years ago wisely guided my doctoral dissertation on Carl von Ossietzky, the martyr of German intellectual resistance. Von Ossietzky received the Nobel Prize for Peace for 1935, when he was in a Nazi jail, and he died in 1938, still in Nazi custody. Let me continue the list of thanks with Leon Wieseltier and Robert Silvers, editors, respectively, of the *New Republic* and the *New York Review of Books,* who over several decades invited me to write a total of well over a hundred review articles on books that, in their majority, dealt with World War II events. There were also stimulating "exchanges" with critics on the pages of the two great journals. Leon Wieseltier is himself a prolific writer; Robert Silvers is the world's most exacting editor, who not only is conversant with the various subjects that new books bring his way but goes into battle with the reviewer over every comma as well as over any conceivable world historical concern.

Two outstanding historians of contemporary Europe, Tony Judt and Jan T. Gross, were kind enough to make me a partner in the preparation of a number of international conferences on immediate post–World War

II Europe, partly sponsored by the Institute of Human Sciences in Vienna and its late leader, Krzysztof Michalski. I also worked with Tony and Jan in writing and editing a successful collection of essays on the politics of retribution in postwar Europe.

Special thanks are due to Bálint Magyar, who put at my disposal a copy of the valuable essay he wrote as a student at Budapest University, in 1971, on the so-called Hungarian Freedom Movement, in which Béla Stollár's "Klotild Street Group" played an essential role. Between 1996 and 1998, Bálint Magyar served as Hungary's minister of education.

For the rest, I list in alphabetical order some of the many who helped me in collecting my thoughts and in writing them down in a reasonable order. Some among these helpers read and corrected my manuscript; others again became the source and inspiration of specific chapters in the book. They are Tarik Amar, Gergely Baics, Csaba Békés, Volker Berghahn, Peter Black, Sally Carr, Holly A. Case, Michael Chad, Mateja Fajt, Jennifer Foray, Tibor Frank, Ben Frommer, Charles Gati, Emily Greble, Paul Hanebrink, Pieter Judson, László Karsai, Andrew Kornbluth, Katherine Lebow, Ann Major, Sanford Malter, Mark Mazower, Dan McMillan, Judith Molnár, Éva D. Peck, Tom Peck, Attila Pók, Ivan Sanders, András Simonovits, Mitja Velikonja, and Nancy Wingfield.

As at first I had no idea what was involved in writing a textbook, I am grateful to Priscilla McGeehon, who introduced me to the idea, and I am now particularly grateful to the wonderful Kelli Fillingim and her associates Victoria Henson, Sandra Beris, and Annette Wenda.

Let me also express my gratitude to Drs. Jerry Gliklich and Bret Taback, both at Columbia University Medical Center, who with great ingenuity and enormous goodwill are keeping the author in good-enough shape to write these lines.

My dear wife, Gloria Deák, assisted me in innumerable ways all the while she was writing her own book.

If a few more people in this country become seriously interested in such subjects as life under foreign occupation, the duties of a citizen toward the occupier and toward his own countrymen, and how the victims of wartime persecution could have been helped by a little more compassion, then my efforts have not been in vain.

ISTVÁN DEÁK
New York, 2014

Introduction

Countries that fell under Hitler's reign in the early and mid-twentieth century experienced armed conflict, foreign occupation, aerial bombardments, persecution, concentration camps, and, what is perhaps less well known, ferocious civil and ethnic wars. It is hard, of course, to generalize about a region that at its greatest extended from the Arctic tip of Norway to the Pyrenees on the French-Spanish border and from the French port of Calais to the highest peaks of the Caucasus. In all of these places, and everywhere in between, German soldiers and policemen were numerous enough to rule the land but not enough to control every town, village, and forest. As a consequence, national governments, local authorities, native populations, and diverse social classes and interest groups, as well as many individuals, were eager, for myriad reasons, to tolerate the inevitable presence of, actively collaborate with, or oppose the ruling Germans. Great industrialists in France, for example, were generally eager to serve and profit from the German war effort, but millions of young Frenchmen resented— and often resisted—the compulsory labor service that would take them to Germany. Others, such as writers, poets, actors, artists, and journalists of France, were drawn in both directions. Much depended on where and when a person confronted the dilemma of passive accommodation, active collaboration, or resistance. The most formidable change in outlook was brought about less by local developments than by the victory of the Soviets over the German Sixth Army at Stalingrad on the Volga River in the winter of 1942–1943. This faraway event caused millions of Europeans to begin to doubt that Germany would win the war, which in turn started a sea change—from accommodation or collaboration to greater and greater forceful opposition to the Nazis.

In all of Europe, only two major groups had no chance to choose between accommodation, collaboration, or resistance. One of these groups was the Polish people, who, except on the level of local bureaucratic and police activity, especially in helping to hunt down Jewish fugitives, were not offered the opportunity to work politically or militarily with the German occupiers. The other group was, of course, the Jews, whom Hitler had collectively sentenced to death. The fate of the ethnic Russians, the third archenemy in the eyes of the Nazis, was, however, quite different. Although millions of them were killed as prisoners of war (POWs) or simply as innocent civilians, hundreds of thousands of other Russians were allowed and willing to serve in the German armed forces.*

Unlike the passive accommodators, who formed the vast majority of the Europeans, both collaborators and resisters tried to use the German presence in their midst to secure their individual and group futures. They also seized the opportunity to rid their country of domestic enemies, be they militant and armed groups or such helpless victims as the Jews.

This book will try to show that whereas the German conquest was the fundamental provocation for drastic changes in European politics and society, the war and the German presence were not the only reasons social upheavals and revolutions engulfed Europe in those years.

Similarly, it would be a mistake to see World War II in Europe as a period when the German soldiers conquered and then, in due time, were driven out by the Allies—whereupon life more or less returned to normal. This may have been true for a few lucky Western and northern European countries, but, in other places, the Germans were not alone in conquering and occupying territory. The Soviets grabbed large areas in Europe during those years, as did Germany's allies, including Italy, Finland, Hungary, Romania, Croatia, and Bulgaria. In consequence, many countries, at least in Eastern Europe, experienced not two but three or four foreign

_____

*In addition to Poles and Jews, fertile Nazi imaginations conjured up other grave threats to the nation, such as the badly handicapped "Aryan" Germans, who were seen as endangering the mental and physical health of the race, and the Roma/Sinti people (colloquially called Gypsies), who were perceived as undermining law and order. But neither of these groups was uniformly under a Nazi death sentence, nor in a position to form a resistance movement. The Nazis also strongly objected to gay men for allegedly endangering the reproductive capacities of the Aryan race and to members of the religious group called Jehovah's Witnesses, who were unwilling to serve the state in any form whatsoever. Both were persecuted but, unlike the Jews, were allowed to escape imprisonment or death by publicly renouncing their practices or faith.

[handwritten margin note: Many povs it seems that Germans aren't to blame]

Something I traunet d [handwritten marginalia]

occupations; people in these areas were forced to choose repeatedly between accommodation, resistance, and collaboration. Consider, for instance, that in today's Ukrainian city of Lvív (previously called Lemberg, Lvov, and Lwow, depending on who was the city's master), it was most advantageous, until World War I, to call oneself a loyal subject of His Majesty the Austrian Emperor Francis Joseph or, between 1918 and 1939, a Polish patriot. But between 1939 and 1941, the survival instinct dictated enthusiastic devotion to the Soviet Union and Joseph Stalin. Between 1941 and 1944, it became a matter of life and death not to offend the German Nazis, while after 1944 the people of Lvív once again had to show boundless admiration for Stalin. (Today, Lvív is in Ukraine, but by the end of World War II many of the city's original inhabitants had been killed, deported, or driven out. In fact, by 1945 all Poles, Germans, and Jews were nearly gone, their place taken instead by Ukrainians and by immigrants from deep inside the Soviet Union.)

Simultaneous with the process of land grabbing was the greatest ethnic cleansing in European history, primarily but by far not exclusively in the form of the "Final Solution of the Jewish Question."* The latter program attempted to eliminate a group of perhaps 9 million people from the face of the earth. The fact that, at the end of the war, only about a third of the Jews in Hitler's Europe had survived, or, to put it differently, nearly two-thirds of them had been killed, was due, on the one hand, to the grim determination of the Germans and their many European helpers to exterminate the Jews and, on the other hand, to Allied victory and the humanitarian impulse of some Europeans. We will therefore examine the various forms of collaboration with and resistance to the German Nazis in the "Jewish Question" by governments allied to Germany as well as by peoples, groups, and individuals. Sympathy for or hostility to National Socialist ideology was only one of many factors in the complex game of determining the fate of the Jews in Europe at that time.

---

*Throughout the text, we shall alternately use the terms *Final Solution, Holocaust,* and *Shoah* to refer to what happened to the Jews of Europe during the war. None of the terms is fully satisfactory because *Final Solution* sounds as if we have adopted the Nazi idea that there was a "Jewish Question" in need of a solution; *Holocaust* is a Greek term meaning "a fiery offering," which is not at all what the Jewish victims were engaged in; and *Shoah,* which in modern Hebrew means "catastrophe," turns mass murder into a tragic incident. Furthermore, the term *Shoah* is not often used in Western books and media.

Although it remains a mystery how one statesman, Hitler, and one nation, the Germans, were able to so drastically alter the face of an entire continent, we must also note that German power was more limited than is generally assumed. With regard to the Jews, for instance, the Nazis would never have succeeded to the extent that they did without the enthusiastic collaboration of many non-German Europeans. Conversely, the survival of many Jews would have been inconceivable without the opposition of many non-Germans to the Nazi presence. Moreover, throughout the war there were countries associated with Germany, such as Finland and Bulgaria, where Hitler's orders had no validity, as well as vast areas, such as German-occupied central Russia and parts of Yugoslavia, from which armed partisans again and again drove out the German troops.

Although the term *accommodation* or *passive accommodation* will occur repeatedly in this book, and although such behavior was characteristic of the vast majority of people in Hitler's Europe, little discussion is needed regarding its definition. Clearly, there were people who tried to get by under foreign occupation, who hoped to survive the war unscathed, and who wished to remain nonpolitical. For them, both collaboration and resistance were unwelcome, even threatening, activities. For many if not most Europeans, the collaborator was a wild-eyed fanatic who tried to get your son to join the Waffen SS (the combat troops of the Nazi SS organization) on the Russian front or to work in a German factory, while the resister was yet another fanatic, likely to be a ragged and unappetizing foreigner who sabotaged train travel and wanted your son to go to the forest and risk being killed there by the Germans or by rival partisan groups.

The nature and character of accommodation varied greatly, as did its boundaries. What if you were doing a good job in a factory producing guns for Germany? What if you were doing a bad job? Did the first make you a collaborator and the second a resister, leaving only those in the middle to practice accommodation? Your work and that of your fellow engineers may have had a crucial influence on German war production.

What about those who during the German occupation simply continued to pursue their harmless peacetime occupations, like Pablo Picasso, for instance, or the world-famous French singer and actor Maurice Chevalier? More than merely performing on the stage in Paris, often before an audience of German soldiers, Chevalier visited French POW camps in Germany, talked to German reporters, and sang for the poor captives. This was a big propaganda coup for Germany, and, as a result, both the

Nazis and the French Resistance saw Chevalier as a collaborator, the first in a positive and the second in a negative sense. After the war he was indicted and tried for treason, and subsequently acquitted, but the United States and Great Britain continued to reject his visa application even after his acquittal.

It also made a great difference where you practiced accommodation; for instance, it was easy to do so in the British Channel Islands, which the Germans occupied from 1940 to 1945 and where the soldiers behaved impeccably. It was more difficult to be accommodating in occupied Russia, where the Germans and their allies routinely burned down villages, drove away or killed all domestic animals, and often shot people indiscriminately. It was also easier to adjust to the German occupation where there were few or no occupiers; it is a pity that there is no statistical data on how many people in Hitler's Europe lived through the war without meeting with a German soldier or policeman.

Despite their best efforts to stay neutral, many among the bystanders could not escape their fate, either. Some were taken hostage and killed by the Germans, others died as innocent civilians in partisan attacks on German soldiers, and still others were forced to take a political stand by local fanatics or died of starvation because, being without influence and connections, they received no help from either side.

World War II spared no one in Europe completely. Admittedly, it was much easier to survive in relative comfort in Denmark, whose inhabitants the Germans treated with kid gloves, than in Poland, where literally no one was exempt from the wrath of the occupiers. Moreover, in Poland both German and Soviet occupiers were keen on exterminating the intelligentsia while brutally exploiting the rest of the population.

This book will show how collaboration and resistance took many forms during the war. The former ranged from offering a glass of water to a thirsty German soldier all the way to assisting the Gestapo—as the most formidable of the German political police force was called—by denouncing, hunting down, torturing, and killing potential and real resisters. Conversely, the latter extended from wearing a patriotic badge hidden under one's lapel to serving and dying in a partisan army, as was the case for hundreds of thousands of Yugoslavs, Poles, and Soviet citizens. And many questions are still open. For instance, how should one judge black-market activities, which weakened German control over the citizens but also often deprived the poor of sustenance? Should a bakers' strike for better pay count as an act of resistance, even though it harmed the bakers' compatriots more than it harmed the Germans, who simply seized the available bread? This, as we will see, is only the beginning of the complications. Were Polish "blue policemen" collaborators or resisters who, during their workweek, hunted down Jews in hiding to hand them over to the German police but on weekends met with fellow anti-Nazis in an attempt to blow up a German military train? And what to think of the Hungarian coal miners, many of whom belonged to their country's National Socialist Party, who went on strike for better wages in October 1940 against the Jewish mine owners? By this act, the miners indirectly prevented some Hungarian heavy industrial plants, equally owned by Jews, from making weapons for the Germans. The strike, directed by Hungarian Nazi leaders, was finally crushed by the Hungarian army units, at the request of the German government.

To be sure, timing played a crucial role in all this: changes at the battlefront made resisters out of collaborators, although many performed both functions simultaneously. After all, in order to be able to cause havoc in the German transportation system at the time of the Normandy invasion, for instance, one had to be a high-ranking French railroad functionary who was enjoying the confidence of the Germans.

Such developments do not mean that there were no genuine anti-Nazis who risked their lives throughout the war in fighting for freedom, for democracy, and, very often, for some form of socialism. There were also those who never wavered in their allegiance to Hitler. As late as April 1945, thousands of young Scandinavian, Belgian, and French volunteers in the Waffen SS gave their lives for him while defending the entrance to the Chancellery Bunker in Berlin.

It should be clear by now that one of our greatest problems will be to define properly the terms *collaboration* and *resistance* as well as to fit specific groups and individuals into these categories. It should also be evident that there were vast regional differences between Western and southern Europe, on the one hand, and Eastern as well as southeastern Europe, on the other hand. And while the German SS committed terrible atrocities in France and Italy, it was never without some provocation by the anti-Nazi resistance. Overall, German war crimes in the West were restrained in comparison with German brutality in Eastern Europe and the Balkans. In Poland, the Baltic countries, the German-occupied parts of the Soviet Union, and Greece and Yugoslavia, there was plenty of partisan provocation for the unleashing of German fury. In those countries the SS and the German army, called the Wehrmacht, also killed for the pleasure of killing or in order to change the local ethnic makeup. It was as if there were two wars: in the West something rather traditional and in the East massive German colonization as well as a racial crusade against Jews, Slavs, and other people whom the Germans regarded as inferior.

It is also important to note that whereas the war in the West started in 1939 and ended in 1945, in the East it often started later but continued beyond 1945, in the form of an armed struggle against the Soviet conquerors as well as bloody conflicts among Eastern Europeans. In Poland, for instance, the last armed anti-Communist resister was killed in 1963. Even more dramatically, while ethnic cleansing was the most lasting outcome of World War II in the East, in Western Europe ethnic cleansing did not take place, except in the form of the Holocaust of Jews achieved by the Germans with varying degrees of local assistance.

The main task of this book will be to deal with questions of collaboration, resistance, and retribution in countries where supreme authority lay in the hands of the German army and other representatives of the Third Reich. This was the case of the Czech lands (then called the Protectorate of Bohemia and Moravia, today the Czech Republic), Poland, Norway, Denmark, the Netherlands, Belgium, Luxembourg, France, Yugoslavia, Greece, the Baltic countries, and the German-occupied parts of the Soviet Union.* Yet World War II Europe did not consist solely of Nazi Germany and the countries that the German military occupied. There was also a large group made up of Germany's politically independent allies: Finland, which was officially a cobelligerent and not an ally, as well as Italy, Slovakia, Hungary, Romania, Croatia, and Bulgaria, all of which had their own heads of state, ministries, diplomacy, armies, police, and national administrations. (Some occupied countries, the collaborationist French government foremost among them, aspired in vain to be accepted by Hitler as his political allies.)

Within the countries associated or allied with Germany, the dilemma of groups of individuals opposed to Nazi Germany was not whether they should obey the Germans—who were often absent from the scene—but

---

*After the war Austria, too, claimed to have been a German-occupied country; in reality, Austria and Nazi Germany had united in 1938 to general rejoicing, and, subsequently, Austrians played leading roles in the German army, police, and occupation authorities.

whether they should obey their own governments. True, these governments were visibly and vocally allied to Germany, but their loyalty to the Nazis was often questionable. In fact, no matter what many history books and cable TV programs say today, none of the allied governments was a puppet of Hitler. Each had a will of its own. Hitler's allies were free to decide whether and how far they would follow the German lead. When they refused German requests, more often than not Germany proved incapable of enforcing its will.

All this meant that by following government orders in countries allied to Germany, individuals or groups were often able either to promote or to harm the German cause. It was fundamentally a question of place, time period, and political as well as military circumstances. It is no wonder then that in the postwar trials, the charge against the newly deposed leaders of these countries was generally not collaboration but treason.

There was also a third category of countries in wartime Europe, namely, the handful of neutrals whose relations with Nazi Germany varied according to time, place, and the interests of their governments. Ironically, Spain and Portugal, whose political systems somewhat resembled those of Italy and Germany, conducted highly cautious policies toward Hitler and Mussolini. On the other hand, democratic Switzerland and Sweden were geographically so close to Nazi power that their leaders considered it necessary to support the German war industry, at least during the first years of the war. Besides, working with Germany brought these countries great material benefits.

What makes these events so historically engrossing is that, during World War II, both collaboration and resistance assumed proportions unheard of in the past, leading to terrible devastation but also to at least partial self-liberation in some of the German-occupied countries. The main reason for the tremendous growth of voluntary citizen participation in the conflict was that, unlike World War I, this was an ideological conflict; profound convictions animated the political activists in both camps. Consequently, when the war was over and the time came for settling accounts, a wave of unprecedented purges swept Europe: millions became the targets of retribution; millions also acted as the initiators and executors of retribution. It is my estimation that post–World War II criminal courts investigated, even if they did not always try and sentence, one in every twenty adult males for treason, war crimes, or collaboration with Germany. Interestingly, quite a few among those who were condemned for their wartime activities were also praised, and sometimes even decorated for their heroic resistance activity. Ardent French collaborator and heinous persecutor of Jews René Bousquet, for instance, was sentenced after the war to five years of *dégradation nationale,* best translated as "national shame and humiliation." Yet he was immediately acquitted by the same court for having "consistently participated in the resistance against the occupier."[1] The post–World War II French government forgave collaborationist police chief Maurice Papon and promoted him to the highest ranks of the civil service, yet in 1998 a French court condemned the same Papon to a long prison term for war crimes committed under German occupation.[2]

Or consider the case of Hungary's uncrowned king, Regent Vice Admiral Miklós Horthy, who, during the war, alternately promoted and opposed German influence in his country, depending on how he judged the probable outcome of the war and who among his close advisers had his ear. Similarly, Horthy both persecuted and protected his Jewish subjects, depending on the turn of military events and the social status and degree of assimilation of the Jews under his reign. In the end, he was neither tried nor imprisoned but at the urging of Stalin was allowed to go into exile in Portugal.[3]

It is indeed amazing how many heads of state, prime ministers, cabinet members, military brass, intellectuals, and even poets and actors were tried in court after the war and how many were hanged. The series of purges actually began very early during the war when in some German-occupied countries the German-approved new governments accused their countries' officers and statesmen of having neglected to take defensive measures against the German threat. Retribution continued after the war, on a much larger scale, either under the aegis of the Western Allies or under that of the Soviet Union. The goal, whether in France or in Yugoslavia, was to rid the country of the remnants of the ancien régime, the old prewar regime, which both collaborationists and resisters had held to be corrupt and incompetent. The result of the trials, it was hoped, would lead to a more honest, less corrupt, and more socially conscious nation.

Even while the war was raging, both collaborators and resisters toyed with the idea of a unified Europe, either under the leadership of Nazi Germany or under that of the United States and Great Britain. Only the Soviets and the Communists in general would not hear of a unified Europe, which they felt the Americans would use against them. This shows that many of the great ideas and issues of the post–World War II era were tackled during the war. Ironically, the new Europe visualized by World War II political activists was finally created less by former collaborators or former resisters, many having been killed during or after the war and generally judged to be utopian dreamers, than by more realistic politicians who had often avoided political commitment during the war.

Throughout this book, we will raise the question, directly and indirectly, of what kind of Europe its inhabitants hoped to have after the war. We will see that there was no consensus on such issues as Europe's future role in the world, the possible unification of the continent, and the nature of the necessary social, economic, and political reforms. Millions of Europeans, more in Eastern than in Western Europe, agreed, however, on the necessity of ridding their respective countries of alien elements, be they foreign occupiers, immigrants, refugees, or domestic minorities. In particular, many Europeans agreed, even in Western Europe, with the Nazi plan, if not the method, of ridding the continent of Jews. In brief, if there was one major European project, it was ethnic cleansing.

Admittedly, ethnic cleansing was less of a burning issue in Western, northern, and southern Europe than in Europe's Eastern and southeastern parts, simply because in the West and the North, ethnic cleansing had already been largely accomplished in earlier centuries through compulsory education, mandatory military service, and, when judged necessary, brute force. In the East ethnic purification began only with the demise, in 1918, of the multinational empires. But in the interwar period and during World War II, xenophobia was the order of the day on the Old Continent.

Everywhere in Nazi-occupied Europe, individuals had to face the dilemma of loyalty, but in this respect, too, things varied enormously. In Denmark where every governmental institution from the monarchy of King Christian X down to the local police precinct survived the German invasion, people had to ask themselves whether it was in the interest of the fatherland and of their own security and welfare to remain loyal to the collaborationist government or whether they should engage in some kind of resistance activity. In Italy in the summer of 1943, the fascist Mussolini government was overthrown; the king and his new government switched allegiance to the Allies in the South of the country; the German army occupied northern and central Italy, and Mussolini formed a new fascist republic.

While all governmental institutions fell apart, Italians had to ask themselves to whom they should pledge loyalty: the absent king or the new fascist government or the anti-German partisan fighters who themselves were divided between Communists, socialists, democrats, and conservative royalists? Meanwhile, German troops occupying much of the country unhesitatingly imprisoned or executed all Italian soldiers they encountered, and in the South, American, British, French, Polish, and other Allied armies, struggling to free Italy from the German yoke, often indiscriminately bombed Italian cities and landmarks. Unlike the Danish people, the Italians during World War II experienced a terrible crisis of society and state.

There has been no comprehensive scholarly treatment of these four related subjects: collaboration, accommodation, resistance, and retribution. There are a handful of studies on collaboration and resistance and many, often excellent, publications on one or the other of the four topics in specific countries, especially in France, Denmark, Norway, and the Low Countries. There are also a few useful essay collections.

Writings on collaboration, for instance, are few in some countries and virtually nonexistent in places such as Belorussia and Russia. The goal of this book is to begin filling this great gap in historiography as well as to make us all aware of what went by the name of collaboration, resistance, and retribution in World War II. Certainly, this exasperatingly complex series of events had a profound influence not only on Europe but on our life today.[4]

In a book attempting to analyze a number of specific developments in dozens of countries, on both the societal and the individual levels, one can have no illusions regarding the validity of generalizations. All-encompassing statistical data are missing: We do not know, for instance, the true number of collaborators and resisters in any one country, and less so in Europe as a whole. Nor are we certain how many Europeans were punished after the war for collaboration with the enemy or for war crimes. Accurate data for a country such as Norway are counterbalanced by the lack of any reliable statistics on the Soviet Union. Yet without some continental generalizations, the narrative would remain repetitive and chaotic. There will be several examples offered in the book in the hope that they will help to create an overall picture in the mind and imagination of the reader.

Following this introduction, the book will cast a brief glance on the history of military occupations and atrocities often caused by the mutual mistrust and fear of soldiers and civilians. We will also look at international attempts to regulate the presence of enemy soldiers in foreign territory. This will be followed by an analysis of why, in 1939, twenty-five years after the outbreak of World War I, the world again faced a general military conflict. Subsequently, in Chapter 2 we shall turn to the early German conquests: the occupation of Austria in 1938, where German troops were greeted as brothers freeing the people from the burden of having to govern themselves; the occupation of the Czech lands in the spring of 1939, where the German occupation was perceived as a national tragedy but one within which the Czech people should make the best of a difficult situation; and the bitterly resisted German invasion of Poland, on September 1, 1939, which marked the beginning of the European war.

Chapter 3 will present an overall picture of the collapse of northern and Western Europe under the German military onslaught and the initial attempt of many in the two regions to live with or even profit from the German presence. Yet as Chapter 4 explains, the generally unexpected and still unexplainable German military attack on its ally the Soviet Union, in June 1941, changed all plans and expectations. Europeans on the right side of politics who had always hated Bolshevism, but whose zeal for the German cause had been restrained by the Hitler-Stalin Pact of August 1939, now had good grounds to offer their hearts and souls to the Führer. Those on the Far Left, who had to stay neutral in the "conflict between imperialist, capitalist powers," namely, the war between Nazi Germany and the Franco-British alliance, now threw themselves with abandon into the "antifascist struggle." The war had suddenly become profoundly ideological.

For the East Europeans, the German-Soviet war presented a nearly insoluble dilemma: where to place themselves in the clash of two threatening giants. Who was the greater enemy in a strange situation in which the small countries were also often each other's bitterest enemies? Chapter 5 tries to explain the particularly difficult situation in which Germany's numerous allies found themselves following Operation Barbarossa, as the German attack on Russia was called.

The German army's first defeat, near Moscow, in the winter of 1941–1942, encouraged the hitherto nearly invisible resistance movements to gather strength and self-confidence, which is the topic of Chapters 6 and 7. Here again we must separate Western and northern Europe from Eastern and southeastern Europe, for while the anti-Nazi struggle and postwar reform were the firm goals of resisters from Norway to France and Italy, the tasks and objectives of those in the East and Southeast were far more complex. Resisters in Paris hoped to restore their country's independence, to punish the traitors, and to bring about a better, more fair postwar society. The same type of anti-Nazi resisters in Lvív in Ukraine first had to decide who their main enemies were: the German occupiers, the Soviet armies, or perhaps their Jewish or Polish neighbors? But no matter where the resister engaged in his or her activities, life was dangerous, the sufferings cruel. In fact, the heroic romanticism of resistance activity turned out to be the stuff more of Hollywood than of reality. Chapter 8 will attempt to show, through three detailed cases, what mindless brutalities the occupiers were driven to by resistance activity. The main victims of resistance were generally neither the occupiers nor the resisters but the civilian population. The last chapters of the book will give specific examples of the postwar retribution as well as attempt some generalizations regarding the unprecedented and never-repeated catharsis and purges that Europe experienced during and after liberation. The positive and negative consequences of the postwar purges in Europe have still not been completely absorbed.

We must finally note that during the two centuries prior to World War II, international efforts were made to humanize warfare so that soldiers would not rob and kill the captured enemy and military commanders would not allow the massacre of innocent civilians. The efforts were certainly not always successful: witness the atrocities committed in the Russo-Turkish War of 1877–1878, the Boer War in South Africa, the colonial wars, and World War I. Yet only between 1939 and 1945 did the atrocities, mass extermination, and mass expulsions come to be seen as ideologically justified, universal necessities. The clash of collaborators and resisters itself instigated a regrettable return to the time-honored habit of savagery. But also, after the war, international organizations tried and sometimes succeeded in enforcing much stronger and more effective humanitarian rules. And even though those conventions were widely ignored in the Yugoslav civil war in the 1990s, this terrible case has remained an exception. In post–World War II Europe, people turned generally to international organizations, not to torture and killing, to settle their disputes. Thus, it can be said that World War II brought not only despair but also a huge wave of hope.

NOTES

1. On René Bousquet, see Lucy Golsan and Richard J. Golsan, eds., *Memory, the Holocaust, and French Justice: The Bousquet and Touvier Affairs* (Lebanon, NH: University Press of New England, 1996).

2. On Maurice Papon, see Richard J. Golsan, ed., *The Papon Affair: Memory and Justice* (New York: Routledge, 2000).

3. On Miklós (Nicholas) Horthy, see Thomas Sakmyster, *Hungary's Admiral on Horseback: Miklós Horthy, 1918–1944* (Boulder, CO: East European Monographs, distributed by Columbia University Press, 1994).

4. For a sampling of books and essay collections on collaboration, resistance, and retribution in Europe, see "Suggestions for Further Study."

CHAPTER ONE

From Brutality to International Conventions to Renewed Brutality

Foreign Occupations in European History

Local populations can survive a foreign military occupation only if the occupation army enforces discipline among the troops—that is to say, if the soldiers abide by their country's military code, and if they regard the locals as fellow human beings worthy of consideration. In return, the occupying power has the right to expect that the locals obey all of what would be considered at least halfway reasonable orders and that they not threaten the lives of the soldiers. No military code, not even that of the German Nazis, authorizes plunder or the slaughter of innocents; in fact, Paragraph 211 of the German penal code, as published in a handbook in October 1943, threatened a soldier guilty of murder with capital punishment without any distinction as to the victim's race, religion, or nationality. Other paragraphs in the code called for the severe punishment of those who incited murder or assisted in the commission of such a crime.[1] Remarkably, the 1943 German military regulations went so far as to threaten with punishment the soldier who carried out such orders of his superiors that were in violation of the law. "The subordinate is punishable as a participant when he knows that the superior's order would have the aim of leading to a military or other crime or violation."[2] The monstrous behavior of German troops during World War II in Eastern and southeastern Europe shows that the military code is useless if the commanders do not bother to enforce it or deliberately disregard it.

Unfortunately, the ideal situation of mutual respect between occupied and occupier existed only intermittently throughout history; more often than not, armies were unruly bands of men whose appearance in foreign lands, whether "friendly" or "hostile," spelled violence and plunder. Occupying armies had to live mostly on the produce of the land, and the land was seldom rich enough to feed its inhabitants, less so a horde of invaders.

Overall, life under military occupation was an unmitigated tragedy. In the European-wide Thirty Years' War between 1618 and 1648, soldiers were mostly indistinguishable from other men carrying implements that could be used as weapons, and, in general, the belligerent powers were unable to provision their troops. Thus, soldiers robbed, raped, and slaughtered; in return, the peasants slew and sometimes skinned the soldiers who were unfortunate enough to find themselves separated from their units.

The great change came in the late seventeenth and early eighteenth centuries with the beginning of centralized administrations and state-directed economic and social policies. For the first time in the history of Europe, economic progress and the growing ability of the royal treasury to collect money from its subjects enabled some governments to create long-lasting rather than temporary standing armies. The mercenaries of the Italian Renaissance princes were usually excellent soldiers, but with the expiration of their contracts, they unhesitatingly switched to the highest bidder or became mere marauders. Eighteenth-century monarchs expected loyalty from their soldiers, whom they were now increasingly able to outfit, feed, and equip with standardized weapons. The king's flag began to be seen not as a mere instrument of visual recognition but as a sacred royal symbol and, increasingly, as a symbol of the state the ruler was governing. Later, mostly in the nineteenth century, the flag became the symbol of the nation.

Soldiers in the new armies were usually commanded by the "cadets," or younger sons of the nobility, for whom service in the military was often no longer an elegant pastime but a destination as well as the source of a modest but steady income. Ordinary soldiers generally came from the poorest strata of society or were such unfortunates whom their communities had wanted to get rid of and had therefore been designated for service. Gradually, however, military service became a general obligation, if at first only for certain strata of society. Over them, iron discipline prevailed, creating a chasm between the draftees, many of whom were not released for twenty-five years, and the "civilians," a new term.

The aristocratic officers who commanded the armies of the eighteenth century formed an unofficial international class whose members were often related to each other and who had nothing but contempt for the "rabble" under their command. Eighteenth-century European wars were limited in scope—unlike those fought in the colonies or on the high seas, where few of the above rules prevailed. Under such conditions, it is small wonder that guerrilla wars, that is, civilians fighting uniformed soldiers from a hiding place, were a rarity.

With all due respect for the danger of hasty generalizations, we can still state with confidence that the more or less successful practice of regulating and humanizing warfare was suspended late in the eighteenth century as a result of the partition of Poland and the French Revolution. Of the two, the second event is far better known, yet the fall of Poland in the late eighteenth century had a more immediate and profound influence on the practice of foreign occupation and resistance to it than the French Revolution.

Starting in 1772 and within the following twenty-three years, Russia, Prussia, and Austria completed the partition of the Polish kingdom, to which Polish patriots reacted with a great rebellion in 1794. The uprising failed, but since then the names of Poland and of the Polish people have been associated with resistance to foreign occupation. Carrying a flag with the inscription "For Our Freedom and Yours," Polish émigrés fought in all of the nineteenth- and twentieth-century wars of national liberation. Sacrificing one's life in the struggle against occupation forces has become part of the Polish national myth. Indeed, in the first year and a half of World War II, Poland was the only country besides Great Britain that did not surrender or join the German Nazis. Not surprisingly, some Poles, especially the poets among them, saw their country as the "Christ of the Nations." Poland, whatever its geographic and ethnic boundaries—an independent Poland in recent history existed only between 1918 and 1939 and then again after 1944—was truly a dangerous place for all foreign occupiers. What a vast difference between the problems of resistance in, for example, Denmark, which had barely known a foreign occupation until 1940, and Poland, which for centuries had experienced nothing but foreign administrations and foreign occupation armies.

The significance of the French Revolution for Europe is neatly summed up in "La Marseillaise," a battle song that became a national anthem as well as the global anthem of resistance. Without the slightest idea of how the Austrian and Prussian troops marching into France in 1792 were going

to behave, "La Marseillaise" called for a fight to the death against the foreign occupiers, whom it called *féroce* and a howling and fearsome horde of
slaves. No quarter was to be given in this holy struggle.

The irony is that in the period between 1792 and 1814, France suffered
no foreign occupation, and thus the French nation had no opportunity to
engage in guerrilla operations. Instead, many ordinary people in Europe
resisted the "ferocious soldiers" of French occupiers. The very term *guerrilla,* meaning "little war," stems from the Spanish struggle against the
French occupation. All of these conflicts were conducted with great ferocity and cruelty by both sides.

The French governments of the revolutionary and Napoleonic conflicts
waged their wars while promising national liberation and enlightened reforms to the enslaved peoples of Europe: the answer in the occupied or
"liberated" countries was the rise of local nationalism. This led to conflicts
not only with the French but also with other local groups; the ideological
conflicts invariably led to the formation of armed irregular units.

The Congress of Vienna from 1814 to 1815, which terminated the Napoleonic Wars, endeavored to return Europe to the hereditary rulers. They,
in turn, promised to combine their forces into a kind of supranational police that would ensure peace and quiet on the continent of Europe. The
resolutions of the congress proved a rare success: peace among the great
powers was interrupted by only the Crimean War in the 1850s. Guerrilla
activities seldom occurred.

Conservative regimes dominating Europe during the first half of the
nineteenth century worried that universal conscription and a three- or
four-year term of service under the flag, demanded by experts as a military necessity, would put weapons in the hands of nonprofessionals. The
specter of millions of trained soldiers and former soldiers with close ties to
their civilian existence haunted the military and political establishment.
Would these civilians in uniform be prepared to fire, if need be, on their
demonstrating or striking brothers and mothers?

The fears were vastly exaggerated: the recruits of the new mass armies,
who were no longer automatons crushed into submission with the sergeant's baton, were often happy and proud to serve. The army, after all, had
freed many of them from the drudgery of rural existence and had brought
the excitement of travel, better nourishment, health care, and a measure of
education. Most important, universal military service brought a sense of
belonging to the nation, actually an imagined community.

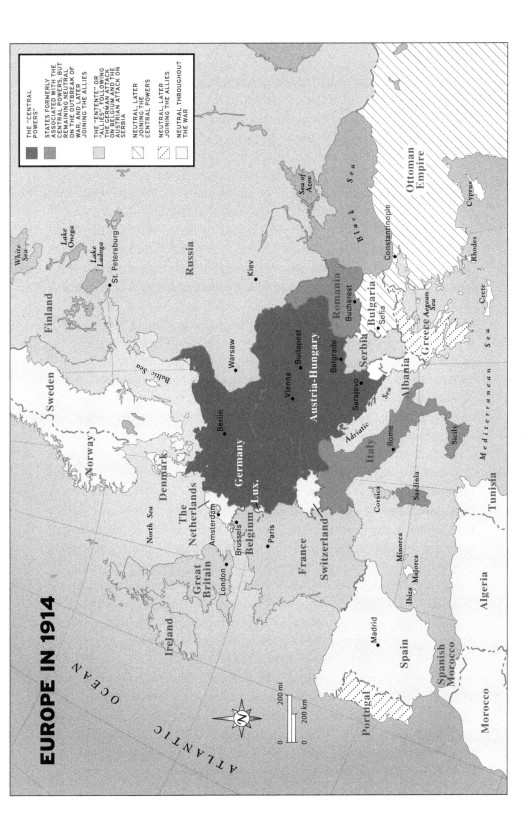

Except for the United Kingdom, European countries introduced universal conscription between the early nineteenth century and the 1870s. Three or four years in the barracks taught the recruit that it was his sacred duty to learn how to kill in the service of his king and nation, yet he was also taught that killing without orders, whether in or out of uniform, was a capital crime. By 1900 Europe possessed several million men trained to be robbers and killers, but only in circumstances carefully delineated by their superiors. To prove their high esteem of trained soldiers, nearly all European states reserved employment to army veterans in the police forces, firefighting, lower administration, the tobacco monopoly, guard duty, and so forth. "Did you serve?" (Haben Sie gedient?) was a standard question used in German private industry when it came to filling "respectable" positions.

The supreme test of the citizens' armies came to pass in World War I when it often became extremely difficult to distinguish between innocent civilians and guerrillas hiding among the local population. Fortunately, by 1914 Europe possessed a series of international conventions and agreements for the regulation and humanization of warfare and the protection of the wounded and prisoners of war. Other clauses in these nonbinding agreements provided for the protection of the occupation forces and even, interestingly, of armed civilians in irregular resistance forces.

The various Hague and Geneva Agreements, initiated by peace-minded thinkers and statesmen but also, for instance, by the Russian czar, forbade the use of particularly devastating instruments of war, such as naval blockades aimed at bringing about starvation in the enemy country, explosive rifle bullets and chemical weapons, and artillery or aerial attacks on cities without a war industry. They further demanded that wounded enemy captives be given the same care as one's own wounded and that prisoners of war not be employed in the war industry. Also, in an unconscious fallback on feudal tradition, the agreements stipulated that captured officers should be treated almost as honored guests and be given the same pay as one's own officers. But while officers and officer candidates could not be required to work, ordinary soldiers and noncommissioned officers among the prisoners could be forced to toil in nonmilitary jobs. And indeed, while a naval blockade became a crucial weapon in the hands of the British, while the Germans felt free to bombard cities from the moment they invaded France and used poison gas as soon as it became available, and while ordinary soldiers died by the hundreds of thousands in Russian,

Austro-Hungarian, and Italian captivity, the belligerents scrupulously observed the privileges of captive officers during the First World War.

The most important innovation regarding collaboration and resistance was introduced by the Fourth Hague International Convention of 1907, whose Articles 42–43 outlined the citizenry's duty to obey enemy occupation forces so long as the latter abided by the terms of The Hague Convention and were able to control the occupied territory.[3] This legalized a limited degree of collaboration, but also legalized resistance, if only in strictly defined conditions: Article 4 of The Hague Convention included guerrillas, militia, and irregular troops among legitimate belligerents but only if they were properly commanded, wore a fixed emblem recognizable at a distance, carried their arms openly, and conducted their operations in accordance with the laws and customs of war. Between 1914 and 1918, neither side respected The Hague Convention regarding guerrillas: resistance fighters regularly operated in disguise, and the military executed captured guerrillas even if they had been "recognizable at a distance." Still, those at The Hague had made an appreciable effort to protect irregular fighters with results that were not entirely negligible.

We must remind ourselves that, during World War I, the Entente or Allied armies (Russia, France, Great Britain, Italy, plus many others) hardly ever succeeded in penetrating German, Austro-Hungarian, Bulgarian, or Turkish territory, that is, the lands of the so-called Central Powers. Consequently, when we talk of foreign occupation, collaboration, resistance, repression, and retribution in the war of 1914–1918, we inevitably mean territories that the Central Powers occupied in Belgium, France, Serbia, Russia, Italy, and Romania. Small wonder that the public within the Central Powers continued to believe that they were winning when, in reality, they had long lost the war to a materially and numerically superior enemy.

No sooner did the war begin than German troops started executing alleged *francs-tireurs* (snipers) in Belgium and France or, as the word itself implies, unattached civilians accused of having fired on the soldiers of invading armies. At the same time, the Austro-Hungarians, Germany's main allies, hanged thousands of Serbian and Russian-Ukrainian civilians, among them Orthodox priests, suspected of spying for the enemy.

Politically, the shootings and lootings benefited mainly the Allies, whose media spread the news of the atrocities committed by the "Huns" (Germans) and their allies, inflaming the French and British as well as, eventually, the American public. After the war, historians and the public, especially in the United States, tended to dismiss the atrocity stories as wartime British propaganda. More recently, however, historians have shown that German atrocities were only too real and that they had been inspired by the German high command's brutal orders as well as by fear and hysteria spreading among the troops. Atrocities in Alsace-Lorraine and Belgium usually began with German troops nervously or accidentally discharging their rifles; it led to panicked soldiers inadvertently firing at one another and then taking revenge for imagined *franc-tireur* attacks by killing innocent civilians.

The issue of collaboration with the enemy was less of a public concern during World War I, at least in Western Europe, than it would become during World War II. In the West, this was because the front lines solidified in 1914 and remained basically unchanged until the last weeks of the war. Higher French and Belgian authorities had fled with the retreating armies; left behind were the local administration, police, and the like, from whom the German occupiers demanded obedience but not any kind of ideological commitment. Whereas suspected opponents were harshly punished, "collaborators" were not rewarded or recruited into the German armed forces. This was not so in the East, where conditions foreshadowed many of the terrible developments in the next great war.

In Eastern Europe in 1914, several ethnic groups were suspected of being hostile and traitorous. The Russian high command believed that all Jews rooted for Germany; the Austro-Hungarian high command assumed that many of Emperor Francis Joseph's Slavic-speaking subjects were siding with their brothers in the Serbian and the Russian armies. Thousands were hanged or shot for mostly imaginary crimes. The dreaded Cossacks, an elite force usually on horseback within the Russian army, forced hundreds of thousands of Jews in Galicia to flee toward Budapest and Vienna; other Jews were killed and their houses looted. In view of such mistreatment, it is not surprising that many Eastern European Jews received the German- and Austro-Hungarian troops as their saviors with whom, among other things, they could communicate in German or in a mixture of Yiddish and German. When the Russians reconquered some territory, as they occasionally did during the war, they persecuted the "hostile" Jewish population with increased ferocity, despite the fact that, meanwhile, hundreds of thousands of Jews had been drafted into the Russian ranks. Nor did the fleeing Orthodox Jews, many among them in their strange garb and with "uncivilized" behavior, earn the love and respect of people in Germany and Austria-Hungary, many of whom resented having to share their starvation rations with the refugees.

In modern history, the first true genocide, an attempt to wipe out an entire people or "race," occurred not in Europe but in the Ottoman Empire, where the Young Turk government and the army high command organized the expulsion and massacre of hundreds of thousands or perhaps even a million Armenian fellow citizens. Armenians were suspected of siding with the invading Russian enemy, and, indeed, many Armenians served in the Russian forces either as subjects of the czar or as irregulars from the Ottoman Empire. Yet nothing justified the deportation to the Syrian Desert of masses of Armenian civilians—including women and children—or their systematic extermination. (Note, however, that Armenians in Constantinople/Istanbul were not harmed.) The Armenian genocide was the first great step, and a very effective one, in the long series of ethnic cleansings that World War I inaugurated.

After the war, in quick succession, several million Greek Orthodox were driven out of Turkish Anatolia, Muslims were deported from Greece and Bulgaria, several hundred thousand Hungarians fled or were expelled from neighboring Romania, and many Poles and Ukrainians changed places. In Ukraine itself, as well as in the Baltic countries, German and Russian soldiers hastily organized national armies. Red revolutionaries and White counterrevolutionaries committed atrocities against civilians, usually with the excuse of preventing or ending some kind of guerrilla resistance. Many of these horrors such as the so-called Greek, Bulgarian, and Turkish population exchanges took place with the permission, nay the encouragement, of the leaders of the great powers assembled in 1919 at Versailles.

Eventually, even Eastern Europe and the Balkans calmed down somewhat. In the various peace treaties dictated by the great powers, victorious Poland, Romania, and Yugoslavia were obligated to subscribe to clauses that protected minority rights. Leaders of the postwar states usually interpreted these clauses as unwanted intrusion into their country's sovereignty and did their best to ignore them, yet the League of Nations was not entirety powerless in remedying abuses committed against ethnic and religious minorities. Following World War II, the Paris peace treaties and the UN Charter left the protection of minorities to the sovereign governments, with the inevitable result of further persecution and expulsions until the much-longed-for goal of ethnic uniformity or purity was almost completely achieved.

[handwritten marginal note: Nazis against Jews were not the first true genocide.]

The post–World War I international community engaged in several new attempts to regulate warfare and to ease the life of civilians in occupied territories as well as that of prisoners of war and especially of their wounded. The seemingly greatest achievement toward regulating warfare was the Kellogg-Briand Pact, signed in Paris on August 27, 1928. Within one year, forty-four nations, including Germany but not Soviet Russia, solemnly accepted the treaty's provisions, renouncing war as an instrument of national policy. Rather than outlawing all wars, however, the pact called the wars of self-defense legitimate, and it did not make waging aggressive wars a criminal offense or contain any suggestion that individuals might be punished for the breach of peace. Unfortunately, not since Attila the Hun in the fifth century has a ruler or a government publicly admitted that it was conducting a war of aggression. Even the Nazis claimed to fight in self-defense.

Hitler's assumption of power and his activist foreign policy in the early 1930s were heralded as a legitimate assertion of a nation's right to self-determination that had been denied at the Paris peace treaties. The enthusiasm with which, in 1936, the German population west of the Rhine River greeted the remilitarization of the region, to be followed by the tumultuous celebration, in 1938, of the German army's entry first into Austria and then into the German-inhabited Sudetenland of Czechoslovakia, seemed to prove the righteousness of the German cause. Even the bloodless occupation, in the following year, of the rest of the Czech lands reinforced this widespread view. The Czechs may have been profoundly disappointed by these developments, but the world registered the fact that the Czechs had not fired a single shot at the occupying German forces.

At last, in September 1939, Great Britain and France declared war on Germany over the unprovoked invasion of Poland and the ruthless bombardment of its defenseless cities. But no help was given to the Poles, nor did many in the West notice that Polish resistance to the occupying power had begun virtually the day after the fall of Warsaw.

NOTES

1. See Otto Schwarz, ed., *Strafgesetzbuch, Nebengesetze, Verordnungen und Kriegsstrafrecht,* 12th rev. ed., 7th Great German ed. (Munich and Berlin: C. H. Beck'sche Verlagsbuchhandlung, 1943). Paragraph 211 on murder is cited on 335–338; the Führer decree of October 8, 1939, regarding the incorporated Eastern regions is on 1010–1012; and the subsequent edicts are on 1012–1019.

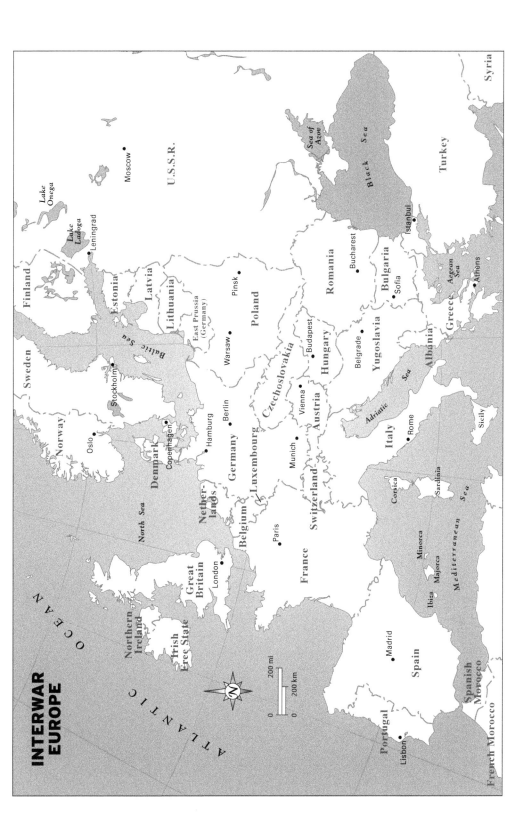

INTERWAR EUROPE

ATLANTIC OCEAN

Northern Ireland

Irish Free State

Great Britain

London

North Sea

Norway

Oslo

Sweden

Stockholm

Finland

Lake Onega

Lake Ladoga

Leningrad

Moscow

U.S.S.R.

Baltic Sea

Estonia

Latvia

Lithuania

Denmark

Copenhagen

Hamburg

Berlin

Germany

East Prussia (Germany)

Pinsk

Warsaw

Poland

Netherlands

Belgium

Luxembourg

Paris

France

Munich

Switzerland

Czechoslovakia

Vienna

Austria

Budapest

Hungary

Romania

Bucharest

Belgrade

Yugoslavia

Sofia

Bulgaria

Albania

Greece

Athens

Aegean Sea

Istanbul

Turkey

Syria

Black Sea

Sea of Azov

Adriatic Sea

Italy

Rome

Corsica

Sardinia

Minorca

Majorca

Ibiza

Mediterranean Sea

Sicily

Spain

Madrid

Portugal

Lisbon

Spanish Morocco

French Morocco

N

200 mi

0

200 km

0

2. Martin Rittau, ed., *Militärstrafgesetzbuch, in der Fassung vom 10 Oktober 1940—mit Einführungsgesetz und Kriegsstrafrechtsordnung* (Berlin: Walter de Gruyter Verlag, 1943), 99.

3. See W. Michael Reisman and Chris T. Antoniou, eds., *The Laws of War: A Comprehensive Collection of Primary Documents on International Laws Governing Armed Conflict* (New York: Vintage Books, 1994), 232–233; Lester Nurick and Roger W. Barrett, "Questions of Guerrilla Forces Under the Laws of War," *American Journal of International Law* 40, no. 3 (1946): 563–583; Kenneth Macksey, *The Partisans of Europe in the Second World War* (New York: Stein and Day, 1975), 17–18; and Major Richard R. Baxter, "The Duty of Obedience to the Belligerent Occupant," *British Yearbook of International Law* (1950): 235–255.

CHAPTER TWO

Austria, Czechoslovakia, and Poland

The First German Conquests

From the point of view of resistance and collaboration, it seems best to divide the history of World War II into three chronological periods. During the first, which lasted from September 1939 to June 1941, most Europeans accepted what appeared to be an irresistible German expansion and decided to live with the German hegemony. Even the mighty Soviet Union and the Communist Parties of the world acted during that period as unofficial allies of Hitler. The second phase opened on June 22, 1941, with Operation Barbarossa, simultaneously a military campaign, a ruthless colonizing venture, and an ideological crusade. The Germans and their many allies invaded the Soviet Union, intending to subjugate, rob, expel, and eventually exterminate a large part of the Eastern European population. Barbarossa was also the time when the Communists suddenly changed course and were now ready to risk life and limb in the struggle against what they called "the fascist beasts." At the same time, Prime Minister Winston Churchill expanded his ambitious program of "setting Europe ablaze" with the help of parachuted special agents and homegrown freedom fighters. Finally, the third phase began with the surrender of the German Sixth Army at Stalingrad in January 1943, a capitulation that alerted Europeans to the possibility of Germany losing the war and to the usefulness, even the necessity, of engaging in some kind of resistance activity. Clearly, then, collaboration must be discussed mainly in the context of the first two or three years of the war. Toward the end, only fools and fanatics remained in the German camp. In this chapter, we will be analyzing events in the three countries that first fell to the Germans, one happily, the other unhappily, and the third by never surrendering.

Between 1939 and 1941, Hitler and the German army went from triumph to triumph, less because of German material and manpower superiority over the other Europeans than because the rest of Europe, with the exceptions of Poland and Great Britain, haphazardly accepted German victory. Some did so in order to avoid a repetition of the horrors of World War I; others hoped to use the German presence for the achievement of national goals that they judged to be more important than the defense of civilization against the new barbarians. It will be one of the aims of this and the following chapter to show that, had they chosen to do so, the combined European forces could have successfully resisted German aggression. The later resistance movements attempted but could not fill the gap left behind by the shortcomings and failures of governments and peoples in Europe during the late 1930s and the early 1940s.

A PERFECT UNION

The German conquest began with the small country of Austria, which was also the first state to find seemingly persuasive excuses, after the war, for having jubilantly surrendered to Hitler. It is one of the great ironies of history that Austria emerged from World War II as a certified victim of German aggression.

Left over from the defunct Austro-Hungarian monarchy late in 1918, German Austria (today's Austrian republic) was built on very weak foundations. Once the center of the great Habsburg empire, also called Austria-Hungary, which ruled over much of Central Europe, the new Austrian state was only a shadow of its former self; moreover, its territorial elements had little unifying tradition and no common purpose to justify the country's existence. The new Austria was simply made up of territories that the other successor states of the Habsburg monarchy had neglected to grab.

The profound difference between the outlook and interests of a country's capital and those of its countryside was quite evident in interwar Austria, which was also the dilemma for many later European resistance movements. Catholic, rural, and archconservative Tyrol, for instance, had no sympathy for Vienna, the Social Democratic–run giant capital of a small country. Two of the republic's three major political parties, the leftist Social Democrats and the rightist German nationalists, wanted the country to unite with the newly created and then progressive German republic; only the so-called Christian Social Party was in favor of an independent, Catholic, conservative Austria. Union with the German republic, called the Anschluss, would have brought the realization of the old German patriotic dream: the creation of a Great German Reich. But fearing a much too strong Germany, the victorious Allies in 1919 categorically forbade such a move.

There were also good economic reasons for so many Austrians to cast their eyes on the German republic. Still, this "unwilling state," as many called it, was an independent republic to which its civil servants, police, and army had sworn loyalty. Thus, when, in 1938, the country's political, military, and administrative elite joined the population in frenzied jubilation over the invading German army, they were violating their oath to the constitution and committing treason.

The dictated peace treaty, signed at Saint-Germain, near Paris, in 1919, had allowed Austria a minuscule army of 30,000 volunteers; obviously, this would have been inadequate to stop the invading German army, but even some symbolic resistance, a few shots fired, would have created a great stir in Europe. But because of the total absence of resistance, no European government seriously protested the clear breach of international law and of the post–World War I peace treaty.

Before the German annexation, thousands of military and police officers as well as civil servants had secretly joined the illegal Austrian SS and SA, plotting to destroy their own country. Those opposed to the idea of an Anschluss were a small minority of devout Catholics, liberals, and Habsburg monarchists who abhorred one or another aspect of Nazism. Because even before 1938 most Austrians had become enthusiastic subjects of the German Führer, one cannot possibly talk of Austrian collaboration with Germany; the vast majority of Austrians saw themselves as German nationals and Austria as a group of German provinces that had at last been able to return to the Reich. During World War II, some 350 former Austrian career army officers served Hitler as generals; hundreds of thousands fought in other German ranks. As people of the Alps, moreover, Austrians constituted the bulk of Hitler's mountain divisions. Austrians were heavily involved in fighting partisans and executing so-called hostages in the Balkans; they also provided an extraordinary number of commanders and personnel to the SS-run concentration and death camps.

After the war, numerous Austrians figured as principal defendants at the international war crimes trials. In Austria itself, the US and other Allied denazification commissions had a hard time distinguishing between those Austrians who had been genuine members of the secret and illegal pre-Anschluss Austrian Nazi Party and those who, after the Anschluss, falsely claimed to have belonged, before 1938, to the illegal Austrian Nazi Party. Was such a lie, the Allies wondered, a punishable offense? And what about such former pseudo–Nazi Party members who claimed, during the post–World War II denazification proceedings, that, as disillusioned former Nazis, they had joined the party only so as to better resist German Nazism? Where did the lies stop and the truth begin?

While the overwhelming majority of Austrians enthusiastically embraced union with Nazi Germany in 1938, many individual Austrians fell victim to Nazi terror, and eventually there would arise a fair number of true Austrian resisters. In 1938 the Gestapo arrested thousands of Socialists, Catholics, and monarchists as well as leading figures of the pre-1938 anti-Nazi Catholic authoritarian state. Many were transported to the Dachau concentration camp; others ended up in the newly created Upper Austrian Mauthausen concentration camp.

Austrian Jews were brutally mistreated from the day of the German entry both by the Gestapo and by the local population. Indeed, with the Anschluss, a new phase began in the Nazi oppression of Jews: until 1938 individual Jews in Germany were thrown in concentration camps, abused, and even killed less because they were Jews than because they were Communists or Socialists. In annexed Austria, ordinary people fell upon and brutalized Jews in the streets of Vienna. In November 1938, during the so-called Kristallnacht (Crystal Night, or Night of Broken Glass), violence descended on the Jews of the entire enlarged Reich, very much including the Jews of former Austria.

WITHOUT FIRING A SHOT

If Austria's case was undoubtedly unique in wartime Europe, so was that of Hitler's first genuine victim, Czechoslovakia. Its special history determined, as we will see, the character and relative weakness of the Czech resistance movement and, conversely, the astonishing strength of the Slovak resistance.

Similar to the post–World War I Austrian republic, Czechoslovakia was an artificial construct. Having seceded from the collapsing Austrian half of the Habsburg monarchy, the western, Czech, half boasted a great historic and socioeconomic tradition; within it, Bohemia formed a nearly thousand-year-old kingdom whose university was one of the oldest in Europe. With the help of great natural resources and a diligent, relatively well-educated population, Bohemia's Habsburg rulers had fostered the industrialization of the Czech lands well before that of the other countries of their realm. As for the eastern, Slovak, half of the new state, there had never been a Slovakia; its territory had for a thousand years formed the northern mountainous part of the Hungarian kingdom. Whereas the Czech lands were economically advanced, Slovakia was poor and rural. The Czech lands had a large Czech, German, and Jewish middle class; in Slovakia the educated element spoke Hungarian and German rather than Slovak. Many Czechs were only nominally Catholic or Protestant; the Slovaks tended to take Catholicism very seriously. Czechs and Slovaks understand each other, but their languages are different.

Czechoslovakia came into being because a number of Czech and Slovak political émigrés had decided, during World War I, that the historic Czech lands should detach themselves from Austria and that the Slovak-speaking areas should detach themselves from Hungary. The émigrés then persuaded some Western statesmen, President Woodrow Wilson among them, that this would be the right thing to do. Indeed, even before the end of the war, the Allies declared the still nonexistent Czechoslovak state a cobelligerent, meaning that the hundreds of thousands of Slovak and Czech speakers in the Austro-Hungarian army now became something like honorary Allied soldiers. Meanwhile, they continued to fight on the side of the Central Powers. During World War I, there were many defections from the Austro-Hungarian army, especially by Czech-speaking soldiers, but the vast majority of Czechs and nearly all the Slovaks served under the Habsburg ruler to the last day of the war. Only thereafter did these defeated and exhausted men begin to grasp that they had just won the war, with a claim to Austro-Hungarian lands. The Croatian, Slovene, Serbian, Polish, Ukrainian, Romanian, and Italian soldiers of His Austro-Hungarian Majesty's armed forces fared similarly; it was only the German- and Hungarian-speaking soldiers who were considered defeated, and they alone were made responsible for the horrors of the war. The resulting mutual resentment among veterans of the same army was a major reason Central Europeans were later unwilling to unite against the Nazi menace.

[handwritten margin note: Very different living styles within the one country that very divided]

Interwar Czechoslovakia was a multiethnic state, in many ways no different from the Habsburg Austro-Hungarian monarchy from which it had emerged. Yet old Austria never claimed to be a nation-state (multiethnic Hungary, however, had made such a claim before 1914), whereas the new Czechoslovak government insisted that theirs was a nation-state with, admittedly, some ethnic minorities. The trouble was that, in reality, Czech speakers, the dominant ethnic group, constituted only one-half of the population; the other half consisted of Germans, Hungarians, Ruthenes or Rusyns and, yes, Slovaks, the latter because the Catholic majority of Slovaks saw themselves as a separate nation. Nazi propaganda later skillfully unmasked the fiction of Czechoslovakia as a nation-state.

The trouble originated with the country's founders, Tomáš Garrigue Masaryk and Edvard Beneš, who had won international support for the creation of a large state by cleverly combining arguments of national self-determination, historic political rights, economic necessity, and strategic considerations. Yet it is also true that, unlike its neighbors who were moving in an authoritarian direction, Czechoslovakia remained, until 1938, a parliamentary democracy in which no one was penalized for belonging to an ethnic or religious minority.

The bill for the original Czechoslovak territorial greed was presented at the Munich conference in September 1938 when the leaders of Great Britain and France surrendered to German pressure and offered to Hitler the German-speaking parts of the Czech lands. Czechoslovakia's military alliance with France and the Soviet Union turned out to be worthless; the Czechoslovak government was not even invited to the conference that decided the fate of their country. Immediately thereafter, Polish troops took over an important industrial section of the Czech lands, while Mussolini and Hitler ordered that southern Slovakia be returned to Hungary. The rest of Slovakia became autonomous.

What remained of Czechoslovakia desperately tried to imitate the authoritarian model so popular in Europe at that time, including the purge of Jews from state employment. The efforts came to naught because, in March 1939, the German army marched into Prague; the Hungarians overran and reannexed Ruthenia, at the eastern end of the former Czechoslovakia; Slovakia proclaimed its full independence, and the Czech lands were made a "protectorate" of the German Reich.

Most probably, Czechoslovakia could have defended itself with the help of its formidable fortifications. Actually, Hitler had originally planned to attack Czechoslovakia and was greatly disappointed when the Western powers forced him to the conference table. Yet he was lucky not to have been allowed to wage war, for, as the German general staff repeatedly pointed out to him, the army would have had a very hard time defeating Czechoslovakia, not to speak of a huge coalition that centered on France. Having been reduced to one hundred thousand volunteers by the peace treaty at Versailles, Germany in 1938 was in the midst of rearmament and would have had to face nearly a million well-trained and well-equipped Czechoslovak soldiers. The Czech armaments industry was one of the best in Europe; after the German occupation, Czech-made tanks, guns, and airplanes proved indispensable to the Nazi war machine for six long years.

Mobilization in Czechoslovakia in the fall of 1938 against a threatening German invasion was deemed a success: the reservists appeared for duty, although no one could tell how many soldiers of German, Hungarian, and Slovak ethnic origin were truly ready to lay down their lives for the country.

Poland was bigger and maintained a larger, although less well-equipped, army than Czechoslovakia: the two countries together may well have been successful against the Nazis. But rather than helping the Czechs, Poland turned against Czechoslovakia at the time of Munich; within a year, Poland disappeared from the face of the earth, and Polish-Czech hostility made cooperation even between the exile communities impossible.

Bitterness about the German occupation but also about what the Czechs viewed as betrayal by the Western powers might explain why so many Czechs tried to make the most of the German presence. They worked hard in the war industry and profited from the unending German demands for its products. Although there would be many Czech resisters, the nation as a whole decided not to sacrifice itself but to await liberation and then to take revenge on all Germans.

For the Protectorate of Bohemia and Moravia, as the Germans called what is today about two-thirds of the Czech Republic, the Reich government created a system that proved acceptable to most Czechs. The Czechoslovak army, or what had been left of it following the country's partition, was dissolved and its arms confiscated. The managers, engineers, and workers of the world-famous Škoda heavy industrial plant and similar industrial enterprises were allowed to stay at their jobs, unless they were Jews. Food rations were better in the Protectorate than in Germany proper, and workers' salaries were more or less the same. Most important,

a point often overlooked by historians, the inhabitants of the Protectorate were not called up for military service, which made the survival rate
among Czech males much higher than among Sudeten German males.
Czech businessmen made vast profits under German occupation, and the
average Czech family lived quite comfortably. Already during the war,
thousands of Sudeten Germans migrated to the Reich; their places were
taken by Czech immigrants from the Protectorate, so the ethnic balance
in Bohemia and Moravia changed in favor of the Czechs even under German rule.

The Czech government, which late in 1938 replaced Edvard Beneš and
other leaders who had fled to England, functioned under the presidency
of the compliant Czech lawyer-bureaucrat Emil Hácha. He was no Nazi;
he did not even have rightist sympathies, but he felt that it was his duty
to serve the Czech people in those tragic years. Ironically, all this made
Hácha and his cabinet members ideal collaborators: they were hardworking, reliable, politically conservative technicians, ready to do the Germans'
bidding while trying their best to protect those in their charge.

The Protectorate's administration remained in Czech hands but under the supervision of both Germans from the Reich and Sudeten Germans who were familiar with the affairs of their homeland. Some Czech
cabinet members worked secretly for Beneš and fellow exiles in London;
when caught, they were shot by the Germans, as was Prime Minister Alois
Eliáš in June 1942. Yet, in general, collaboration with the occupiers was a
smooth affair. Perhaps we should instead call it cooperation or accommodation; after all, collaboration implies a certain degree of ideological affinity or at least a shared long-term goal, yet this was not the case with most
Czechs, who were simply biding their time. In this model satellite, there
were only few enthusiastic and committed collaborators. Even the Czech
fascists, a small political party, were not in favor of the German occupation, nor did they have the ear of the German occupiers.

If the Czech lands produced the first collaborators and accommodators, they also produced some of the characteristic early resisters, brave individuals who maintained radio contact with the London exiles, engaged
in minor acts of sabotage, or were patriotic university students who ended
up in concentration camps. As long as the Soviet Union was an ally of
Germany—that is, until June 1941—the Czech Communist underground
praised "the brave German workers in uniform" and was critical of the

"Western imperialists." Now, however, the Communists became highly active in the "antifascist" resistance.

Following the German occupation of Prague, in March 1939, the Czechs actually had two governments: one in Prague, under German supervision, and the other in London, made up of Czech and Slovak exiles. The latter claimed to be the only legitimate government of momentarily nonexistent Czechoslovakia. Yet international recognition was not easy to come by; after all, it was the British government that at Munich had abandoned the Czechoslovak government and forced President Beneš into exile. When, however, the war was becoming more and more fierce, and finally even the Soviet Union joined the fray, all the Allied governments recognized the legitimacy of the Beneš regime. By 1942 the Polish, Norwegian, Dutch, Belgian, Luxembourgian, French, Greek, and Yugoslav exile governments were also in London and were accorded all the honors, if not all the power, of an Allied government. All were painfully aware that they and their followers were being housed and provided for by the British authorities, but whereas Polish, Norwegian, Dutch, and Belgian exile governments could use their exile armies and navies or their vast overseas colonies as bargaining chips in negotiations with the British leaders, others, especially the Czechoslovaks, had to strengthen their position vis-à-vis the Allies by adopting some desperate measures. The assassination of Acting Reich Protector Reinhard Heydrich in Prague was a means to that end.

The killing, in June 1942, of Heydrich, one of the vilest mass murderers in Nazi history, had been planned by the Czechoslovak government in exile in order to show the world that the Czech and Slovak peoples hated the German occupiers. The attackers were Czech and Slovak soldiers trained in Great Britain who parachuted over the Czech lands via the British air force. They acted in the name of the Czech resistance, but they were not of the Czech resistance. Unfortunately for President Beneš and his companions, bloody German revenge—as we shall see later—did not end massive Czech cooperation with the German occupiers. Following the arrests and execution of many of its members, the resistance movement remained isolated, now with even fewer active participants. As a result, the Czech lands and the Czechs themselves survived the war with far fewer casualties than any other country in Central and Eastern Europe.

Slovakia, which in 1938 had become autonomous, less than a year later proclaimed its independence; from then on, and despite the claims of some

[handwritten marginalia: How did two governments work? How was Germany okay with this?]

historians, it functioned not as a puppet state but as Nazi Germany's first but not last Slavic-speaking military ally. Slovakia's subsequent history differs fundamentally from that of Austria and that of the Czech lands. In Slovakia, and in other countries allied to the Third Reich, both friends and enemies of Nazi Germany faced a special dilemma: how to behave toward the national government that stood between them and Germany. Who, indeed, was a Slovak fascist's main friend: his own government or Hitler's empire? Conversely, who was the Slovak resister's main enemy: Father Jozef Tiso's anti-Semitic and wildly nationalist government or the German Nazis? Should one try to ally oneself, albeit temporarily, with the enemy of one's enemy? Such a triangular situation was very common in Europe in those days. The strengths and weaknesses of Germany's alliance systems and the dilemmas of the local resisters and collaborators will be discussed in the chapter on Hitler's allies.

TO THE LAST BULLET

Similar to Czechoslovakia, Poland emerged from World War I an independent state; previously, it was divided between Germany, Austria-Hungary, and Russia. The dilemma of the new-old state can easily be imagined: among other things, during World War I, Polish soldiers fought each other in the trenches; hence, liberation and unification, or, rather, reunification, took place under extremely difficult conditions. Fortunately for the Poles, the Western Allies were so keen on building a bulwark against both German revanchism and Russian Bolshevism that they readily overlooked problems such as that the leader of national resurgence, Józef Piłsudski, had started his wartime career in the service of Austria-Hungary.

In an attempt to reclaim Poland's historic borders that, before the First Partition in 1772, included much of Eastern Europe and much of today's Russia and Ukraine, reborn Poland strove to expand its rule far beyond its ethnic boundaries. This led to a war, in 1919–1920, against the Russian Bolsheviks, which the Poles won, arousing the undying hatred of Stalin as well as a huge ethnic problem at home. Ukrainians, Belarusians, Lithuanians, the generally unassimilated Jews, and Germans made up more than one-third of the population. Poland treated its minorities worse than Czechoslovakia did: as a result, Ukrainian resentment became particularly dangerous. Still, following the age-old East European tradition of finding easy scapegoats for one's troubles, many Polish leaders and much

Image 2.1. Monsignor Jozef Tiso, president of independent Slovakia during World War II, in the company of German diplomats. Tiso was hanged by the judgment of a Slovak court after the war. Source: Corbis.

of the public focused their resentment on the harmless and powerless Jewish minority.

Interwar Poland had a functioning multiparty parliament, which included minority representation, but it slipped from time to time into authoritarian military rule. Some of its soldiers and politicians harbored great-power ambitions, forgetting that Poland was much weaker than its Soviet and German neighbors, let alone a combination of the two.

Confident that they would benefit from the promised political and military support of France and Great Britain, the Polish government in August 1939 defied Hitler's demand for territorial revisions. On August 23, the so-called Molotov-Ribbentrop Pact, signed in Moscow, provided for Poland's fourth partition. This monstrous agreement, from whose implications the world has yet to recover, contained a secret clause dividing all of Eastern Europe between Hitler and Stalin.

The unjustified German military attack on Poland, on September 1, was followed by British and French declarations of war. Yet the two great powers never seriously attempted to challenge the extremely weak Western German defenses.* In fact, by vastly and deliberately exaggerating the German strength, and by advocating a purely defensive strategy, the French high command took the first step toward the surrender of Western European democracies to the "Third Reich." The Polish army fought with traditional bravery, but it had already lost the war against the Germans when, on September 17, the Soviet Red Army entered the fray, occupying the entire eastern half of Poland and capturing tens of thousands of unsuspecting Polish soldiers. Caught between the two invaders, only about one hundred thousand Polish soldiers managed to flee through then neutral Romania and Hungary to take up the fight in the West. This was the beginning of Polish exile armies fighting against the Nazis in Norway, France, Belgium, and the Netherlands; over Great Britain in the air; and later in Italy as well as under the command of the Soviet Red Army. In addition, the Polish navy played a major role in combating the Germans on the high seas.

In the fall of 1939, much of western Poland was incorporated into the German Reich; the central provinces, including Warsaw and Cracow, were renamed Generalgouvernement (Government General) and were subjected to the absolute rule of a German plenipotentiary. Meanwhile, the Soviet Union officially annexed the eastern half of Poland. Ethnic Poles in western Poland were expelled to the Government General, especially those who appeared "racially inferior," or when a German coveted their business or land. Those younger Poles who were allowed to stay in the former western Poland were drafted into the German army and suffered the fate of all

---

*In September 1939, during the so-called Saar Offensive, which was the only military action the Western Allies undertook on behalf of Poland, 110 French and British divisions advanced on 20 German divisions; still, within a few days and after suffering only a few casualties, the Allies withdrew to their starting lines.

Question 3 of why resulted in a little fighting: limited action between the two countries

Wehrmacht soldiers. Those in the Government General were considered slave labor and were shot or hanged under the slightest pretext.

German treatment of the Poles was infinitely crueler than the treatment that the German authorities meted out to the Czechs, another Slavic-speaking nation. This shows that although all Slavs were considered inferior to the Germanic peoples, not all Slavs were treated the same: some were allowed to function as Germany's valuable allies, while others were perceived as enemies to be persecuted and eventually deported or killed.

In what used to be eastern Poland, the Polish population was lorded over by local Ukrainians, Belarusians, and Jews. Other Poles were

Why was their treatment so much harsher?

deported to Russia, together with masses of captive soldiers and such Ukrainians, Belarusians, and Jews whom the Soviet authorities judged to be too "polonized" or too "bourgeois." Only a minority of the deportees survived the war. Yet at least under Soviet rule, a cunning Pole could get himself accepted as a Communist or a sympathizer; in the Government General, no collaboration was invited or tolerated. True, the services of some journalists, minor businessmen, and local policemen were used, but their lives were as precarious as those of the rest of the population. There never were any Polish SS men or Polish concentration camp commanders and guards. Finally, unlike the Czech protectorate, occupied Poland had no president, no government, and no native high officials; the latter were all in exile, at first in Paris and later in London. Under German rule, all Poles had to work for wages and food rations that were barely sufficient to keep body and soul together.

If life for Poles was harsh under German rule, life for the 3 million Polish Jews was simply a preparation for death. Some Poles make much of what they call Jewish collaboration with the German occupation forces, meaning those Jews who headed the so-called Jewish Councils that the Germans had created, served in the Jewish police (which was armed only with batons), or acted as spies and agents of some German intelligence service. But these individuals simply tried to prolong their lives and those of their families; they were not committed collaborators. The same principle applies, as we shall see, to the Jewish resistance: a non-Jew in Europe could generally choose between collaboration and resistance, between passivity and activism; Jews could at most choose between a quick death and a delayed death. Most had no choice whatsoever.

What we have learned so far is that Poland's battle-scarred history almost naturally led to the creation of a massive anti-Nazi resistance movement, that Polish life under German and Soviet rule was tragic, and that each major historical event during the war only exacerbated the hatred Poles felt for Germany and the Soviet Union. Yet there were also bloody conflicts between Polish Communists and non-Communists as well as between Poles and other ethnic groups. Clearly, then, the bulk of the Polish wartime story belongs not here but in the chapters on the resistance movements.

CHAPTER THREE

Defeat and Submission

Europe's Honeymoon with Hitler, 1939–1941

Poland's tragic demise, in September 1939, was followed by a relatively uneventful seven months, the so-called Phony War between Great Britain and France, on the one hand, and Germany, on the other. The astonishingly quiet international scene was disturbed only by the Soviet Red Army's attack on Finland, which was motivated by the desire to extend Soviet power all the way from the Baltic Sea to the Black Sea. Between November 1939 and March 1940, in the so-called Winter War, a country of 4 million stood up to a country of 170 million with, at first, nothing but Finnish successes. At last, after suffering terrible losses due to bad leadership and poor morale, the Soviets prevailed, forcing a peace treaty and some territorial concessions on Finland. The latter had won the admiration of both warring camps.* What the public tended to overlook was that no Scandinavian country hastened to the aid of their Finnish neighbor, not even in diplomacy, mainly because Nazi Germany was at that time an ally of the Soviet Union and no Scandinavian government wished to aggravate Hitler. Within a year and a half of the Winter War, Denmark and Norway suffered German occupation; Finland became embroiled in an even more savage second war with the Soviet Union; and Sweden alone remained neutral, at the price of acting as Nazi Germany's indispensable supplier of iron ore, steel, and machinery.

---

*In the winter of 1939–1940, it became clear, for instance, that the British public would rather fight the Soviet Union than Germany; indeed, plans were made for sending the British Expeditionary Force to assist the Finns, but the German invasion of Norway put an end to such dreams.

The Winter War gave Hitler the correct impression that the democratic states of Europe would never seriously contemplate combining their forces against aggression. Instead, they would try to avoid conflicts; failing that, they would separately surrender. But they also gave Hitler the incorrect impression that the Soviet Union was hopelessly weak, a "clay colossus without a head," as he called it,[1] and mortally dangerous to the Reich.

Today it is hard to fathom why the countries of northern and Western Europe, economically among the most advanced in the world, with exceptionally healthy populations, would make no effort to prepare for the eventuality of war. Norway had at that time 3 million inhabitants, Denmark nearly 4 million, the Netherlands almost 9 million, Belgium well over 8 million, and France 40 million; each could have mustered a formidable army. Moreover, the Netherlands, Belgium, and France possessed immense colonial empires; the matériel and manpower resources (colonial troops) available in the three empires far surpassed the means available to Germany. French armament production was superior to that of the Germans almost until the outbreak of the war; the French navy was bigger than the German navy, to name just a few comparisons.

According to contemporary military thinking, modern industrialized countries practicing universal conscription could train and mobilize 10 percent of their population for war. For Belgium, this would have meant a trained force of 800,000 and for the total forces of Norway, Denmark, the Netherlands, Belgium, Luxembourg, and France 7 or 8 million men in uniform. Together, they could have created the best-trained and best-equipped army in the world, added to which would have been the certainty of British and British Commonwealth intervention on their behalf. Their combined armies would not have had to engage in symbolic resistance; they could have defeated Nazi Germany. Or their combined stance would have persuaded Hitler not to engage in aggression.

All this may sound outlandish, and in reality it was, indeed, very different. Having been neutral during World War I, Norway, Denmark, and the Netherlands tried to preserve their neutrality by conspicuously limiting the size of their armed forces. Amazingly, the Netherlands, a wealthy country with nearly 9 million loyal inhabitants and a huge colonial empire, had only twenty-six armored vehicles and not a single tank to oppose an eventual German invasion. Yet the Dutch general staff had firm evidence, from documents that had fallen into their hands, that, in the case of a war with France and Great Britain, the German army would march into the Netherlands—as it indeed did in May 1940. Some German generals, who back in 1938 started plotting to overthrow Hitler, repeatedly informed the British—and through them all the affected countries—that the Führer was planning to attack them. Instead of engaging in mutual consultations, the Danes withdrew their already meager forces from the German border, making clear to all that they had no desire to defend themselves. As for the Norwegians and the Dutch, they kept emphasizing their neutrality even after the German forces had begun moving against them.[2]

Perhaps the saddest case of the loss of self-confidence was that of Belgium, which, in 1936, publicly proclaimed its neutrality and threatened to oppose the French and British with arms were they to enter Belgium in the case of war. Back in 1914, full-fledged Belgian cooperation with Great Britain and France prevented a German victory. In 1940, when the Germans attacked Belgium, again without any provocation, the French and British troops were allowed into Belgium so late as to make them worthless. Worse even, they were trapped when the king of the Belgians, Leopold III, threw in the towel after a few days of fighting.

Before World War I, the French government and military were so systematically preparing for revenge against Germany that they had virtually no plans for defense; the prevailing ideology was "attack, always attack." In August 1914, when the German army's right wing furiously advanced through Belgium toward Paris, the French high command threw millions of men against the German left wing, suffering defeat and terrible losses. Only when it was nearly too late did the French and the British Expeditionary Force change tactics and finally stop the German advance on the Marne River, near Paris. Having drawn the wrong lesson from World War I and ignoring changes brought by tanks and airplanes, the French now put their faith in the so-called Maginot line of fortifications that had not even been extended along the Franco-Belgian border. In May 1940, the Germans easily broke through the Franco-British front and circumvented the Maginot line. In brief, between April and June 1940, the German army conquered all of northern and Western Europe with only small losses. It also acquired an industrial base and port installations that from then on made Germany appear invincible.

The reasons for this collective debacle have been insufficiently recognized, yet there can be no doubt as to the defeatist attitude of the Western and northern European governments, military, and peoples when confronted with German Nazi aggression. In France, especially, many right-wing political leaders and big businessmen preferred Nazi rule to what they wrongly perceived to be the threat of a Communist takeover. As some said, "Better Hitler than Stalin." What made things worse was that in these countries, the political Far Left also agitated against rearmament and "war preparations," expressing their hatred for the "bourgeois French republic." Following the Molotov-Ribbentrop Pact, the Communist leadership in France virtually went over to the Nazi side, spreading propaganda against "the imperialist war within the capitalist camp" and preaching mass disobedience. The Communist slogan "Fight War and Fascism" was used for strikes against the French war industry. Add to this propaganda the general desire for peace, the widespread admiration for the real and pretended social and economic achievements of German National Socialism and Italian Fascism, and the contempt for the "corrupt republic" as well as the near-incredible incompetence of the French commanders. Yet even these factors do not explain the Western and northern Europeans' unwillingness to combine their actions and to prefer ruin, foreign occupation, and national humiliation to armed resistance.

The theoretical question of collaboration assumed real urgency following the surrender of France on June 22, 1940, and the formation of a new national government under Marshal Philippe Pétain. The latter promised to complement the surrender with a "national revolution" aimed at creating a rejuvenated and pro-German France.

Before going into any detail here, we must note that cooperation with Nazi Germany, or at least the toleration of the German presence, was facilitated by the initial exemplary behavior of the German occupation forces. Whether at Narvik, in the far North of Norway, or at Bordeaux in southern France, the German soldiers were instructed to be polite, to observe local customs, and to pay for merchandise—although it would be paid in occupation currency of doubtful value. In other words, the soldiers behaved as the best of tourists. Myths of Nazi brutality and immediate popular repudiation of the German presence, propagated by political exiles in Great Britain, reflected wishful thinking. These stories were contradicted by the photographs of blonde Danish girls arm in arm with German soldiers and elegant *Parisiennes* appearing at the Longchamp horse races in the company of German officers, as well as the initial smooth cooperation between occupier and occupied.

Why did the Germans treat those nations gently that had so easily accepted their own dishonor and defeat? The reason was simple: Hitler had no interest in colonizing the North and the West; he had fought the war there reluctantly. He was not even certain whether he wished to reannex the former German province of Alsace-Lorraine, in northeastern France. The area of Nazi colonization, of total conquest, lay not there but in the East. For this end, the Nazis needed—and generally received—the willing cooperation of the Western and northern Europeans.

Obviously, generalizations can be carried too far; there was, after all, a good deal of difference between the geographic positions, national traditions, past politics, and ethnic problems of, for example, Norway and Belgium. Despite the initial general German restraint, the treatment meted out to the defeated countries varied substantially, depending on such factors as the perceived race of the inhabitants, the circumstances of the country's surrender, its strategic and economic importance, the willingness of the local population and of its leaders to cooperate, and, last but not least, which German power group had succeeded in obtaining control of the place to the detriment of other German power groups. As it turned out, none of the conquered countries denied cooperation with the occupiers, but none completely satisfied the German requirements, either.

TOWARD A "GREAT GERMANIC" BROTHERHOOD?

Undoubtedly, "race" was an important consideration in Nazi eyes: Norwegians, Danes, the Dutch, and the Flemish-speaking majority of the Belgians were Germanic peoples, closely related to the German Volk. As for the small Grand Duchy of Luxembourg at Germany's southwest border, which the German army also occupied in May 1940, they were seen simply as Germans speaking one of the many German dialects.

The German Nazis were especially keen on seeing in the Norwegians the idealized "Nordic Aryans": tall, athletic, blond and blue-eyed, and therefore admirably suited for interbreeding as well as for participation in the great German national enterprise. Never mind that, in their majority, the Germans themselves were not blond and blue-eyed: in Nazi ideology, the Norwegians stood for the much-admired Viking tradition, that of the bravest of the brave among warriors and sailors.

In the Nazi view, Danes fell into the same racial category as the Norwegians, except that whereas the Norwegian army had put up a short but brave resistance to the German invasion (with, in fact, British, French, and Polish military assistance), Denmark had surrendered without firing a shot. Moreover, while the Norwegian king Haakon VII and his government had fled to Great Britain and only the Norwegian army capitulated, King Christian X of Denmark immediately signed the surrender document. Government, parliament, and every single state and municipal institution continued to function. As a consequence, the Norwegians were subjected to the arbitrary rule of a German high commissioner, assisted by the self-appointed prime minister, Vidkun Quisling. (As is well known, the early collaborationist Quisling unwillingly gave his name to the practice of voluntary and ideological cooperation with the occupying enemy.) The Danes, on the other hand, were allowed to preserve their own system of government and their laws, a choice example of accommodation with the occupier paying immediate dividends.

Occupied Norway was run by native civil servants under close German supervision; Denmark continued under its old form of government, and, in March 1943, it was even allowed to hold fair and open parliamentary elections. While the Social Democrats received the highest number of votes, the Danish Nazi Party had to be satisfied with a little more than 2 percent of support. In Norway relations between occupiers and occupied were rather tense from the beginning; in Denmark near-ideal conditions prevailed for the Germans who were lucky enough to be stationed there. Whereas in both Norway and Denmark there were thousands of collaborators as well as volunteers for the SS, only in Denmark did the government become an official ally of Nazi Germany: in November 1941, the Danish government entered the so-called Anti-Comintern Pact, whose goal was to destroy the Soviet Union and communism.* The Danish government outlawed the Communist Party and arrested many of its members. Signing the Anti-Comintern Pact seemed to be a clear declaration of agreement with the war goals of Hitler, yet, in reality, the Danish government did its best to mitigate the devastating propaganda effect of its own pro-German action.

Let us note here that the Anti-Comintern Pact, signed by Germany and Japan in November 1936, was later signed by Italy, Hungary, Manchukuo

---

Comintern is the abbreviated form of the term *Communist International,* a theoretically supranational organization of the world's Communist Parties and of such left-wing Socialist Parties that recognized the leadership of Soviet Russia and of Lenin as well as, later, Stalin. Founded in 1919, the Comintern, whose headquarters were in Moscow, was disbanded in 1943 in order to demonstrate the unified will of all antifascists. In reality, the hegemony of Stalin and of the Soviet Union continued for quite some time over the world's Communist Parties.

(a Japanese puppet government in Manchuria), Spain, Finland, Romania, Bulgaria, Croatia, Denmark, Slovakia, and Nanjing China (another Japanese puppet government), making it look as if Hitler and his allies half dominated the world. The strange thing about it all was that the target of the alliance, the Soviet Union, became Germany's most important unofficial ally in 1939, and even after Germany had attacked the Soviet Union in 1941, Japan continued to maintain friendly relations with its supposed archenemy.

After the war turned against the Germans, more and more Danes dared to defy the occupiers: the strikes and anti-Nazi demonstrations caused the occupying authorities in August 1943 to proclaim a state of siege; the Danish police were put under surveillance, and the Danish army was dissolved. It looked like the end of Danish autonomy, but, in reality, the somewhat reshuffled Danish government and civil service continued to run the country to the end of the war under generally sympathetic German plenipotentiaries. The complex game played by the Danish government was characteristic of many other European countries, yet Denmark was and remained in German eyes a model satellite, similar to the Protectorate of Bohemia and Moravia and another, smaller, area of Europe whose identity we shall reveal later.

If we compare all this with the savage oppression that the Germans visited upon Poland in the same period—ruined cities, starvation, thousands arbitrarily imprisoned or shot, Polish resisters tortured and killed in Auschwitz—then it will become clear that the German occupation was far from meaning the same thing in all places. Allied propaganda spoke of the uniform suffering of captive nations; in reality, life in Hitler's Europe was more divergent than perhaps at any time in history.

Strategically, Norway was so crucial for the Germans as to cause the stationing there of an almost unbelievably large occupation force of three hundred thousand soldiers. Denmark, although an invaluable source of agricultural and industrial products, was never threatened by an Allied invasion or even by an Allied commando raid. Thus, there were times when the occupation forces amounted to only a few thousand soldiers.

The different surrenders of Norway and Denmark created dilemmas for every politically conscious citizen. Whom was a Norwegian patriot to obey: his king and government, who were calling for resistance from the safety of England, or the civil servants at home, who were responsible for the everyday running of affairs and whose aim was to keep the country as calm as possible in order to improve general conditions? And what was a patriotic Dane to do when witnessing his government's kowtowing to the occupiers and thereby securing for him and his family an undisturbed and often prosperous existence?

Finally, just a few words—to be expanded later—on the connection between collaboration with the enemy and the chances of Jewish survival; note, however, that in both Norway and Denmark, Jews were a negligible presence, making up far less than 1 percent of the population. Yet whereas in Norway the local authorities and the population were, with the exception of some in the resistance movement, uninterested in saving the lives of most of the country's seventeen hundred Jewish citizens, in collaborationist Denmark the government and the population—as well as the local German occupation forces—succeeded in protecting the lives of nearly all of their eight thousand Jewish inhabitants. What conclusions can be drawn from this will be discussed in the chapter on the European resistance movements. It should be enough to say here that cooperation—for instance, in efficiently producing heavy guns for the occupier—did not exclude secretly fighting the occupier, even with arms. Conversely, many mortal enemies of Nazi Germany did not hesitate in lending assistance to the Nazis in the hunt for Jews.

Another important and highly developed democratic Western European country conquered by the Germans was the Netherlands. There the extent of military resistance to the fully unprovoked German attack fell somewhere between that of Norway and Denmark. Queen Wilhelmina and her government fled to England; the army then surrendered, and the Dutch settled down to life under the leadership of their civil servants and city mayors. The Germans saw the Dutch as a Germanic people who, the occupiers hoped, would "Nazify themselves" and would eventually join the Reich. Because the Netherlands had less strategic significance than Norway, few German troops were stationed there. As in Norway and Denmark, the German soldiers must have felt privileged to be assigned to that location.

To a certain extent, the Netherlands was a special case, because Hitler entrusted the country not to the German army or the SS security police but to Artur Seyss-Inquart, the pre-Anschluss leader of the underground Austrian Nazi Party. Entrusted with dictatorial powers, the new viceroy then tried to educate the Dutch for future membership in the Third Reich. Meanwhile, in Belgium the Wehrmacht ruled supreme.

Native Nazi Parties were active in all these countries both before and during the war, but none ever gained a mass membership, nor were the Germans interested in bringing them to power. They preferred to rule through experienced conservative, old-regime politicians and obedient bureaucrats. Interestingly, however, in the Netherlands a new organization called Nederlandse Unie (Dutch Union) arose, which attempted to bring about revolutionary changes in national politics. Created by anti-Communist and conservative middle-class elements, Nederlandse Unie hoped to turn the Netherlands into a one-party state, not at all sympathetic to Nazism but not democratic, either. At the end of 1941, the German authorities put an end to this experiment, and the traditional political parties took over, acting in the underground.

In the Netherlands, nonideological collaboration was practiced by the so-called secretaries of state who, in the absence of the royal government, ran the everyday affairs and by the national administration at large, which fulfilled the Germans' political and economic demands. Among other things, governmental offices collected and kept accurate statistics on the country's Jews. Dutch precision and reliability also infected the Jewish Council (Judenrat or Joodse Raad) created by the Germans, whose respectable members performed impeccably under their German superiors. Strict obedience to German commands was also the order of the day at the Jewish Council in Warsaw, but there the council members faced the choice between collective death and trying to satisfy the Germans by offering Jewish skills to the war industry. In the end, as it turned out, economic cooperation saved only a few lives, which was still better than none. But in Amsterdam, in 1940, members of the Jewish Council did not have to fear immediate extermination; there is really no excuse for their servile submission to the Germans to whom they gave the name and data of every Jew in the Netherlands.

Nor did the Dutch Communists behave any better, at first. Similar to the French and other Communists, they agitated in their underground publications not against the Nazis but against "the imperialistic struggle between two capitalist states to achieve European and even world domination." The Communists also continued to excoriate the Social Democrats for supporting "the conflict between German and British imperialism." It is true, however, that many individual Communists changed to the anti-Nazi side well before the German attack on the Soviet Union.

As for Dutch industry and agriculture, their initial collaboration with the occupiers was complete: during the war, the total value of Dutch goods exported to Germany amounted to about 8.5 billion guilders (at the time, US$3 billion), of which almost two-thirds was for military goods.

No doubt, there was also such a thing as a heroic and widespread Dutch resistance, which we will discuss in the chapters on the European resistance movements; still, when contemplating the Netherlands story, we cannot help feeling that the democratic countries' extensive collaboration with Nazi Germany would have not happened without their earlier military surrender to Nazi Germany.

THE BELGIANS AND THE FRENCH UNDER GERMAN RULE

So far, we have been talking only of collaboration in such "Germanic" countries that the Nazis saw as likely candidates for complete *Eindeutschung,* that is, Germanization. Belgium was a different case because next to its Flemish, Germanic-speaking majority, it contained a large minority of French-speaking Walloons whose upper classes were vastly overrepresented in the administration, the armed forces, and the universities. The language of the royal house, as it was of the intellectuals, was primarily French. Some conservative and far-right Walloon leaders liked to brag that they were of Germanic origin, but this did not endear them to the German Nazis, who could never really decide whether the French, and French speakers in general, were corrupted, even "mongrelized," misfits or exciting and enviable creatures whom one should try to imitate for the elegance and beauty of their women, the marvels of their cuisine, and the general refinement of their lifestyle. Paris, especially, both attracted and repelled the occupiers.

The occupation of France and French collaboration make for a unique story, in part because these events are so well researched and, in part, because, far more so than the Netherlands and Belgium, France remained an empire, a great colonial power, with a large navy and a substantial colonial army and police whose existence the German occupiers had to take into account.

Following the long Phony War, Germany attacked France on May 10, 1940, and even though some French troops fought on for six weeks, with 120,000 casualties, the battle had been lost within the first two weeks. Among other catastrophes, a large part of the French army as well as the

Image 3.1. German troops marching down the Champs-Élysées in Paris. Source: Bundesarchiv, Bild 183-S58183 / photo: o.Ang.

entire British Expeditionary Force were encircled by the German tank divisions in Belgium: luckily, between May 27 and June 4, nearly 200,000 British and 140,000 French soldiers managed to escape to Great Britain. This famous battle at Dunkirk (in French, Dunkerque) on the French coast saved Great Britain and should have solidified the alliance of the

Question 7

two nations. Instead, nearly all the French soldiers chose to be repatriated, and Brigadier General Charles de Gaulle, who had flown to England to continue the fight from there, found himself without followers. The French had had it with the war.

The Germans rightly referred to their campaign as *Blitzkrieg,* a lightning-fast war: on June 16, the prowar French prime minister resigned in favor of the World War I hero Marshal Philippe Pétain, who immediately announced that he would sue for an armistice. The latter was signed on June 22 under humiliating conditions, and on July 1 the French parliament voted extraordinary powers to Pétain, making him head of state. Thus, unlike Poland, Norway, the Netherlands, and Belgium but very much like Denmark, France came out of defeat with its own head of state and government, even an army of 100,000 men—which was exactly what the Allies had granted the German republic in 1919.

Defeated France was divided into five parts: the so-called Occupied Zone, which included two-thirds of continental France, with Paris as its center, and extended along the Atlantic coast all the way to the Spanish frontier; two departments in the North, which came under the German military authorities in Belgium; the Free or Unoccupied Zone, which included most of southern France; a narrow strip along the Italian border, which was occupied by Italian troops and where Jews found asylum until Italy's attempt to surrender to the Allies in September 1943 when it was occupied by German troops; and, finally, the French empire, which included much of northern, central, and western Africa as well as Indochina, French Guyana, and some islands in the Pacific and the Atlantic Ocean.

The politically and economically most important territories were the Occupied and the Unoccupied Zones; travel between the two was very difficult, and the Germans never really made clear how much power the Vichy government would be allowed to exercise over the Occupied Zone. Authority in the latter was uneasily shared by competing German occupation organs and the French police and administration. Yet nothing illustrates better the awkward situation in which France found itself during the war than that although the home country was divided into small parts, the Germans never took over any of France's colonial possessions, nor did a single French warship fall into German hands.

Unlike the other defeated Western European states but somewhat similar to the Czech state in 1939, the new French government immediately went beyond just trying to live with surrender and foreign occupation; it

started a "national revolution" that would enable the new state, or so it was hoped, to find its place in a German-dominated Europe. Under Pétain, all those who had disliked the republic and the republican institutions, and who felt that France had been on the wrong track since the Enlightenment and the French Revolution, stepped forward. Their goal was to restore a mythical pre-Revolutionary France based on traditional Catholic values. The new government, settling in the resort town of Vichy in the Unoccupied Zone, declared that moral decline spread by godless Marxists, liberals, Freemasons, and especially Jews had undermined France and was responsible for the military defeat. This so-called Vichy regime hoped to purify France and bring back the age of the medieval king Saint Louis IX and of "La Pucelle," the virgin Joan of Arc. Thus, fascinatingly, the idea of national purification, of purges, originated not from the triumphant anti-Nazi resisters following the defeat of Nazi Germany but from the first collaborators in defeated and occupied France.

Some of those in charge at Vichy were morally flexible old-regime politicians and technicians, others were adventurers and opportunists, and still others came from among the many soldiers, aristocrats, and Catholic clerics who had been feeling neglected and oppressed in republican France; their grievances went back to the turn of the twentieth century, when the case of Captain Alfred Dreyfus, a Jew, had divided society. Then and for a long time thereafter, two camps faced each other: in one were the progressives, the anticlericals, the free-thinkers, and other liberals who accused the army high command of having scapegoated a Jew in the mysterious case of military espionage on behalf of the German Empire. In the other camp were those who, even after Dreyfus's innocence had become crystal clear, claimed that the army's prestige was more important than justice toward an individual. Step by step, the so-called Dreyfusards won the battle and purged many real or suspected anti-Dreyfusards from the political and military leadership. Now, in 1940, the anti-Dreyfusards and their descendants could have their revenge.

Characteristically for Hitler's Europe, such Frenchmen who actually swore by Hitler—in other words, the pro-Nazi fanatics—were generally kept away from the seat of government. They assembled in Paris, in the German occupation zone, where Otto Abetz, the Francophile German ambassador, might have innocently created the illusion among the French radicals of a great and militantly fascistic France one day marching alongside Nazi Germany. Many Frenchmen believed Abetz: in the words of the French fascist philosopher Pierre Drieu La Rochelle, "Only Germany can assure hegemony in Europe. She is at its center, her population is double that of any other European nation, she holds and can keep critical strategic points, but most of all, she possesses the greatest organizational, material, and spiritual resources in the world."[3]

Unfortunately for the French fascists, Ambassador Abetz had to share power with a number of German military, political, economic, and SS/Gestapo authorities; put another way, the German Embassy in Paris constituted just one center of power in the vast web of complex, intriguing, and mutually hostile occupation organs. Such was the reality of German power in all the occupied countries but especially in France. In their majority, the

German leaders, from Hitler down, would not think of putting French fascists and Nazis in power. What if one day they became the ideological rivals of the German National Socialists?

The pro-Nazi French radicals in Paris were a variegated lot made up of ex-Communists, professional anti-Semites, fascists, dogmatic pacifists, and self-centered journalists, writers, and poets. Some were highly talented, such as writer Louis-Ferdinand Céline, although one wonders how anyone can feel enthusiastic about the writings of a person who hated all "non-Aryans" and who after the war became an unabashed Holocaust denier.

What the Paris radicals had in common was their hatred of the defunct Third Republic that had not sufficiently appreciated their talents and the contempt they felt for the conservatives and opportunists at Vichy. They admired Nazi ideals and policies, and they aspired to create a racially clean, rejuvenated France. They abominated the Jews and, particularly, the Eastern European Jewish immigrants and refugees whom they saw as vermin, the ultimate corrupters of the noble French nation, especially of young French women.

The Paris radicals were a noisy lot, and although they had no real power, they succeeded in whipping up public animosity toward the Western Allies, the Soviets, and the Jews. Because the latter alone were available as scapegoats for the defeat of France, the radicals heaped relentless abuse on them and their non-Jewish "hirelings." Never mind that in both world wars, French Jewish soldiers suffered a proportional number of losses in dead and wounded and that many French Jews had given proof of their ardent patriotism. So did Captain Dreyfus, for that matter, who professed his undying loyalty to the fatherland even when chained to his cot for years on end on Devil's Island.

Effective and direct assistance to the German occupiers was the specialty not of the Paris radicals but of the government at Vichy. The term *collaboration,* to denote working voluntarily with the occupying power, originated from Marshal Pétain, who, after the handshake with Hitler at a meeting at Montoire-sur-le-Loir, in October 1940, proclaimed, "I enter, today, into the way of collaboration." Thus, a perfectly innocent term came to denote, first, the hopes of a profoundly humiliated nation and, later, cowardly treason. Naturally, there was to be no equality between the two countries: the French had to pay a huge indemnity as well as bear the astronomical costs of foreign occupation. They were also to deliver food, other goods, and, later, forced labor to Germany for almost no pay.

At first, French collaboration was greatly assisted by a dramatic incident that occurred, in July 1940, at Mers-el-Kébir, a French North African naval base. Worried, probably without reason, that the French would allow their warships to fall into German hands, thereby causing Britain to lose its naval superiority and thus the war, Prime Minister Churchill ordered the admiralty to neutralize the French fleet at any cost. But when British battleships appeared at Mers-el-Kébir, the French commander refused either to join the British in the war or to scuttle his ships. Thereupon, British naval guns sank a French battleship and destroyed or at least badly damaged many other French warships. In turn, the French shot down at least one British warplane. More than eleven hundred French sailors were killed by their former allies, an outrage that reawakened the old antagonism between the two nations. Now the collaborators had a powerful argument against British perfidy; Pétain was widely celebrated, nay adulated, as the defender of the nation, and few listened to or even heard of de Gaulle's initial London broadcasts. Rarely did a nation's collective mood change as dramatically as it did in France at that time.

French collaboration took many forms during the honeymoon years of the German occupation: Pierre Laval, the prime minister under Pétain and a former Socialist, guided the country steadily in the direction of ever-better relations with the Third Reich, but he actually never surrendered France's great-power status. It is still not clear what Laval, whom everybody regarded as a master of political intrigue, had in mind regarding his country's future. For instance, all through the war, Vichy's military intelligence apparatus secretly but efficiently combated the infiltration of German agents into the Unoccupied Zone.

The US ambassador to Vichy concluded that Laval's, and especially Pétain's, goal was to shield France from excessive German demands.* But if this was the case, then Vichy was not too successful: German exactions caused hunger and untold misery among poorer people in France, anti-British propaganda emanating from Vichy seemed to know no bounds, and a minor war for the possession of Syria was fought in the summer of 1941 between British and Free French forces, on the one side, and Vichy French as well as German troops, on the other. Moreover, as in so many

---

*Amazingly, the United States was able to maintain diplomatic relations with "neutral" Vichy France until May 1942, long after Germany and its allies had declared war on the United States.

Image 3.2. The French head of state Marshal Philippe Pétain receiving the Cardinals Suhard and Gerlier, archbishops of, respectively, Paris and Lyon, in the company of Minister President Pierre Laval, Vichy, 1942. Unlike Suhard, Cardinal Gerlier publicly denounced Laval's anti-Jewish measures and was later declared one of the "Righteous Among the Nations" by Yad Vashem in Jerusalem. Source: Bundesarchiv, Bild 183–2010–0325–502 / photo: o.Ang.

other countries in Hitler's Europe, Vichy took anti-Jewish measures in advance of German requests. Jews were deprived of their rights and property, and thousands of Jewish refugees from the East were pushed across the German border, often despite German protests.* Meanwhile, the war and the callousness of the world made Jewish overseas emigration impossible. In 1941 and 1942, the French police arrested and deported thousands upon thousands of Jews, many among them born in France, to Germany, which then sent the Jews to the death camps.

*Overeager action against the Jews was one of the foremost ways for Germany's allies to demonstrate their loyalty to Hitler. The massacre of Jews in Eastern Europe, for instance, began with the mass murder of Jews in the Soviet territories that Romanian troops occupied, beginning in June 1941. Almost simultaneously, the Hungarian authorities pushed at least fifteen thousand Jews of "doubtful nationality" across the Ukrainian border. The German occupation authorities protested this one-sided move, but because the Hungarians refused to reaccept the expellees, the German SS found no better solution to the dilemma of "overcrowding" than to kill all the Jews in the region.

Aside from those in the highest level of society who loved to socialize and to do business with the German occupiers, contacts between the French and the Germans were mostly on the level of man-woman relations. With more than 2 million French soldiers in captivity, German soldiers sometimes took their places in women's lives. By far not all these relations were of the famous *collaboration horizontale* variety, so much discussed by the resistance and by the US media after the war, but, of course, prostitution also flourished, as it would later in Allied-occupied Germany. Unlike the American GIs later, however, ordinary German soldiers had no chocolate, nylon underwear, expensive cigarettes, and rare medicines to offer.

COZY ISLANDERS

There was one more place in Hitler's Europe where the issues of accommodation versus collaboration are of particular interest: the Channel Islands. The reason their case is interesting is that those who lived there under German supervision were His British Majesty's proud subjects. Their story

Image 3.3. German soldiers enjoying their time with French women. Source: Bundesarchiv, Bild 101I-058–1761–19 / photo: Harren.

allows us to express some doubts regarding the determination of the British people to oppose an eventual German invasion to the bitter end, which is what the country's leaders and later countless studies, novels, plays, and British as well as Hollywood films claimed.[4]

The Channel Islands, with, as their main constituting elements, the islands of Guernsey and Jersey, were a British Crown dependency, dating back to the Norman Conquest. It was legally not a part of the United Kingdom; many of its inhabitants still spoke local languages, yet all saw themselves as quintessentially British. Because of their proximity to the French coastline, the Channel Islands were considered of no strategic significance; men of military age and thousands of children were evacuated to Britain as soon as the German military campaign began. One small island, Alderney, was left with only six inhabitants; on another, Sark, the entire population stayed put under the rule of their formidable "seigneur," the Dame of Sark. In view of the inevitable German invasion, the British government instructed the islands' leaders, in June 1940, to practice "passive cooperation," which they assiduously did over the next five years.

It is hard to conceive of a more effective propaganda weapon in German hands than the photograph of unarmed German soldiers in Guernsey and Jersey being smartly saluted by a bobby, the famous British policeman, or of a typically British-looking city street in which smiling locals shake hands with the German invaders. The Germans' goal was to demonstrate that, in case of their landing in Great Britain, such peaceable scenes would ensue rather than the determined struggle on the beaches that Churchill had so confidently predicted in his fiery parliamentary address in June 1940, a few weeks before the German invasion of the Channel Islands.

The elected administrators and aldermen of the Channel Islands readily cooperated with the German commanders: they consented without murmur to the conversion of Alderney Island into a lethal concentration camp for Russian and Jewish slave laborers, they carefully prepared lists of the handful of local families who were of fully or partly Jewish origin, and they handed the families over to the Gestapo. Most of these Jews later died in concentration or death camps. The Dame of Sark, who happened to speak fluent German, treated the German invaders as welcome guests; British officials arrested real and potential resisters. It is also noteworthy that the women of the islands gave birth to some nine hundred German British children.

Image 3.4. A British "bobby" giving information to a German officer in the occupied Channel Islands. Source: Times/News Syndication.

All of this is particularly disturbing in view of Churchill's call for the European resistance movements to fight the Nazi occupiers, which inevitably carried a lethal risk for uninvolved civilians. In fact, there were some brave resisters, mainly women, on the Channel Islands, but what is significant is that the British government never even tried to set the Channel Islands "on fire." These dangerous games were left to other Europeans. After the war, there was some talk of punishing the so-called Jerry-bags, women who had had German lovers or such islanders who had denounced resisters to the German authorities. In the end, however, not a single islander was tried or punished for collaboration, war crimes, or treason.

While the Germans were occupying half of Poland as well as Western and northern Europe, and while the Soviet Union used its friendly relations with Germany to grab Estonia, Latvia, Lithuania, eastern Poland, and parts of Romania and Finland, Italy's dictator, Benito Mussolini, was desperate to show that he was equal in popularity and power to Hitler. Yet the dismal failure of the last-minute Italian offensive against collapsing France a few months earlier should have taught him not to take any more risks.

THE PITFALLS OF COLLABORATION IN THE BALKANS

In his quest for an empire to parallel that of brotherly Germany, Mussolini decided, in October 1940, to attack and occupy Greece from the Italian base of Albania. To general amazement, the small Greek forces counterattacked and pushed the half-million-strong Italian army back into Albania. This reminded the world of the Finnish miracle a year earlier against Soviet troops during the Winter War. The British help to the Greeks and the appearance of British soldiers in the Balkans made a German intervention inevitable. By then, Hitler had already given up his halfhearted plan to invade Great Britain; he was now preparing to settle accounts with his unofficial ally the Soviet Union. It was to be the war of all wars, which would extend German power deep into Asia, create the "necessary living space" for the German race, and put an end to Nazism's ideological rival, communism.

Italy's Greek adventure had come as a most unwanted complication for the Führer when, in April 1941, the Yugoslavs virtually repudiated their alliance with Germany, and he decided to solve the entire Balkan problem. This, as many historians argue, caused a fatal few weeks' delay in Operation Barbarossa, the plan to attack and overwhelm the Soviet Union.

The Balkan campaign was another German miracle: in less than two weeks, the Yugoslav army surrendered, and in the following few weeks the Germans occupied all of Greece, ejecting the British Expeditionary Force even from the island of Crete. This left Britain without a toehold in Europe; as of May 1941, Hitler had no enemies but only allies and friendly neutrals on the European continent. Yet, as it turned out, his troubles had just begun.

[handwritten marginalia: Question 13]

[handwritten marginalia: Question 14]

German victory brought to the fore in the Balkans the question of accommodation, collaboration, and resistance, but, unlike in Western and northern Europe, with a number of additional complications. One factor was the often undeveloped mountainous terrain and the myriad islands near the coasts of Greece and Yugoslavia, both of which allowed for every conceivable semilegal and illegal activity. The other complication was that, unlike the Danes or the Dutch, the inhabitants of the Balkans were not peaceful people; the many hundreds of years of struggle for or against the Ottoman-Turkish overlords had taught them to trust only their weapons and their own families and clans. But the main problem was the ethnic, religious, and political multiplicity of the Balkans. Whereas Greece had only a few (though by far not insignificant) ethnic minorities, the Yugoslav kingdom consisted of Serbs, Croats, Slovenes, Bosnian Muslims, Macedonians, Montenegrins, Albanians, Hungarians, Germans, Italians, Jews, Vlachs, and others. It was also divided by language, religion, political history, and tradition. South Slavic–speaking Serbs, Croats, Bosnian Muslims (called Bosniaks), and Montenegrins could at least understand each other; the Slovenes spoke a different Slavic language, and the Albanian, Hungarian, German, and Italian inhabitants of Yugoslavia spoke completely different tongues. The South Slavs themselves were divided by religion, historically a crucial distinction: Croats and Slovenes were mostly Catholic; Serbs, Montenegrins, and Macedonians followed the Eastern Orthodox rite; and the Bosniaks were Muslim. Some, including the Serbs, Coats, Montenegrins, Albanians, and Hungarians, could boast of a tradition of great medieval kingdoms; Germans and Jews were immigrants of a later date; Bosniaks once formed the landowning class in their region, as opposed to the Croatian and Serbian serfs. The Slovenes, Germans, and Hungarians of the Yugoslav kingdom were relatively well off; those in the South, such as the Kosovo Albanians, felt neglected by their wealthier cocitizens.

In April 1941, the Yugoslav army collapsed, in part because some extremist Croatian politicians exploited the arrival of German troops to proclaim a Croatian fascist state. Thus, similar to what had happened to the soldiers of the Austro-Hungarian army at the end of World War I, a large segment of the defeated and captured soldiers of the Yugoslav army learned that they had suddenly become allies of the victorious enemy.

By the end of the German *Blitzkrieg* in the Balkans, Hungary, Bulgaria, and even the Italian puppet state of Albania had annexed parts of Yugoslavia, but the bulk of Yugoslavia and all of Greece came under either

Image 3.5. Ante Pavelić (on the left), who became independent Croatia's fascist dictator following the German conquest of Yugoslavia in April 1941, and German foreign minister Joachim von Ribbentrop. Source: Bundesarchiv, Bild 183–2008–0612–500 / photo: Henkel.

German or Italian control. The ensuing holy confusion can only be imagined: Croats, Serbs, and Greeks had their own collaborationist government, but only Croatia was genuinely independent.

German, Italian, Hungarian, and Bulgarian soldiers occupied every part of the Balkans, regardless of whether there was a local native government allied to Germany. Nowhere did the new political boundaries coincide with the ethnic, religious, and linguistic boundaries. The Croatian fascist, so-called Ustasha, state included millions of Serbs and Bosniaks; the parts of Yugoslavia that Hungary reannexed to the historic mother country had an absolute majority of Serbs and other non-Hungarian ethnic elements; and the Muslim Bosniaks had to live within the militantly Catholic Croatian state. One could continue the causes for unrest and discontent ad infinitum. Soon the revolts against the occupation forces began, but in each case the revolt also had an ethnic and religious connotation. The revolts then turned into civil wars in which the German, Italian, Hungarian, and Bulgarian occupiers played often secondary, though mostly a very bloody, role.

There was to be a final complication: the rise and extraordinary activism, in both Yugoslavia and Greece, of the Marxist-Leninist Communist movement. In Yugoslavia it triumphed over all other groups and parties; in Greece it would, in all likelihood, also have won the game had the British army of liberation not intervened, in 1944, on behalf of the Greek anti-Communist forces.

Under such circumstances, an accommodationist attitude was nearly impossible; those who tried to live their own lives and simply obey orders became, sooner or later, suspect because of their real or presumed ethnicity, their religious affiliation, their mother tongue, or a combination of these elements. Survival required that one belong to one or more groups and that one fight with arms if necessary. Let us imagine a Hungarian farmer in northern Yugoslavia, who until 1918 had been a Hungarian subject, then was a Yugoslav citizen, and in 1941 again became a Hungarian citizen. In the same year, he reported to the Hungarian gendarmes that his Serbian neighbor was sheltering a suspicious-looking and possibly armed man. Was that farmer acting as a Hungarian patriot and law-abiding citizen, or was he a traitor to the Yugoslav state and the Serbian nation? In reality, the farmer's motivation was none of the above: he had denounced his neighbor mostly because he desired his wealthier neighbor's land, house, and cattle. Chances are that the Serbian neighbor would have been shot by Hungarian soldiers in 1941 and the Hungarian farmer by Yugoslav partisans in 1945.

Was the Serbian nationalist guerrilla fighter who killed both Communist partisans and German soldiers a collaborator or a hero of national resistance? How to judge Greek politician Ioannis Rallis, who agreed to be prime minister of Greece under the Germans in order, as he later claimed, to alleviate the famine and fight the Greek Communist guerrillas? No doubt, according to traditional Western standards, Rallis was a collaborator; still, we must note that at the end of the war, the British liberators made use of the Security Battalions that Rallis created in order to defeat the Communists. Let us wait until we come to the chapters on resistance before casting judgment on those who tried to survive and in so doing killed or were killed in the Balkans.

It is indeed legitimate to call the Norwegian prime minister Vidkun Quisling a "quisling," that is, a collaborator; it does not seem that his serving the Germans benefited the Norwegians in any way. It is more difficult to condemn the three consecutive Greek prime ministers who served the Germans and, until the fall of 1943, the Italians and who argued in postwar

YUGOSLAVIA UNDER FOREIGN OCCUPATION, 1941-1945

courts, not without justification, that the situation in Greece had been so desperate that it was better to collaborate with the occupiers than to let one's own people die of starvation. Yet, arguably, Rallis and his colleagues failed to improve the situation. In brief, their followers saw the three as tragic heroes; their more numerous critics saw them as mere poltroons.

The question of collaboration becomes even more difficult to resolve in Eastern Europe, where there were several aggressors and occupiers and where would-be collaborators had to decide which of the occupiers they wished to serve. Those who tried to stick to one occupier were more likely to suffer death than those who switched their allegiances in favor of the ruler of the moment. But there were no guarantees: survival was more a matter of luck than of some particular talent for servility and intrigue. The wars in the East, especially the one against the Soviet Union, were total.

NOTES

1. Cited in Joachim Fest, *Hitler,* translated by Richard and Clara Winston (New York: Vintage Books, 1975), 646.

2. On all of this, see, for instance, L. de Jong, "The Dutch Resistance Movement and the Allies, 1940–1945," in *European Resistance Movements, 1939–45: Proceedings of the Second International Conference on the History of the Resistance Movements Held at Milan 26–29 March 1961* (Oxford: Pergamon Press, 1964), 341.

3. Quoted in Jacques Sémelin, *Unarmed Against Hitler: Civilian Resistance in Europe, 1939–1943,* translated by Suzan Husserl-Kapit (Westport, CT: Praeger, 1993), 5.

4. Of the growing literature on the Channel Islands during World War II, see particularly Madeleine Bunting, *The Model Occupation: The Channel Islands Under German Rule* (New York: HarperCollins, 1996); and K. M. Bachman, *The Prey of an Eagle* (Channel Islands: Guernsey Press, 1972). The latter is a compilation of the author's letters written during the German occupation.

CHAPTER FOUR

The Invasion of the Soviet Union and East European Collaboration

On June 22, 1941, the German army launched a surprise attack on the Soviet Union in which it was soon joined by Finnish, Romanian, Hungarian, Slovak, Croatian, Italian, and Spanish regulars as well as by volunteers from nearly every European nation. The campaign was proclaimed a crusade against "godless Bolshevism," while nearly everyone, whether friend or foe, predicted another one of Hitler's lightning-fast victories.

The initial German move, code-named "Operation Barbarossa," included more than 3 million troops, five thousands tanks, more than ten thousand artillery pieces, and three thousand aircraft.*

Why Stalin had refused to believe precise warnings from many quarters is one of the grand mysteries of modern world history. Within a few weeks, the Germans and their allies captured 4 million Red Army soldiers and conquered territories inhabited by some 75 million people, all this against an enemy that, at least in theory, enjoyed great numerical superiority in trained soldiers, tanks, guns, and aircraft.

Interesting how this was much was put into operation. What if it failed?

---

*Except for the statistics kept by the US and British armies, data on World War II battle strengths, casualties, and material gains or losses are remarkably inconsistent; often they are mere guesses. This is particularly true for the Eastern front, where accurate records were very difficult to keep and each side forged statistics for propaganda purposes. We do not even have precise figures on the number of German troops and matériel involved in the initial attack on the Soviet Union.

Operation Barbarossa, the most devastating military campaign in history, has been the subject of countless books and documentaries; it concerns us here mainly because it opened the way to collaboration and resistance on a scale with which nothing in Western or northern Europe could be compared. The costs of Operation Barbarossa in suffering and death were unimaginable but will not be systematically discussed here. On the British Channel Islands, as we have seen, mutually correct behavior made life more than tolerable for both occupier and the occupied population. In the Balkans and in German-occupied Soviet lands, trying to accommodate the foreign occupier was rarely a viable solution: those with the smallest chance of survival were people who just tried to get by.

The German army crossed the Soviet borders under explicit orders and often with the individual soldiers' firm resolution to be merciless with the Bolsheviks, the Jews, and all others judged to be subhuman. During the conflict, the Germans and their allies systematically starved to death, shot, or gassed at least 3 million Soviet prisoners of war. On his side, Stalin declared both retreat and surrender to be capital offenses. As the Soviets had not signed the Geneva Convention, the Germans had an apparent excuse for mistreating and killing whomever they wished. When the Soviets belatedly offered to respect the humanitarian clauses of the convention, the German Foreign Office did not even bother to reply.

In the summer of 1941, while the German tanks advanced as fast as the terrible Russian roads permitted, millions of Red Army soldiers were left behind the advancing front line. Their choice was either surrender, which they feared would bring death in German captivity, or try to reach the rapidly withdrawing Soviet lines, which—as many were to find—could bring execution by their own suspicious authorities. As a consequence, many stray Soviet soldiers fled to the limitless forests of the region and engaged in banditry for survival. This was soon given the name of "partisan activity," with its practitioners being proclaimed heroes of the "anti-Hitlerite, anti-fascist struggle." Countless thousands of partisans were subsequently killed by rival groups or by hostile armies; others were slaughtered by angry peasants whose meager food supply and remaining livestock had been confiscated. Clearly, in such a world, few people were able to engage in the kind of "passive cooperation" that, for example, the Channel Islanders practiced.

Historians agree that had the German Nazis decided to behave reasonably, millions of Soviet citizens would have joined them, and they might have won the war. After all, the Soviet lands that the Germans first conquered were the three independent Baltic countries or lands that had belonged to anti-Communist Poland, Romania, or Finland. By 1941 people in those lands had experienced a year or two of Soviet rule, which meant not only being subjected to a thoroughly illegitimate occupation but also persecution for such alleged crimes as having been a nobleman, army officer, official, teacher, non–Eastern Orthodox clergyman, intellectual, businessman, bourgeois, or "kulak" (a purported well-to-do farmer). As a result of the arrests and deportations to the interior of the Soviet Union, the Baltic countries lost a large part of their social and professional class, while hundreds of thousands of mostly Polish speakers were deported from eastern Poland. At Stalin's explicit orders, some 20,000 Polish career and reserve officers (the latter in professional occupations when not in uniform) were shot in the back of the head at Katyń and elsewhere in the Soviet Union. Among them were some 800 Polish Jewish reserve officers.

CAUGHT BETWEEN TWO GIANTS

Until quite recently, few in the West wanted to believe what the former Soviet archives have since shown, namely, that in Stalin's Soviet Union, millions had been persecuted, deported, and often killed not only because of their real or supposed political opposition, or for having the wrong social origins, but for belonging to the wrong ethnic group. In this respect, there was scant difference between the Nazi and Soviet practices; the victims, such as the Polish intelligentsia, were murdered en masse by both Germans and Soviets.

The Stalinist destruction of the ethnic minorities began in 1932 with the famine, the so-called Holodomor (Death by Hunger) in Ukraine, that many historians consider to have been aggravated, if not caused, by Stalin's cruel order to wipe out the Ukrainian kulaks. Hunger and typhus led to about 4 million deaths. The Soviet policy of destruction continued with the so-called Great Terror in 1937, in which the political police (first called the Cheka, then the GPU [State Political Directorate], and later the NKVD [People's Commissariat for Internal Affairs]) exterminated a large part of the Soviet Communist Party leadership. In addition, the high- and middle-level commanders of the Red Army were executed or sent to the Gulag (the name of Soviet concentration camps), which functioned as a state within the state. Finally, a great many Polish-, Japanese-, Chinese-, and German-speaking citizens of the Soviet Union were shot, deported, or detained. Not many historians provide such exact and therefore debatable data on the number of victims of the Soviet terror as Timothy Snyder, who writes about 111,091 Polish-speaking citizens of the Soviet Union executed, accused of espionage for Poland, and of 681,692 recorded death sentences in the Great Terror, but all experts agree that the numbers were horrendous.[1] The turn of other ethnic groups came later, mostly during and after the war when masses of Estonians, Latvians, Lithuanians, Soviet Germans, Poles, Crimean Tatars, Kalmyks, Chechen-Ingush, and others were deported from their homelands to camps in the East, where many perished. What makes these deportations historically unique was that some of these ethnic groups were sent east in cattle cars in their entirety. Communist Party secretaries and decorated war heroes were not excepted.

At the news of the German invasion on June 22, 1941, the Soviet political police massacred thousands of prison inmates in western Ukraine, the former eastern Poland, and the Baltics; as a consequence, the German armored columns were presented with the spectacle of piles of dead in the prison courtyards. Now it was the turn of locals to engage in an orgy of violence against suspected Communists and, even more, against Jews. At first, the Germans were there merely to take pictures of the pogroms.

Many in the Baltic countries and the Ukraine had awaited the Germans as saviors and liberators; the most efficient German propaganda crews, following the example of army photographers on the Channel Islands, showed Ukrainian peasant women in national costume offering the customary bread and salt to dust-covered German motorists advancing toward L'vov (today Lvív) and Kiev (today Kyiv).

Even among the Soviet POWs, many, including some generals, were willing to offer their services in the struggle against Stalin. Amazingly, the very same German Waffen SS (fighting SS) and Wehrmacht commanders who had ordered or at least tolerated the mass starvation of Soviet war prisoners were ready to accept other Soviet soldiers as fellow combatants. Moreover, in some areas, Russian civilians were permitted to organize anti-Soviet partisan units. Mostly, however, collaboration had an ethnic character: Ukrainians, Belarusians, Estonians, Latvians, Lithuanians, Caucasians, and members of some Asian nationalities were assembled in ethnic units and served the Germans as Waffen SS volunteers, armed

Image 4.1. Bosnian Muslim volunteers of the Waffen SS at prayer. Members of the so-called Handschar Division, the first non-Germanic, Slavic-speaking unit under Heinrich Himmler, participated in the fight against the Titoist Communist partisans. Source: Bundesarchiv, Bild 146–1977–137–20 / photo: Falkowski.

militiamen, policemen, concentration camp guards, low-level administrators, professionals, workers, and laborers. German policy toward foreign volunteers changed repeatedly. At first, the SS would recruit only "Nordic" types, or "Aryans," whatever these terms meant; later, however, the necessities of war caused Heinrich Himmler to take into the SS the most varied nationalities and "races," including Slavic speakers and Muslims. There were Ukrainian, Estonian, Latvian, Lithuanian, Bosnian Muslim, Scandinavian, Dutch, Walloon, and French Waffen SS divisions, brigades, "legions," and battalions, most of them bearing the names of historical heroes. It is difficult to keep track of these units because some represented wishful thinking more than reality and because their names, numbers, and affiliations changed repeatedly. Even practicing Jews of the so-called Karaite sect were allowed to serve in the Waffen SS after Himmler had been persuaded by a Jewish rabbi that the Karaites were racially Turkish and not Semitic.

A Russian liberation army was also created within the German Wehrmacht and survived to the end of the war, although its name and composition changed again and again. It has become best known as the Vlasov Army, after the highly decorated Soviet general Andrei Vlasov, who at first defeated large German units near Moscow but, after his capture, volunteered to create an anti-Communist Russian army. Individual German officers, among them some of Baltic German origin, advocated arming as many Russians as possible in the fight against the Bolsheviks; others were aghast at the idea of giving arms to those whom one wanted to destroy or at least to send behind the Ural Mountains following victory. A zealous advocate of the idea of arming Russian POWs was Claus Count von Stauffenberg, the immortal hero of the German resistance movement who early on speculated that perhaps Germans and Russians could work together to get rid of both Hitler and Stalin.

Some units composed of Soviet citizens turned out to be robbers and murderers, such as certain Ukrainian SS units whose members delighted in massacring Jews and Poles. Others included the so-called Kaminski SS brigade, whose commander, a former Soviet engineer, made his name odious by helping to drown in blood the Warsaw Polish uprising in the fall of 1944. It appears that he was later executed by a firing squad on German orders.

Many, probably the great majority of Soviet citizens, joined the German service in order to avoid death by typhus or starvation in the POW camps; they often tried to avoid fighting against fellow Russians and changed back to the Soviet side when it became clear that Germany was losing the war. But running over to the other side was not easy: the Soviets generally shot those among their citizens who had been in German service. Remember that letting oneself be captured by the enemy counted as a capital crime in Stalin's Soviet Union. Yet altogether more than 1 million Soviet citizens served in the German armed forces. The most notorious of all were the so-called Trawniki men, Soviet POWs who had volunteered to serve the SS plan to create a "living space" for German colonists in Poland. Trained at Trawniki in western Ukraine, thousands of Trawniki men tortured and shot hundreds of thousands of Jews under strict German supervision. In the words of historian Peter Black, "Even with the deployment of minimal German staff this plan was feasible. Trawniki men not only served as foot soldiers of the Final Solution; they also represented prototypes for the enforcers of the world that the Nazis intended to construct."[2] The presence of so many non-Germans in the German army and the simultaneous presence of so many non-Russians and even non-Slavs in the Red Army made this war a mind-boggling spectacle.*

Did all of this amount to voluntary collaboration with the enemy? The answers are yes, if we consider how the Soviet courts treated those they called collaborators, and no, if we take into account that the majority of those who entered German service were doing it for survival. Yet in the case of Bronislav Kaminski, for instance, who had been a civilian when he volunteered to set up a fighting brigade and to administer an entire district for the Germans, we can definitely speak of collaboration.

Matters were further complicated by the dilemma that those in the Soviet Union faced whose conquerors were not Germans but one of Germany's allies. Some of the conquerors, such as the Italians and Spaniards, had no colonizing ambitions; their ordinary soldiers and even their officers were motivated, at most, by their hatred of communism. Indeed, members of the Spanish Blue Division and the Italian Eighth Army occasionally attempted to protect the inhabitants against German depravations. Some of the soldiers helped persecuted Jews. At the other end of the spectrum, Romania attacked the Soviet Union in June 1941 in order to reconquer territories that the Soviet Union had seized a year earlier. Now the Romanians grabbed these as well as additional lands. Romanian colonizing and recolonizing policies spelled disaster for the local Jews and for many Ukrainians, all of whom were accused of having collaborated with the Soviet occupiers.

Ukrainians and Russian speakers in the Romanian-occupied region were at least allowed to offer their services to the Romanian authorities; Jews had no such opportunity. In fact, between 1941 and 1944, Romanian soldiers and gendarmes killed nearly three hundred thousand Jewish civilians.

As elsewhere in Europe, much depended on what the occupying power wished to do with the occupied territory. As a general rule, and despite their noisy liberation propaganda, the Germans did not grant independence or even autonomy to any of the nations and nationalities formerly under Soviet rule.

Some of Estonia's, Latvia's, and Lithuania's right-leaning politicians had fled to Germany in 1940 to escape Soviet deportations; a year later, they returned with the German tanks and attempted to set up local as

---

*The writer of these lines remembers well the Asian soldiers in German uniform riding small Mongolian horses in Hungary while they were driving skeletal Red Army prisoners before them. In one case, he witnessed Soviet prisoners and their Wehrmacht guards speaking the same Asian language without their officers being able to understand what they were saying.

well as national administrations. Yet nothing on the national scale was tolerated; the three Baltic countries were incorporated into a much larger German occupation zone called Kommissariat Ostland, under a German Nazi administrator, while awaiting the entire Ostland's incorporation into the German Reich. Local collaboration was gladly accepted, but political equality was not granted. Still, many of those who had survived Soviet annexation were enthusiastic about what for them was German liberation. Local anti-Semites, as we have said, started Jewish pogroms even before the arrival of the German troops, and later each Baltic country set up its own Waffen SS divisions. Some became much-decorated fighting units. Estonian, Latvian, and Lithuanian local authorities vigorously cooperated with the Germans. Finally, a still painful issue in the Baltic countries was that many of their young men volunteered for guard duty in the concentration camps, which involved participation in mass executions. Without the Baltic volunteers and the Ukrainians in the same type of units, the technical execution of the "Final Solution of the Jewish Question in the East" would have been far less effective. Moreover, we must state categorically that only the assistance of masses of Estonians, Latvians, Lithuanians, Ukrainians, Romanians, Hungarians, Slovaks, Frenchmen, Dutch, Poles, and many other Europeans made the Holocaust possible.

THE WORST PLACE TO BE: UKRAINE DURING THE WAR

The situation was particularly dire in Ukraine, whose 40 million nationally conscious inhabitants had hardly ever known independence and had suffered more foreign occupations than perhaps any other European nation. Although a very old term, the name *Ukraine* came into common use only in recent times. There once existed powerful principalities in the region, and the early medieval principality of Kievan Rus gave its very name to Russia. What concerns us here, however, is that in the twentieth century, Ukraine underwent numerous political changes that profoundly influenced the culture and politics of its inhabitants. Divided before World War I between Austria-Hungary and czarist Russia, Ukraine was redivided in the interwar years, this time between Poland and Soviet Russia. In the 1930s, the Soviet part of Ukraine was devastated by famine and the Stalinist terror, with the latter administered by such Ukrainian Communists as Nikita Khrushchev. The aim was to eliminate all those even vaguely suspected of Ukrainian nationalism. In 1939 the Polish part of

Ukraine was annexed to Soviet Ukraine; two years later, both western and eastern Ukraine were overrun by the German army.

In June 1941, German newsreels offered the surprising spectacle of blonde and blue-eyed Ukrainian peasant maidens waving to the German troops. Were these then the despised Slavic Untermenschen (subhumans)? The scene bewildered even Heinrich Himmler, who had been convinced that no Slav, whether Ukrainian or not, could look like a Nordic type and be an "Aryan." But the Germans soon lost their chance of winning over the entire population by their refusal to disband the much-hated, though somewhat more efficient, collective farms. The Germans also confiscated food and livestock to feed the home country, and they deported young people to Germany to work (for pay, in fact) in the farms and factories. From the Ukrainian nationalist point of view, there was, however, a huge advantage to compensate for the many losses: just as in the Czech state, German occupation policy was involuntarily beginning to make Ukraine a monoethnic country. It is no wonder, then, that Ukrainian militiamen and civilian volunteers powerfully assisted the Germans in the massacre of Jews, Poles, and real or suspected Communists.

Ukrainians were a patriotic people, but they interpreted national interests in so many ways as to make a civil war under German occupation inevitable. Between 1939 and 1941, a great number of young men were drafted into the Red Army, and they now shared the lot of other Red Army soldiers by fighting and dying at the front, starving in POW camps, or joining the partisans in the forests. Other young Ukrainians changed from one miserable condition to another repeatedly, or they fought as partisans not only against the German occupiers but also against the Communist partisans. Still others cooperated with the Hungarian troops then occupying large parts of Ukraine in fighting the Communist and Soviet partisans, but they also combated the German soldiers. Patriotic Ukrainian partisans themselves were divided along ideological, tactical, and political lines; all this and much more took place while the Red Army and the German army alternately devastated the land, blew up railroad lines and bridges, burned houses and barns, poisoned wells, stole food and cattle, planted millions of land mines, drove off the civilian population, bombed the cities, booby-trapped the ruins, and operated concentration camps. Ukraine was, as Timothy Snyder writes, the very heart of the "bloodlands."

Who indeed was a collaborator in Ukraine? The question cannot be answered with the clarity available in Norway, for instance, where the

[handwritten marginal note: I find this weird, why would they deport them, then pay them?]

population was divided into resisters, quislings, and a large majority of cautious bystanders. In Ukraine and in much of Eastern and southeastern Europe, there were proportionally fewer bystanders, and the situation was complex in the extreme. Still, there is a clear distinction between, for instance, a Ukrainian town mayor who prostrated himself before the Nazi occupiers and a university student who died in a gun battle with the Gestapo. The distinction is less clear in other cases, such as those who fought the German and Soviet occupiers simultaneously. What should we say about such Ukrainians, and they were many, who alternately harassed, robbed, or even killed Germans, Soviet partisans, Jews, local Communists, political rivals, and Polish peasants? It all depended on the circumstances and the imagined interests of the Ukrainian fatherland. From the point of view of universal morality, what distinguished one Ukrainian from another was that some were able to preserve their human dignity and their capacity for compassion, while others behaved like the vilest of criminals. There were those who hid a Jew at mortal risk to their lives and those of their family, and there were those who denounced the Jew and his or her protector to the German authorities for a pithy remuneration.

TOWARD A TURNING POINT IN THE CONFLICT

While these internal Ukrainian conflicts were raging, the German army occupied Kiev, the Ukrainian capital, and advanced rapidly to the gates of Leningrad (today St. Petersburg) and Moscow. But then the advance slowed because of desperate Soviet resistance and because of the fall mud. By the winter of 1941, the German army—lacking winter clothing and equipment, thanks to Hitler's belief in a speedy victory—was retreating on many fronts. The reputation of the German soldiers for invincibility was decidedly weakened.

The summer of 1942 saw another major and seemingly decisive German push to Stalingrad (today Volgograd) on the Volga River as well as to the Caucasus Mountains and Baku, with its all-important oil wells. It was at this point that German power was geographically at its greatest, with the swastika flag flying over Hammerfest at the northernmost tip of Norway, on the peaks of the Pyrenees at the Franco-Spanish border, all around starving and besieged Leningrad, and on top of Mount Elbrus, the highest peak in the Caucasus. How did Germany, a country of some 80 million inhabitants, manage to achieve such miraculous successes? Explanations

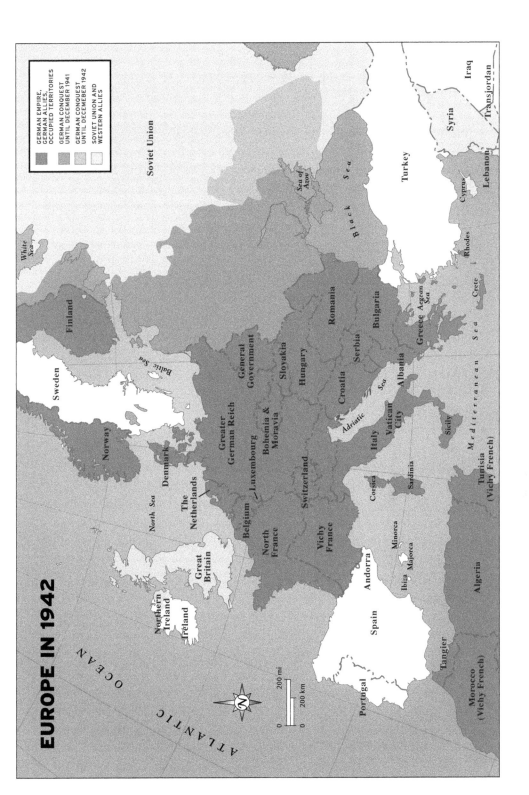

EUROPE IN 1942

Legend:
- GERMAN EMPIRE, GERMAN ALLIES, OCCUPIED TERRITORIES
- GERMAN CONQUEST UNTIL DECEMBER 1941
- GERMAN CONQUEST UNTIL DECEMBER 1942
- SOVIET UNION AND WESTERN ALLIES

ATLANTIC OCEAN

Soviet Union

White Sea

Finland

Sweden

Norway

Denmark

North Sea

Baltic Sea

Northern Ireland

Ireland

Great Britain

The Netherlands

Belgium

Luxembourg

Greater German Reich

General Government

Bohemia & Moravia

Slovakia

Hungary

Switzerland

North France

Vichy France

Croatia

Serbia

Romania

Bulgaria

Albania

Greece

Italy

Vatican City

Sicily

Sardinia

Corsica

Adriatic Sea

Aegean Sea

Crete

Rhodes

Cyprus

Black Sea

Sea of Azov

Mediterranean Sea

Turkey

Syria

Iraq

Transjordan

Lebanon

Spain

Andorra

Portugal

Tangier

Morocco (Vichy French)

Algeria

Tunisia (Vichy French)

Minorca

Majorca

Ibiza

N

0   200 mi

0   200 km

range all the way from the idealism inspired by the most evil of all political theories, National Socialism, and the magic charisma of the Führer to the prowess and devotion of the German soldier. But the major reasons for the blinding German successes can be ascribed to the other Europeans who would rather surrender than cooperate with their neighboring rivals against the Nazi onslaught. Worse even was Stalin, who had convinced himself that the Germans would not attack the Soviet Union. Yet the same Stalin was able to rally millions of people behind the idea of defending the Soviet fatherland. The Red Army did stop the onslaught of the Nazi armies, but at the price of terrible casualties due at least in part to the intrigues and suspiciousness of their strong leader and his underlings.

The unique insights and military-political savvy of Hitler are the subject of thousands of books and millions of articles, but so are his mistakes as well as the greed and abject servility of his generals. Yet there was one more factor helping to explain both German victories and their later decline, a factor generally ignored or easily dismissed by historians. This is the important role played by Hitler's European allies in at first reinforcing and later weakening the Nazi war machine. Italians, Romanians, Hungarians, Bulgarians, Slovaks, Croats, and Finns were Hitler's most important collaborators while still causing some of his worst headaches and defeats.

One might wonder why so many of Europe's still independent countries—Italy, Hungary, Romania, Slovakia, Bulgaria, and Croatia—chose, in 1940–1941, to enter the war on the German side. After all, they must have understood that in case of Hitler's victory, Germany would establish total hegemony in Europe. Possible reasons range from fear of German violence, competition among rivals for Nazi favor, haste not to fall behind in the scramble for territorial conquest, and respect for German intellectual and technological superiority. There were also shared beliefs in anti-Semitism, hatred of Soviet communism, enthusiasm for some variety of National Socialist ideology, and hope for a united Europe even though under German Nazi supremacy. Slovakia and Croatia, as we already know, won their independence thanks to German aggression on their mother country. Father Jozef Tiso's Slovakia, formerly a part of the Czechoslovak republic, had proclaimed itself a sovereign country in 1939, and Croatia, formerly a constituting part of the Yugoslav kingdom, had become a fascist state under Ante Pavelić in April 1941. A few months later, both Slovakia and Croatia joined in the war because they knew that their independence would end with the collapse of the Third Reich. Finland entered the war,

[handwritten marginal note: How could they be important yet give headaches? Our story?]

in June 1941, mainly to regain the lands lost to the Soviets in the Winter War. Finally, all these countries were driven by economic necessity: having been cut off from all other markets, they felt they had no choice but to line up with Germany.

Why did fascist Italy conclude the closest possible alliance with Nazi Germany in the so-called Pact of Steel of 1939? Certainly, Benito Mussolini's megalomania and his desire for relatively poor and underdeveloped Italy to achieve strategic and economic equality with Nazi Germany were some of the main factors. But Mussolini was not an anti-Semite, and back in 1915 this former Social Democratic journalist had vociferously demanded that his country make war on the "Teutonic" enemy, Austria-Hungary and the German Reich. The answer to the dilemma must be that Mussolini and his cohorts were dazzled by German successes.

It cannot be our purpose to list every possible reason why individual countries entered the German alliance, but we can try to arrive at some generalizations and look at the consequences of the alliances. In the course of this analysis, we will move all the way to 1945, in this way dealing more comprehensively with the phenomenon of state-level (as opposed to individual or group) collaboration during the war.

By the time Italy (in 1940) and Finland, Romania, Hungary, Bulgaria, Slovakia, and Croatia (all in 1941) entered the war on the German side, they had lost their faith in the ability of the great Western democracies to protect their economies and political independence. They had also lost their belief—provided that they had any—in democracy, the parliamentary system, and multiparty elections. In the general European rush away from free trade and the free exchange of ideas, these countries were among the first to set up authoritarian regimes. The only exception was Finland, which, as we should again remind ourselves, never officially allied itself with Nazi Germany but was a cobelligerent in the military campaign against the Soviet Union. Finland preserved its well-functioning multiparty parliamentary system throughout the war. With the exception of one or two minor states, none of Germany's allies was an absolute dictatorship of the National Socialist type.

By the time Hitler came to power in Germany in 1933, Italy had been a fascist one-party state for nearly a decade. Yet King Victor Emmanuel III preserved enough constitutional authority to be able, in 1943, to rid himself of Benito Mussolini as the national leader (Il Duce) and as prime minister, but only after it became clear that Italy had lost the war.

Romania, Hungary, and Bulgaria had preserved from the pre–World War I liberal age a halfway genuine parliament and political parties ranging from the far right to a moderate left-of-center orientation. The Communists had long been forbidden. Of course, in all three cases, the ruling political party made sure that it would never lose an election. As in Italy, so in Romania and Bulgaria, ultimate authority rested in the hands of the king; in Hungary the ruler was a so-called regent. All three heads of state occasionally dismissed their generally more powerful prime ministers, and there was, in general, some space for maneuvering among ruler, government, and parliament.

As for Slovakia and Croatia, they were both German creations emerging from the ruins of Czechoslovakia and Yugoslavia, respectively, the first in 1939 and the second in 1941. Both were one-party right-wing dictatorships, although in Slovakia disagreements within the ruling Fascist Party between so-called moderates and radicals provided for some lively controversies.

Let us now investigate the policies of Germany's always enterprising, never completely reliable, and incessantly quarreling allies.

NOTES

1. Timothy Snyder, *Bloodlands: Europe Between Hitler and Stalin* (New York: Basic Books, 2010), 103, 107. See also Robert Conquest, *The Nation Killers: The Soviet Deportation of Nationalities* (New York: Macmillan, 1970); and, for a brief account, Lyman H. Legters, "Soviet Deportation of Whole Nations," in *Encyclopedia of Genocide,* edited by Israel V. Charny (Santa Barbara, CA: ABC-Clio, 1999), 2:521–523.

2. Peter Black, "Foot Soldiers of the Final Solution: The Trawniki Training Camp and Operation Reinhard," *Holocaust and Genocide Studies* 25, no. 1 (2011): 45.

CHAPTER FIVE

Germany's Many Allies

A Blessing or a Curse?

The question we will investigate in this chapter is how Germany behaved toward its European allies and how these allies in turn behaved both toward Germany and each other. My argument is that, far from having been the puppets of Hitler's Germany, as most journalistic articles and even some historical studies claim, Italy, Finland, Slovakia, Hungary, Romania, Croatia, and Bulgaria were, to a large extent, masters of their own fates. Moreover, Germany's allies served as an inspiration to several of the countries that Germany had defeated and occupied, which then aimed at securing sovereign status in Hitler's Europe, similar to that enjoyed by Germany's official allies. As a consequence, it was not always easy to distinguish between Germany's allies and such defeated and occupied countries as the Czech protectorate, Denmark, and France. Germany's official allies, and even some of the occupied countries, preserved throughout the war such a degree of independence as to be able to exercise strict control over, for example, their own Far Right, pro-Nazi opposition. Moreover, they decided how they would handle the "Jewish Question," turning the German insistence on a "Final Solution" to their own advantage. They were also largely able to determine their relations with their similarly pro-German neighbors, and in so doing they often defied the German Nazis. In other words, regarding German policy in Europe, it was often a case of the tail wagging the dog.

Occupied Poland, the Netherlands, Belgium, Serbia, Greece, and the three Baltic countries of Lithuania, Latvia, and Estonia were less lucky because they were either granted only a puppet national government, as was the case in German-occupied Serbia and Greece, or allowed no national government at all.

Regarding Germany's official allies, we may briefly consider the following four theses: first, that the German alliance system was murky, confusing, and open to diverse interpretations; second, that the independence of Germany's allies gave them the freedom to maneuver but also made their leaders and their citizenry responsible for the war crimes and crimes against humanity they committed; third, that many of Germany's allies were hostile to each other to an extent unheard of in history; and fourth, that Germany's allies used the war as an effective instrument for ridding their country of ethnic and religious minorities. In other words, nearly all engaged in some form of ethnic cleansing.

Before beginning a more detailed discussion of these troubled relationships, we should remind ourselves of the chronology that forces us to differentiate between three time periods. During the first phase, the alliance system gradually came into being due to the widespread conviction that Germany would win the war and that one must curry the Führer's favor. The second period began in the late fall and winter of 1942 with the battles of El Alamein and Stalingrad and lasted until late in the summer of 1944, during which every one of Germany's allies, except Croatia, put out feelers to Germany's enemies with a view toward an eventual surrender. The king of Italy even attempted, but only half succeeded, in the late summer of 1943 to join the Anglo-American alliance. The third and last phase began in the late summer of 1944, when Romania, Finland, and Bulgaria changed sides, while the Hungarian leadership refused to surrender, causing the country to end the war as Germany's last ally. Meanwhile, fascist Slovakia and Croatia rejoined their mother countries, Czechoslovakia and Yugoslavia, respectively, thus becoming integral parts of these triumphant "antifascist" powers.

Regarding the first thesis, the very term *Germany's allies* intrigues and baffles because, unlike during World War I, when the Central Powers consisted of four distinct sovereign monarchies (Germany, Austria-Hungary, Bulgaria, and the Ottoman Empire), the Nazi alliance system in World War II was much larger but also much less definable. Who, after all, were Germany's real European allies? It is customary to regard two international treaties, namely, the Anti-Comintern Pact, aimed at a large German-led coalition against Soviet communism and originally signed only by Germany and Japan in 1936, and the Tripartite Pact of 1940 as the foundations of the Nazi alliance system. The problem is that the Tripartite Pact was joined neither by Croatia, which was Germany's staunchest ally in the Balkans, nor by Finland, Germany's second most important partner in the war against Russia. It is true that the Anti-Comintern Pact included both Croatia and Finland, but then we also find Denmark, a country occupied by Germany, and Spain, a neutral state, among its signatories, which renders the political and diplomatic value of the Anti-Comintern Pact debatable. But, as we have already indicated in Chapter 3, what makes a mockery of the Anti-Comintern Pact is that its target, the Soviet Union, was Nazi Germany's main ally until June 1941.

One could actually argue that both Denmark and Spain were in reality German allies: Denmark, because it provided Germany with invaluable industrial and agricultural goods while it served as a much-coveted safe haven for German troops in need of rest and recreation, and Spain, because it sent an entire army corps (called the Blue Division) to Russia to fight on the side of the Germans. In this respect, neutral Spain was more useful to the Third Reich than Bulgaria, an official ally, which refused to commit troops to the war against Bolshevism and would not even break diplomatic relations with the Soviet Union. Going one step further, we may wonder whether Spain, Denmark, Vichy France, Belgium, the Netherlands, the Czech protectorate, or even Switzerland and Sweden were not more useful to the German war effort than such official allies as fascist Croatia and Slovakia, in which internal revolts necessitated German military intervention and cost the lives of thousands of German soldiers. Or how useful to Germany was its greatest ally, fascist Italy, which the German leaders increasingly saw as an intolerable burden?*

There were also Ukraine and the three Baltic countries that—unlike Serbia, Greece, and the Czech protectorate—were not allowed to form a government under German domination, but in which a substantial part of the population actively supported the German war effort. They sent so many young men into German service as to allow the formation of several

---

*Dr. Joseph Goebbels noted in his diary, "[The Italians] are not fit to serve on the Eastern front; they are not fit for North Africa; they are not even fit for the anti-aircraft batteries at home. The Führer is right to wonder why they are making war at all." Peter Gosztony, *Deutschlands Waffengefährten an der Ostfront, 1941–1945* (Stuttgart: Bernard und Graefe, 1981), 216.

Baltic and Ukrainian Waffen SS divisions. Why not consider them Germany's allies?

All in all, then, we must admit that the German alliance system was complicated, informal, and confusing. Thus, historians are certainly right in granting the status of German allies only to such countries that had negotiated an alliance treaty with the Third Reich, namely, Italy, Finland,* Slovakia, Hungary, Romania, Croatia, and Bulgaria. Still, we should keep in mind that other countries offered more valuable assistance and caused less trouble to the Nazi leaders than some of Germany's official allies.

The second question is whether Germany's allies possessed enough freedom of action to be more than an extension of German policies. The answer to this must be a categorical affirmation of their power of self-determination in such fundamental issues as whether to conclude an alliance with Germany, if and when to enter the war on the side of Hitler, and how much assistance to offer the Nazi war effort. Again and again, the decision was not that of Germany but that of the governments allied to the Nazis. Consider, for instance, that in June 1941, Italy, Finland, Romania, Hungary, Slovakia, and Croatia decided, with little or no German prodding, that they would join in Operation Barbarossa against the Soviet Union. Italy's decision to jump into the campaign derived, according to historian Peter Gosztony, "from Mussolini's megalomaniac wish to show his presence everywhere where the Germans have established themselves."[1] Other countries joined for fear that their neighbor would enter the war before them and thus would be the first to reap the fruits of a German victory. In particular, Romania, Hungary, Slovakia, and Croatia eyed each other with the greatest suspicion when joining in the fray.

As another sign of their independence, the countries allied to Germany were at some point able to limit or even to cease their contribution to the war. In 1941 Finns and Romanians were alone in sending large armies to the front; in 1942 the Hungarians, Italians, Slovaks, and Croats also made a major effort, but following the debacle at Stalingrad in the winter of 1942, the very same countries withdrew almost all their battered combat troops from the front lines and only the Finnish and Romanian contributions remained basically unchanged. On all these developments, the German high command had astonishingly little influence. For lack of anything better, German generals consoled themselves with the thought that Germany's

---

*Finland, to repeat, was a cobelligerent, not an ally.

Image 5.1. King Boris III and Hitler at the signing of Bulgaria's entry into the pro-Nazi Tripartite Pact in March 1941. Center background: Martin Bormann, Hitler's powerful private secretary. Right background: Field Marshal Wilhelm Keitel, the subservient head of the German armed forces. Source: Corbis.

allies were of little use in any case. But why, then, one might ask, did the Germans insist, in 1942, that much larger allied armies appear at the front, and why did the generals assign to these troops long sections of the front that, with their miserable weapons, they could not defend? Let us remember also that allied Bulgaria, whose troops enjoyed a great reputation for bravery during the First World War, refused to send a single soldier to the Russian front.

The most convincing proof of political and military national independence was the relative ease by which Finland, Romania, and Bulgaria seceded from the war in August and September 1944. For instance, the Germans tried but failed to find a single Romanian general willing to set up a countergovernment following King Michael's surrender to the Soviet Union. In fact, the Romanian, Finnish, and Bulgarian armies proved willing to turn on their German ally from one day to another.

Interesting

Question 3

Question 4

THE ALLIES OF GERMANY AND THE "FINAL SOLUTION"

Germany's allies were independent enough to decide how far they would go in cooperating with the Nazis in the so-called Final Solution of the Jewish Question, an issue that the Germans considered the ultimate test of loyalty on the part of their allies. Jews within these countries were persecuted or tolerated, kept alive or killed, less according to German wishes than according to what the respective statesmen thought was in the interest of their country. Thus, the Bulgarians never gave in to German pressure and refused to hand over their Jewish population. Yet the same authorities sent the Jews of the Bulgarian-occupied provinces in Greece and Yugoslavia to the German-run Treblinka death camp. The Romanians engaged in their own monstrous Holocaust in Romanian-occupied northern Bukovina, Bessarabia, Transnistria, and Odessa, but they refused to hand over to the Germans the Jews in the Romanian provinces of Walachia, Moldavia, and southern Transylvania. Slovakia in 1942 deported about fifty-eight thousand of its eighty-nine thousand Jews to the German gas chambers in Poland but subsequently, in a change of policy, refused to surrender the others. But then the Germans and their Slovak helpers killed thousands more following the suppression of the Slovak anti-Nazi uprising in 1944. Altogether, almost four out of every five Slovak Jews perished in the Holocaust.

In Italy the Germans were able to grab Jews only following the collapse of Mussolini's regime in the late summer of 1943, and even then the municipal authorities, priests, nuns, and the general population successfully hid the great majority of Jews. Also, so long as Mussolini was in power, the Italian army fiercely protected the Jewish refugees in the Italian occupation zones of France, Croatia, Slovenia, Albania, and Greece.

It is quite amazing, in retrospect, how weak the Germans proved to be vis-à-vis their allies regarding the "Jewish Question." A telling example is the case of Jewish citizens of various countries allied to Germany who were residing in German territory. In 1943, when put under German diplomatic pressure, Croatian, Slovak, and Romanian governments consented to the deportation to the East of their Jewish nationals from the German Reich, and Adolf Eichmann did indeed send these Jews to the death camps in due course. But Italy and Hungary simply forbade such action, even while the two countries were adopting strong anti-Jewish measures at home. The purpose was to assert national independence and to show the world that they were not Hitler's marionettes. Italian diplomats were especially famous for trying to recover and save some "accidentally" deported Jewish Italians. They were never satisfied with such routine German explanations as that the family in question "had emigrated" or had "left without leaving a forwarding address." Of course, as these people had been gassed, none was ever seen again. Unfortunately, the protection extended to the Italian Jews resident in Germany came to an end with the attempt of an Italian surrender in September 1943, and the same happened to Hungarian Jews residing in the German Reich after the German army occupied Hungary in March 1944. In fact, it was at least in part because Hitler feared that Hungary had fallen under Jewish influence and would want to change sides in the war that he ordered a preventive invasion and thus a direct intervention in the "solution of the Jewish Question" in that country.

In Hungary, despite drastic anti-Jewish legislation, most of the original 800,000 Jews (including some 100,000 Christians whom the law considered racially Jewish) were living under more or less normal conditions at the time of the German invasion. Thereafter, the Hungarian authorities collected more than 400,000 Jews and sent them to their deaths at Auschwitz. But in July 1944, Regent Admiral Miklós Horthy suspended the deportation of the Jews of Budapest and of those Jewish men who were doing labor service within the Hungarian army. True, Adolf Eichmann managed to smuggle two more trainloads of Jewish victims from Hungary to Auschwitz, but then he was ordered out of the country. He returned only in October, following an SS-led coup d'état against the Horthy regime. The coup then brought Ferenc Szálasi's Arrow Cross Party into power. Now mass deportations began again under Eichmann's guidance, but soon thereafter the Arrow Cross ordered the creation of two major ghettoes in Budapest. In the vain hope of receiving diplomatic recognition from some neutral countries, the Arrow Cross regime defied Eichmann—although most probably not Heinrich Himmler, who was trying to negotiate a personal treaty with the Western Allies. All in all, about 125,000 of Hungary's Jews survived in Budapest, and even more elsewhere.[2]

All through the war, Hungarians, Slovaks, Romanians, and Bulgarians anxiously watched each other, often complaining of each other's too conciliatory or too harsh treatment of the Jews. They also had to divine who would win the war and whether Great Britain and the United States were taking the Jewish issue seriously enough to punish the persecutors of Jews

Question

Find this interesting because they first were against this but now are doing what they were against.

Question.

after the war. As we know, not much was forthcoming from London and Washington until June 1944, when President Roosevelt finally delivered a strong warning to Regent Horthy. By then, it was too late for the Jews of the countryside in Hungary, but the warnings of Roosevelt, of Pope Pius XII, and of the king of Sweden helped to at least prolong if not always save the lives of the Budapest Jews.

In sum, Germany's allies solved the Jewish Question in their own ways, their actions characterized by a mixture of brutality and leniency, cynicism and occasional humanitarian considerations, as well as by a desire to assert national sovereignty.

Further proof of the independence of Germany's allies was their tendency to take their cues from Mussolini, not only with regard to the Jewish Question, but in all other respects. When Italy fell apart, the other German-allied countries lost their only beacon of light aside from Germany.

Hitler's allies had no choice but to trade with Germany; this allowed them to secure freedom of movement in military and political matters. Also, their own prosperity depended on producing for and trading with Germany, at least so long as the Germans were able to give something in return.

MUTUAL JEALOUSIES AND SUSPICIONS

The main worry of the governments of most countries allied to Germany was not the war itself but rather how the war and its end would affect their relations with their neighbors. Every major political and military step taken by Germany's allies was predicated on the fundamental consideration of relations with one's neighbors. The aim of the alliance members was to preserve, to gain, or to regain territory and, as a next step, either to get rid of their ethnic minorities or to make them politically impotent. Hence, there was no end to the headaches for Germany, whose basic aim was to keep order among its allies and to secure their economic and, hopefully, military assistance, as well as the German decision everywhere to support the well-established conservative elites and not the unruly extreme rightists. The latter were used only when no one else was available, which was what happened in Italy in the fall of 1943 and in Hungary in October 1944.

In disputes among allies, Nazi Germany and Italy (until the fall of 1943) tried to act as impartial arbitrators: witness the Second Vienna Award of

August 1940, which divided Transylvania between Hungary and Romania, as much as possible along ethnic lines. Certainly, the new borders were more judicious than the ones drawn up at the Treaty of Trianon in 1920 and again at the Paris Peace Conference in 1946. One must also consider the often frustrated efforts of a German-Italian military commission to arbitrate the mutual hatred of Romanians and Hungarians in divided Transylvania. However, as historian Holly Case has demonstrated, the "German-Italian Officers' Commission" was nearly powerless against the activist authorities in the two countries.[3]

In independent Croatia, the German military plenipotentiary, the former Austro-Hungarian general Edmund Glaise-Horstenau, and even local representatives of the SS, complained in vain about the murderous fury of the Croatian Ustashe against their Serbian Orthodox neighbors.

I wonder whether any alliance system, besides that of the Axis powers, has ever included as many mutually hostile allies. True, the statement does not apply to Finland, which had no German allies as neighbors. It was in East Central Europe and the Balkans that Germany's allies confronted each other. Bulgaria had coveted and now secured various provinces from Romania, Greece, and Yugoslavia; these were all territories that Bulgaria had lost as a result of the second Balkan war and the peace treaty following the First World War. Elsewhere in the Balkans, Catholic Croats, Bosnian Muslims, Orthodox Serbs, Montenegrins, Macedonians, Kosovans, and Albanians fought a many-sided civil war. Their armed conflicts had been precipitated by foreign invasion in 1941, but thereafter the presence of German, Italian, Bulgarian, and Hungarian occupation forces only complicated the ethnic struggle, which was finally put to an end not by the Germans or the Italians, but by Tito's supranational Yugoslav Communist partisans.

At least in the Balkans, not all warring partners were official allies of Germany; in Central Europe, however, the three enemies—Hungary, Romania, and Slovakia—were. Here is a characteristic anecdote preserved by Count Galeazzo Ciano, fascist Italy's foreign minister. In his famous diary, this is what he wrote for May 11, 1942, a short time after Hungary declared war on the United States:

> Hungarian uneasiness is expressed by a little story, which is going the rounds in Budapest. The Hungarian minister declares war on the United States, but the [American] official who receives the communication

is not very well informed about European matters and hence asks several questions: He asks: "Is Hungary a republic?"

"No, it is a kingdom."

"Then you have a king."

"No, we have an admiral."

"Then you have a fleet?"

"No, we have no sea."

"Do you have any claims, then?"

"Yes."

"Against America?"

"No."

"Against Great Britain?"

"No."

"Against Russia?"

"No."

"But against whom do you have these claims?"

"Against Romania."

"Then, will you declare war on Romania?"

"No, sir. We are allies."[4]

Ever since the formation, in 1921, of Yugoslavia's, Romania's, and Czechoslovakia's so-called Little Entente alliance, the primary concern of the three countries was how to protect their newly acquired lands from Hungarian revisionism. At first, the signatories cared less about Germany until, following Hitler's rise to power, the Little Entente slowly disintegrated. Slovakia, which in March 1939 had declared its independence with German support, kept nurturing a grievance over Hungary's seizure, also with German support, of what used to be southern Slovakia in Czechoslovakia. In the same month, the Hungarians reannexed Ruthenia, or Subcarpathian Rus, again with German permission, after defeating the local Rusin nationalists, thereby cutting off direct communication between Slovakia and Romania. Even worse for Slovakia, there was now a common Hungarian-Polish border. A year and a half later, Hungarian diplomacy achieved its greatest success by persuading Germany and Italy to return northern Transylvania to Hungary.

While the Hungarians set up their administration in Cluj (Kolozsvár in Hungarian, Klausenburg in German) (the Transylvanian principality's historic capital), the Soviets seized Bessarabia and northern Bukovina, again with German consent, all good reasons for the Romanians to resent Nazi Germany's hostile actions. But because Romania's traditional protector, France, had been defeated and was occupied, the Romanians had no choice but to join the German alliance, proof that in modern Europe the loss of a geopolitical patron inevitably leads to the search for a new one.

Less than a year later, in March 1941, the last link in the Little Entente broke when Yugoslavia first joined the Tripartite Pact and then reneged on its commitment, causing Hitler to wreak untold destruction on that country. In April, Hungary joined the German military attack on Yugoslavia, recovering some more territories lost as a result of World War I. Thus, by June 1941, when Slovakia, Romania, Croatia, and Hungary were entering the war on the German side, the three successors to the Little Entente had territorial claims on Hungary as well as some other parts of the region. Meanwhile, the Hungarians still felt grievously deprived of vast regions of what they had liked to call, before 1918, the Hungarian Empire. In brief, both for Hungary and for its neighbors, the newfangled Pax Germanica represented but a brief lull in a protracted and many-sided struggle.

It is interesting to contemplate how many times Germany's allies came to blows. For example, in March 1939 Hungarian troops entered Slovakia, forcing the latter to cede a small part of their country. At about the same time, Slovak and Hungarian airplanes battled each other in the skies and bombarded each other's territory. In September of the same year, the Hungarian government denied permission to both Germany and Slovakia to use the Hungarian railroads for troop transports against Poland. Characteristically, the Hungarians would have allowed the Germans (but not the Slovaks) to pass through—but only in exchange for German diplomatic support of a Hungarian military attack on Romania. How the Hungarians imagined that they would succeed against the Romanian army, which was many times the size of their own, remains a mystery, but what is certain is that all through the Second World War, the Romanian and Hungarian governments made preparations for attacking each other.

In August 1940, following the Second Vienna Award, Hungarian troops occupied northern Transylvania. It seems that local Hungarian commanders provoked clashes with alleged Romanian guerrillas so as to make the reconquest more of a heroic saga. A year later, while the Romanian and Hungarian armies were advancing together against the

Bolshevik enemy, as part of the same German army group, troops of the two countries clashed at their common frontier.

During the war against the Soviet Union, one of the German high command's important concerns was how to separate Romanians from Hungarians, an especially difficult task as, for some unknown reason, Romanians, Italians, Slovaks, Croats, and Hungarians were assembled within the German Army Group South. In the winter of 1942–1943, on the Don River, only the Italian Eighth Army kept apart the Hungarian Second Army and the Romanian Third Army. As both sides made amply clear, any cooperation, even any meeting between the two allies, was out of the question. A year later, when Hitler planned the military occupation of Hungary because of the Hungarian government's secret, or not-so-secret, attempts to secede from the war, Marshal Ion Antonescu offered 1 million Romanian soldiers to help in the occupation of Hungary. The Führer rejected the offer because he wanted to change the Hungarian leadership but not cause the Hungarian army and people to turn against him; this was a plan in which he eminently succeeded in March 1944. Romanian soldiers did, indeed, march into Budapest, not in March 1944 but in January 1945, and not as allies of Germany but as allies of the Soviet Union.

During the bulk of the war years, Romanians, Slovaks, Hungarians, and Croats denounced each other for plunder, corruption, and maltreatment of the civilian population. Romanians and Slovaks accused the Hungarians of having arrived at a modus vivendi in their zone of occupation with local anti-Nazi and anti-Soviet Ukrainian guerrillas, as well as fraternizing with Poles and Jews.

Not even the terrible debacles of the winter of 1942–1943 could bring together the allies, even though all complained bitterly of mistreatment by German troops during the precipitous withdrawal from the Don region. It was reported again and again that during the flight in subzero temperatures, Germans had seized the horse-drawn wagons of their allies, thrown the wounded into the snow, evicted soldiers from their night quarters in miserable peasant huts, and shot those who protested. Hungarian, Romanian, Italian, and Slovak soldiers who tried to hoist themselves on a German truck had their fingers crushed. There were reports of gunfights with the Germans, but no known account shows the allies teaming up against the brutality of the German soldiers.

Romania seceded from the war on August 23, 1944, a turn of events more devastating for Germany than the defeat at Stalingrad. Whereas

Stalingrad, despite the terrible losses in men and equipment, had not led to the collapse of the German front in the East, Romania's turning against Hitler fragmented the German southeastern army groups and allowed the Soviet army to occupy the Balkans.

A sign of growing German impotence by 1944 was that the German high command could do nothing about Romanian generals ignoring German instructions well before the fateful day of August 23. Actually, the gradual disentanglement of Romanian troops from the German embrace occurred well before Romania's surrender to the Soviet Union.

For a fleeting moment, the surrender of Romania appeared to the Hungarian high command not as an unmitigated disaster but as a golden opportunity for reconquering southern Transylvania and for planting the national flag on yet another Carpathian range. While the Red Army raced from Bessarabia through Bucharest to the southern Carpathians and the Romanian army was regrouping, two Hungarian armies entered some southern Transylvanian cities, set up a military administration there, and ordered the Jews to wear the yellow star. Ghettoization also began immediately. Unfortunately for the Hungarians, Red Army units arrived in southern Transylvania within a few days, and the Hungarians had to withdraw into Rump Hungary (as defined by the Treaty of Trianon), there to be followed by Soviet and Romanian troops. By December Soviets and Romanians were besieging the Hungarian capital. By not joining the Romanians in the change of sides, Hungarians lost the last opportunity to avoid the near-total destruction of their country; their mutual enmity had prevented any kind of cooperation between the two so-called allies.

All in all, the German alliance brought varying results to its members. The Finns gained nothing by joining in Operation Barbarossa; instead, they were forced to give up more territory to the Soviets than they had following the Winter War of 1939–1940. They also had to subject their foreign policy to the Soviet Union. But at least domestically, Finland was completely spared Bolshevization.

Slovakia and Croatia considered their participation in the war as an exercise in sovereignty. This was all the more beneficial to the two countries as, after the war, they were reintegrated into Czechoslovakia and Yugoslavia, respectively, thus escaping punishment for their wartime behavior. Ultimately, Slovaks and Croats achieved their national purpose of ridding themselves of their German and Jewish fellow citizens as well as "inheriting" their properties. But whereas Slovakia was left with only a thoroughly intimidated Hungarian minority, Croatia's problems with Serbs and Muslims were far more serious and in the 1990s led to an internecine war. Still, what is important in nationalist eyes is that both Croatia and Slovakia are free and that the vast majority of their inhabitants are of Croatian and Slovak nationality, respectively.

Despite all the clever maneuvering of its king and politicians, Bulgaria did not escape the ravages of war. American bombers repeatedly devastated the capital, and following an unjustified Soviet declaration of war in September 1944, the country suffered military occupation, a Communist takeover, and one of the most ruthless political purges in history. Moreover, Bulgaria had to declare war on Germany, which had caused it no grief in the past. The 100,000 soldiers of the Bulgarian First Army fought their way to Central Europe, suffering enormous casualties, yet at the subsequent peace treaties Bulgaria had to consent to territorial losses.

Romania's change of sides hastened the end of World War II in Europe by several months, yet the conflict cost the Romanian people 500,000 dead, two-thirds of them by fighting on the side of the Germans, one-third by fighting against them. With the peace treaty of 1946, Romania regained northern Transylvania but not Bessarabia and northern Bukovina. The country also subsequently fell under the sway of one of the most brutal Communist dictatorships. Finally, Romania did not even become purely Romanian, because, unlike other countries in Eastern Europe, it had not expelled its German minority and because there remained more than 1.5 million Hungarians as well as many smaller ethnic groups in the country.

The principal loser of both world wars was Hungary. Not only did the German alliance bring a degree of devastation to the country that only those of Poland, Russia, and Germany surpassed, but it was not allowed to keep any of the provinces it had regained between 1938 and 1941. Instead, at the end of the war, Hungary was obliged to give up even more territory to Czechoslovakia—again in complete defiance of the principle of ethnic self-determination. Furthermore, it is hard to see in what way the killing of hundreds of thousands of generally assimilated Jews and the postwar expulsion of more than 200,000 generally assimilated Germans had profited the country. Certainly, extreme Hungarian nationalists see it as a gain, for it had put an end to ethnic diversity. Yet, in reality, the country suffers badly for having lost its two most dynamic minorities.

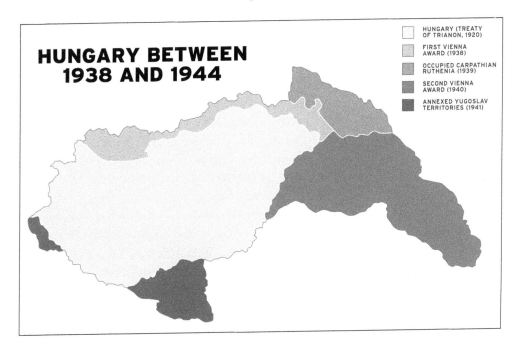

HUNGARY BETWEEN 1938 AND 1944

- HUNGARY (TREATY OF TRIANON, 1920)
- FIRST VIENNA AWARD (1938)
- OCCUPIED CARPATHIAN RUTHENIA (1939)
- SECOND VIENNA AWARD (1940)
- ANNEXED YUGOSLAV TERRITORIES (1941)

ETHNIC CLEANSING

The attempt of Eastern Europeans to assimilate or to expel their ethnic minorities is as old as nationalism. However, the Jews were hit much harder than other groups because of traditional religious prejudice, the total absence of a foreign protector, and the Jews' own tradition of trusting and obeying the authorities. Culturally and religiously, the Jews were the "other," yet many among them had become enviably prosperous and successful. Among the countries allied to Germany, Jews were both numerically and proportionally well represented in Slovakia, Romania, and Hungary, much less so in Bulgaria and Croatia, and very little in Finland.* After 1918 the Jewish presence became statistically crucial in the new states of Eastern Europe because their assimilation into one or

---

*It must be noted here that in all of Hitler's Europe, the Finnish army alone drafted Jews into its combat units; in fact, more than three hundred of them served in the war against the Soviet Union, making these Jews unwilling fellow fighters of the German armed forces. See Hannu Rautkallio, "Finland," in *Encyclopedia of the Holocaust,* edited by Israel Gutman, 4 vols. (New York: Macmillan, 1990), 2:493.

another nationality could tip the balance for or against the new dominant nation. In both Slovakia and Romania, Jews were pressured either to choose the new dominant nation or to declare themselves of Jewish nationality. But no matter what nationality the Jews chose, the notion spread in anti-Semitic circles, whether Romanian, Slovak, or Hungarian, that the Jews were traitors. In Transylvania they suffered the double jeopardy of being both Hungarians and Jews; in Bessarabia, which the Soviets had seized in 1940 and the Romanians reconquered in 1941, Jews suffered the double jeopardy of being Jews as well as being seen as Soviet-friendly Communists. This lent false legitimacy to the massacre of Jews by the Romanian soldiers and gendarmes in Bessarabia and other Romanian provinces formerly under Soviet occupation. It also eased the conscience of the Hungarian authorities, in the event they possessed such a thing, when sending the Jews of northern Transylvania to Auschwitz. The unforeseen consequence was that every Jew the Hungarians deported to the death camps meant one less Hungarian in the area that would soon again be a Romanian province.

The attempted annihilation of the Jews was only the first step in the process of ethnic purification, a popular measure in all countries, whether allied to or defeated by Germany. As Heinrich Himmler infamously said, the time had come "for the cleansing of the soil among the peoples [*völkische Flurbereinigung*]."[5]

Hungarians, Romanians, and Slovaks were, of course, not the only ethnic cleansers. Nazism's East European victims, such as the Poles and Czechs, also ended up ridding themselves of their Jews and their entire German minority. President Edvard Beneš enunciated, while still in exile in London, "We are preparing the final solution of the question of our Germans and Hungarians since the new republic will be a Czechoslovak nation state."[6] Amazingly, this murderously racist program was approved in 1945 at Potsdam by all the great powers. Altogether, up to 13 million Germans fled, were expelled, or were killed in the postwar years. As a result, today's Eastern Europe is not only largely *judenfrei* (free of Jews) but also largely *deutschenfrei* (free of Germans). In addition, millions of Poles, Ukrainians, and others were driven out of their homes and transferred elsewhere. In short, while fascism, Nazism, and communism seem to have been transitional phenomena, the consequences of ethnic cleansing will remain with us forever.

Image 5.2. Miklós Horthy, former Austro-Hungarian admiral who, between 1920 and 1944, was regent (governor) of Hungary, at the annual St. Stephen's procession near the Royal Palace in Buda. Source: Bundesarchiv, Bild 102–12190 / photo: o.Ang.

HITLER'S "STRONGMAN" ALLIES

Who were the men at the head of the countries allied to Germany? Actually, it is not too difficult to draw a collective portrait of Benito Mussolini of Italy, Reverend Jozef Tiso of Slovakia, Admiral Miklós Horthy of Hungary, Marshal Ion Antonescu of Romania, Ante Pavelić of Croatia, and King Boris III of Bulgaria. Historians call them "strongmen," leaders whose power exceeded the customary democratic restraints set upon the authority of heads of state. Yet with the exception of Croatia's Ante Pavelić, none was an absolute dictator, their authority being restrained at least to a degree by some kind of a constitution. In fact, all were born and grew up in more or less well-functioning multiparty parliamentary systems that they helped to weaken or whittle away in the antidemocratic interwar years.

Although by far not all the strongmen were professional soldiers, they usually appeared in uniform and preferably on horseback—including

Finland's Marshal Carl Gustaf Emil von Mannerheim, who was commander of the armed forces but was also his country's unofficial leader. Admiral Horthy and Marshal Antonescu were career military men, but Pavelić, although by profession a lawyer, and Mussolini, a journalist and a politician, were nearly always seen wearing military garb. Jozef Tiso of Slovakia always wore his priestly cassock, which is also a uniform, and Czar or King Boris III of Bulgaria often wore either the uniform of a Bulgarian field marshal or that of the honorary colonel of one or another foreign guards' regiment.

Tiso, Horthy, and Boris III shared power with a prime minister they had selected and appointed; Mussolini, Antonescu, and Pavelić were their own prime ministers, but the first two of the three, as we have already said, recognized the sometimes theoretical, sometimes real higher authority of their kings. The Duce governed in the name of King Victor Emmanuel III; Antonescu acted as national leader (*conducator*) at first under King Charles II and then under King Michael I. The two strongmen later paid a heavy price for having failed to get rid of their king; in August 1943, Mussolini was arrested at Victor Emmanuel's orders, and in August 1944 young King Michael personally arrested Marshal Antonescu.

How to judge the "strongmen"? How useful or harmful were they to humankind, their people, and their countries? Regarding the interests of humanity, the judgment must be harsh, for they had allied their countries with Nazi Germany, one of the most destructive political systems in world history. Germany's allies contributed millions of soldiers and enormous resources to the common war effort. Yet one may also argue that Italy's participation in the alliance did more harm than good to Germany, for it led to unwanted, unnecessary, and wasteful wars in the Balkans and in northern Africa. The other allied armies were more useful to Hitler, although their equipment and morale were greatly inferior. Moreover, as already made clear, Germany's allies could make life very difficult for the Germans, and ultimately most of them were able to turn their backs on Hitler.

The next question to be considered is whether there were better alternatives for these countries than these German-friendly governments. Would other, better, statesmen have been able to avoid at least some of the death and destruction? Three selected cases might show that an anti-Nazi alternative earlier than 1944 would have been difficult but not impossible to achieve.

The first case is that of the Yugoslav royal government, which rather reluctantly joined the Tripartite Pact on March 25, 1941. Among other things, the pact allowed the crossing of German troops on their way to Greece. Two days later, some Yugoslav generals, aided by British secret service agents, overthrew the government, thereby choosing conflict with Germany. In April a combined German, Italian, Hungarian, and Bulgarian force invaded and systematically dismembered the country. One may certainly argue that had the coup d'état not taken place, Yugoslavia could have remained more or less neutral in the war.

Another case is the overthrow of Mussolini by monarchal and left-wing elements in August and September 1943, which precipitated a German invasion of such parts of Italy that had not yet been occupied by the Western armies. It also led to the death of thousands of Italian civilians and soldiers and the partial extermination of Italy's Jewish population. Italy's volte-face turned out to be of little use to the Allies, who still had to slog their way up the Italian peninsula while the Germans disarmed and captured the entire Italian army. With Mussolini still fully in power, Italy might conceivably have suffered less from a German occupation and the ravages of war.

The third case is that of Hungary, which the German army invaded and occupied, in March 1944, under the valid suspicion that Regent Horthy and his ministers were attempting to extricate their country from the war. There was no resistance to the German occupation, yet within a little more than a year nearly 1 million Hungarians, including 500,000 Hungarian Jews, were killed and the country left in ruins. The dean of historians of the Holocaust, Randolph Braham, speculates that had the Hungarian government not secretly negotiated with the Western Allies—of which Hitler was well informed through his spies in the Hungarian government—it is conceivable that the German occupation may have been avoided and more Jewish and non-Jewish Hungarians could have survived.[7] Braham's thesis is challenging, but there is no proof of its validity; furthermore, one might well counterargue that unquestioning Hungarian military and political collaboration would have prolonged the war, which in turn would have led to more Jewish deaths.

As already mentioned, the Germans did not and could not force the Italian, Finnish, Hungarian, Romanian, Slovak, Croatian, and Bulgarian governments to enter the war; they had all joined of their own volition. Whether the strongmen could have continued to keep their countries out of the war is impossible to answer; one can only point to the geographic factor. Far-away Bulgaria, with its traditional pro-Russian sympathies, could and did avoid participation in the Russian campaign, yet it still ended up being heavily bombarded by the Western Allies. Hungary, which was next door to the greater German Reich and had benefited from German help in recovering some of the territories it had lost as a result of defeat in World War I, would have found it much more difficult not to engage its troops in the Eastern campaign. In any case, the Hungarians did not even wait for Barbarossa to join in the war. In April 1941, having recently concluded the Treaty of Eternal Friendship with Yugoslavia, Hungary attacked Yugoslavia in harmony with the German campaign. The aim was to recover, at least in part, the lands that Yugoslavia had seized at the end of World War I. In brief, Hungary's was the typical case of a small country profiting from a major strategic decision made by a gigantic neighbor, in this case Nazi Germany.

It is noteworthy, however, that not everybody in Hungary was pleased with his or her country's blatantly opportunistic repudiation of a "Treaty of Eternal Friendship" with Yugoslavia. The Hungarian prime minister, Count Pál Teleki, committed suicide over what he called in a letter to the regent "an infamous act." Yet Teleki himself had been a dedicated nationalist. Two months later, Hungary joined in the attack on the Soviet Union for fear of lagging behind in the race for Hitler's favor. When Regent Horthy, in October 1944, finally tried to "jump out" of the war, as the term went at that time, Germany's nearness and the treason of the officer corps combined to thwart the attempt.

But were the strongmen up to the task? Decidedly, none possessed a great mind; none was a political giant.

Benito Mussolini, a former Social Democratic journalist, had become a rabid nationalist during World War I. After the war and a peace treaty that did not satisfy Italian imperialist ambitions, he founded the Fascist Party, which with populist propaganda, expansionist ideology, and brutal practices allowed him not only to become prime minister in the early 1920s but also to establish absolute power in Italy. Mussolini had the reputation of possessing a fast-moving and forceful intellect, but his demagoguery, megalomania, and undue pride always got the better of him. He was overthrown and arrested in August 1943. Liberated shortly thereafter by German parachutists, he founded a short-lived Italian fascist republic that engaged in a ferocious civil war with other Italians. He was captured and executed by Italian partisans in the last days of the war.

Slovakia's Jozef Tiso was a country priest who believed in God with the same fervor that he demonstrated in his hatred for Jews, Hungarians, Communists, Socialists, liberals, Freemasons, and Czechs. All these people, he believed, conspired to undermine Christian ethics, the Holy Mother Church, and the independence of his beloved Slovakia. Toward the end of the war, much of his army and administration rebelled against him, and he remained in power only at the end of German bayonets. Arrested at the end of the war, Tiso was hanged by orders of a Slovak court in 1947.

Admiral Miklós Horthy of Hungary had been one of the not so numerous landlocked Hungarian youth who joined the Austro-Hungarian navy and made a quick career thanks to his ambition, talent, and some sort of governmental affirmative action program favoring Hungarians in the fleet. Called upon to serve as an aide-de-camp to Emperor-King Franz Joseph, an appointment of which he remained forever proud, he always claimed to follow in the footsteps of the wise old ruler. Yet when the Dual Monarchy collapsed in 1918 and his naval career came to an end, he learned to be a chauvinist and a racist. Like so many of his contemporaries, he blamed the liberals, Jews, and Communists for the military collapse and the political revolutions. He would never admit that the dissolution of the Dual Monarchy in 1918 had been the result of economic exhaustion, hunger, military defeat, and the unbridled chauvinism manifested by the leaders of the monarchy's eleven ethnic groups.

As a former admiral and the victor in a minor naval encounter during the war against French and Italian warships, Horthy made himself the head of a new "national army" agitating not against the Romanian, Czechoslovak, and South Slav forces invading Hungary but against the Communist revolutionary government of Hungary. While the Romanian troops occupied Budapest, his officers' detachments in western Hungary engaged in killing Jews and suspected Communists, mostly poor peasants who had dared to turn against the landowners. Horthy's anti-Semitism and fear of the lower classes stemmed from the experience of the 1918–1919 Hungarian democratic and Communist revolutions, yet there was also enough in him of an officer in Habsburg service, and of a gentleman, to constantly hesitate between violent counterrevolutionary radicalism and moderate politics. By 1941 he had presided over the introduction of a series of anti-Semitic laws aiming at the takeover of Jewish-owned factories, banks, shops, and offices and the ultimate expulsion of Jews, yet he also maintained friendly relations with some great Jewish businessmen and generally wished to protect "patriotic," that is, assimilated, Jews. Horthy profited from an alliance with Hitler to recover some of the territories Hungary had lost to Czechoslovakia, Romania, and Yugoslavia after World War I, but he also feared German ideological and political influence in Hungary. He showed genuine foresight when he predicted, early in the war, that British and American naval superiority would ultimately prevail, but did not dare draw the necessary consequences from this prediction. Easily influenced by his friends and advisers, Horthy often took wildly contradictory stands. In 1944–1945 he at first did not protest the Germans troops marching into Hungary, but by early fall he tried to withdraw the country from the war. This was prevented by a German SS-led coup d'état that made him a prisoner of the Germans. A man of great personal charm and mediocre mind, Horthy ended his life in Portuguese exile.

Ion Antonescu of Romania, who, too, was a soldier, had always been a conservative ultranationalist.[8] He was also greatly ambitious, daring to overrule his commanders during World War I and later defying Charles II, his king—not that the latter did not deserve defiance with his irresponsibility, immorality, and corrupt practices. Antonescu hated Communists, Jews, and Hungarians, with the three being identical in his eyes. In the late 1930s, he unhesitatingly associated himself with the even more nationalistic and violent fascist party, called the Iron Guard. Unlike Regent Horthy or Boris III, he gave the fascist salute at public meetings, and in 1940 he formed a coalition government with the Iron Guard, encouraging the latter to engage in pogroms against Jews and the Roma people. A few months later, using his comfortable personal relations with the Führer and the latter's fear of political radicalism among Germany's allies, Antonescu literally exterminated the Iron Guard leadership and thenceforth governed alone. Yet he did not do away with the institution of monarchy. In June 1941, he sent his armies against the Soviet Union as well as organized Romania's own, unique, Holocaust of the Jewish people. At his direct orders, thousands of Jews, including decorated war veterans, women, and children, were crammed into trains that then aimlessly traveled the countryside until nearly everybody suffocated inside. The survivors were then robbed and killed by the Romanian gendarmes and the local populace. In fact, greed and robbery were supreme everywhere, including the city of Odessa, where Romanian soldiers and gendarmes tortured, hanged, shot, burned alive, flayed, or blew up with hand grenades some thirty thousand local Jews. Antonescu had insisted that no Jew remain alive in the city.

One would have supposed that Antonescu was simply mad, but then, as earlier indicated, he reversed himself in 1942 and refused German demands for the surrender of Romania's remaining Jews. By 1944, under his rule, Romania had become a safe haven into which Jews escaped from persecution elsewhere. By then also, Antonescu had begun betraying his friend Hitler by secretly negotiating with the Western Allies for surrender. But now young King Michael and the army high command took matters in their own hands, and, as we already know, in August 1944 Antonescu was easily arrested. He was executed after the war.

Ante Pavelić of Croatia was a fanatical nationalist in an age of fanatical nationalism; he abominated Jews, Communists, Serbs, and the Eastern Orthodox Church. During his rule, between 1941 and 1945, hundreds of thousands of Serbs were killed in Croatia for their nationality or their religious affiliation or both. Hundreds of thousands of Eastern Orthodox were forcibly converted to Roman Catholicism, mostly by zealous Franciscan monks. Against this backdrop, some important German delegates protested in vain. Pavelić also had the Jews and the Roma killed, even though his own wife was half-Jewish and the wives of some of his most important underlings were of fully Jewish origin, as had been, incidentally, the founder of his own political party. Having totally ruined his country, Pavelić in the spring of 1945 left his followers and his army in the lurch and escaped to Argentina, where he continued his political activity. Badly wounded by an attacker in 1957, he died in Madrid two years later.

King Boris III of Bulgaria belonged to a family of German princelings, as did most of the European crowned heads, which did not prevent him from using the title czar, meaning "Caesar" or "emperor," quite an ambitious denomination for the ruler of a small country that had just lost two consecutive wars. Boris himself learned to survive rightist, military coups d'état, and several assassination attempts as well as an anarchist-Communist bombing attack, which, in 1925, killed 150 members of the Bulgarian political and social elite assembled in a cathedral. In turn, several thousand Communist and Peasant Party members were killed. During World War II, Boris cautiously kept Bulgaria out of the war with the Soviet Union but could not avoid an ultimately catastrophic declaration of war on the Western Allies. Although his role in preventing a Bulgarian Holocaust is still debated, it seems certain that the survival of all the 50,000 Bulgarian Jews was due not only to some Bulgarian politicians and church leaders as well as the Bulgarian people but also and very much so to the king. Boris died of heart failure in August 1943, but rumor had it that he had been murdered at the orders of Germany. It is customary among journalists and memoir writers to refer to him as "Boris the Wily," which is still better than to be called a fanatic, a description that fits men such as Ante Pavelić and Ion Antonescu.

Finally, Marshal Mannerheim governed Finland with a great deal of personal and constitutional restraint. No doubt, he was influenced by his Swedish aristocratic background, his long service in the Russian czarist army, and his fight against the Communists in Finland's terrible civil war of 1918.

How did the populations of these countries fare during the war? As a basic rule, we can say that having their own army, police, and administrative apparatuses allowed the governments to maintain law and order and to provide for their populations better than the countries under German occupation. Germany's allies were also far more able than others to despoil their neighbors in order to enrich, or at least to better feed, their own citizenries. Yet there were no absolute rules: the tightly German-controlled national government of the Bohemian and Moravian Protectorate could feed the population and was able to maintain order better than independent fascist Croatia, where civil war reigned. Occupied but democratic Denmark was a paradise compared with Mussolini's Italy, where the government mismanaged the already frail economy and where young men were sent to die in the wars of Ethiopia, Greece, North Africa, and Yugoslavia. Toward the end of the war, thousands of Italian POWs died in Soviet and German captivity, while women and children suffered from Allied bombardment, German terror, and the depredations of German, American, British, Polish, Australian, Moroccan, Brazilian, and French West African soldiers.

Judging by tourist standards, wartime Europe's liveliest cafés, the best cuisine, and the seemingly most carefree population could be found neither in Berlin, which was being constantly bombed, nor in Paris or Rome, where the food supply was notoriously short. The most desirable places, aside from neutral Stockholm, Zurich, and Istanbul, were Budapest, until the German occupation in March 1944; Bucharest, until the arrival of the Red Army in August 1944; and Copenhagen as well as Prague, both under permanent German occupation and liberated only in the last days of the war. Two of these cities were capitals of countries allied to Germany, two lived under German occupation, but all had accepted German predominance.

One of the most terrible places during the war was undoubtedly Warsaw, where, following the suppression of the great Polish uprising in the early fall of 1944 and the razing by the Germans of the entire city, the remaining inhabitants lived like troglodytes in cellars and sewers as well as being starved. During the siege of Leningrad between 1941 and 1944, nearly 1 million civilians died of cold and starvation.

We are left with two final questions: What type of individuals and groups were most keen on seeing their governments collaborate with the Third Reich? How much suffering did the armies of Germany's allies visit on other peoples during the war? There is little scholarly study on these subjects, but let us engage in some speculation.

Italians felt more affinity for other speakers of Romance languages and thus for the French than for the Germans. Besides, Germany and German-speaking Austria had been the great enemy during World War I. But then there were also those in Italy who perceived a close affinity between Italian Fascism and German National Socialism.

Romanians, too, speak a Romance language, and the Romanian political and military elite had been trained largely in French schools. Without French assistance in the nineteenth century, an independent Romania would not have existed. On the other hand, the mighty Romanian fascist Iron Guard professed unconditional admiration for the Führer.

Ever since Chancellor Bismarck's days, Hungarians tended to look at the German Reich as a defender of their independence against Austrian and Habsburg encroachments and the Russian and Pan-Slavic menace. More important, it was by Hitler's grace that their country recovered some of the lands it had lost after the First World War. The officer corps in particular cherished the memory of the "comradeship in arms" when Germans, Austrians, and Hungarians stood "shoulder to shoulder" against the Russian, Serbian, and Italian enemy. On the other hand, Hungary's cultural elite much preferred to cast its eyes on Paris; the aristocracy was famous for its Anglophile attitudes, and the Jews, who made up an inordinately large part of the educated classes and were the primary bearers of

German culture in Hungary, had no choice but to dread Hitler's Germany. Members of the large German minority in Hungary and Romania both tended and were pressured by Reich German representatives to identify with their ancestral home and even to join the Waffen SS.

Anti-Semites from every layer of society admired and envied the Germans for their ability to solve the "Jewish Question." Lovers of smart uniforms and of war were inevitably drawn to the German cause. Young people, especially in Eastern Europe, tended to admire, nay to worship, the demigods of the SS Panzer divisions; the thousands who volunteered for the Waffen SS from nearly every European country paid with their lives for the admiration.

Within specific social groups, big industrialists and large landowners favored the closest possible cooperation with Nazi Germany where great profits could be made. Even Jewish factory and mine owners earned fabulous sums in Hungary and Romania from producing goods for the German army. Besides, working for the German war industry, as owners, engineers, or workers, appeared to be the best guarantee of Jewish survival.

As befits semiauthoritarian or, perhaps better, semiparliamentary countries, Germany's allies conducted no public opinion polls; during the war, the press and the radio were centrally controlled, as they were everywhere else in Europe. Consequently, it is hard to know what people believed in and where their hearts belonged. It is worth noting, however, that in Hungary's 1939 parliamentary elections, which were based on a restricted male and an even more restricted female suffrage but were genuinely secret, the cautiously pro-German Government Party and the much more pro-German radical Far Right parties together received more than 80 percent of the votes. On the Left, a Jewish-supported bourgeois party and the worker-supported Social Democrats garnered only a handful of mandates. The famous "Red" working-class districts in Budapest voted overwhelmingly for National Socialist candidates. The fact is that, in 1939, the majority of Hungary's voters favored cooperation with Nazi Germany, welcomed anti-Jewish measures, and demanded that the government attempt to recover some, if not all, of Hungary's lost lands. One might indeed argue that the notion of an alliance with Nazi Germany met with popular approval in Slovakia, Hungary, Croatia, Romania, Bulgaria, and even Finland, at least in the first years of the war. Only in Italy was the public generally loath to fight on the German side.

In general, it was from Hitler's Germany that the majority of people expected the realization of national goals, the improvement of living conditions, modernization, social reform, and, last but not least, permission and encouragement in the enterprise of robbing and expelling the Jews.

As for the second question, how the armies allied to Germany treated the populations in the occupied countries, the answer must be sadly negative: there is no indication that the Hungarian or Romanian or even Finnish soldiers treated the local Russian population and the Soviet minorities any better than did the German soldiers. The Romanian army, as already explained, organized its own Holocaust in the territories it occupied. On the other hand, Italian soldiers were famously kind to Jews and even hid many in their barracks in Yugoslavia and France.

Time was short for all this, however. Following the battles of Stalingrad and El Alamein, an increasing number of Europeans decided to oppose the German presence, at first with symbolic gestures, then with words and political action, and finally with arms. Beginning in 1943, *resistance*—not *collaboration*—was the watchword of the politically conscious Europeans.

NOTES

1. Peter Gosztony, *Hitlers fremde Heere: Das Schicksal der nichtdeutschen Armeen in Ostfeldzug* (Düsseldorf: Econ Verlag, 1976), 100.

2. The most substantial source on the Final Solution in Hungary is Randolph L. Braham, ed., *The Politics of Genocide: The Holocaust in Hungary*, 2 vols. (New York: Columbia University Press, 1994).

3. Holly A. Case, *Between States: The Transylvanian Question and the European Idea During World War II* (Stanford, CA: Stanford University Press, 2009), 150–174.

4. Galeazzo Ciano, *Ciano's Diary, 1939–1943,* edited by Malcolm Muggeridge (London: Heinemann, 1947), 467–468.

5. Cited in Norman M. Naimark, *Fires of Hatred: Ethnic Cleansing in Twentieth Century Europe* (Cambridge, MA: Harvard University Press, 2001), 67.

6. Cited in Kálmán Janics, *Czechoslovak Policy and the Hungarian Minority,* Social Science Monographs (New York: distributed by Columbia University Press, 1982), 72.

7. See Braham, *Politics of Genocide,* 1:233–234.

8. See Iosif Constantin Dragin, *Antonescu: Marshal and Ruler of Romania, 1940–1944,* translated by Andrei Bantas (Bucharest: Europa Nova, 1995); and Dennis Deletant, *Hitler's Forgotten Ally: Ion Antonescu and His Regime, Romania, 1940–44* (New York: Palgrave Macmillan, 2006).

CHAPTER SIX

The Beginnings of German Decline

The Growth and Many Dilemmas of the
Resistance Movements

In the summer and fall of 1942, German power was at its height; all the more dramatic were the great reversals that ensued in the late fall of the same year. From that time on, the road led inevitably to the total defeat of National Socialist Germany. Yet even though the German generals must have known that the war would be lost, they continued to obey the Führer, some for another year, most of them to the bitter end. It is possible to argue, however, that the Casablanca Conference, which took place in January 1943, and at which the Western Allies resolved to demand Germany's unconditional surrender, made it more difficult for German generals to end the war. Unconditional surrender meant delivering one's soldiers as well as oneself to the good graces of the enemy. True, decent treatment could be expected from the Western Allies, but at the time of the Casablanca Resolution the British and the Americans did not have even a foothold in Europe. Meanwhile, the relentlessly advancing Soviet Red Army troops were likely to act wildly revengeful once they reached Germany. Whatever the cause of the German refusal to surrender, we must remember that of the 50 million people who were killed in the war, about 40 million died during the last two and a half years of a six-year war.

The battles of El Alamein and Stalingrad, fought mainly in the fall and winter of 1942 are legendary events, and they have been described thousands of times. It should be enough to say here that at El Alamein, in Egypt, British and Commonwealth troops defeated the famed German general Erwin Rommel's German and Italian troops, shattering Hitler's dream of reaching the Suez Canal. The battle marked the beginning of the end of the Axis presence in North Africa, and British historiography is justly proud of the great victory won so far from home. As Churchill stated, "Before El Alamein we never won a battle, after El Alamein we never lost one."

In Russia, following the Battle of Stalingrad, the Germans could no longer hope to interrupt traffic on the Volga, Europe's longest river that connected Russia to the oil wells of Baku on the Caspian Sea. Instead, they had to evacuate the entire Caucasus region as well as other huge areas of their southeastern front. The armies of their Hungarian, Italian, Romanian, Croatian, and Slovak allies had been largely wiped out. From then on, Hitler's armed forces had no choice but to retreat or to surrender; unfortunately, except for those in North Africa, only a few chose to surrender.

Meanwhile also, with Pearl Harbor, the conflict had become globalized. Japan's war, although fought separately, mainly because Japan and the Soviet Union had remained on friendly terms until August 1945, nevertheless had an immense influence on the European conflict. The Battle of Guadalcanal, which took place in part on the high seas and in part on an island in the Pacific between August 1942 and February 1943, ended in a clear American victory. Thereafter, Japan, just like Germany, was on the defensive and could no longer hope for victory.

It is worth noting here the crucial differences between the size of the battles in the Pacific and in North Africa, on the one hand, and in Russia, on the other. By its very nature, the Battle of Guadalcanal involved "only" tens of thousands of American and Japanese combat troops, marines, air crew, and sailors. The Battle of El Alamein involved some 300,000 Axis and Allied soldiers and caused the deaths of maybe 10,000 among them. On the other hand, the Battle of Stalingrad, fought between August 1942 and February 1943, was fought by well over 2 million Axis and Soviet soldiers, of whom nearly 1 million died—if not on the battlefield, then in POW camps; it is small wonder that the world, especially the Europeans, perceived the Battle of Stalingrad as the real turning point in the war.

As it should be clear from the above, by 1943 the time had come for the Europeans to prepare for, or even to hasten, the departure of the German troops; the hitherto modest resistance movements began to blossom. But before we go into some detail here, we must ask ourselves what the goals of the wartime resisters were. Their primary aim was to oppose those in

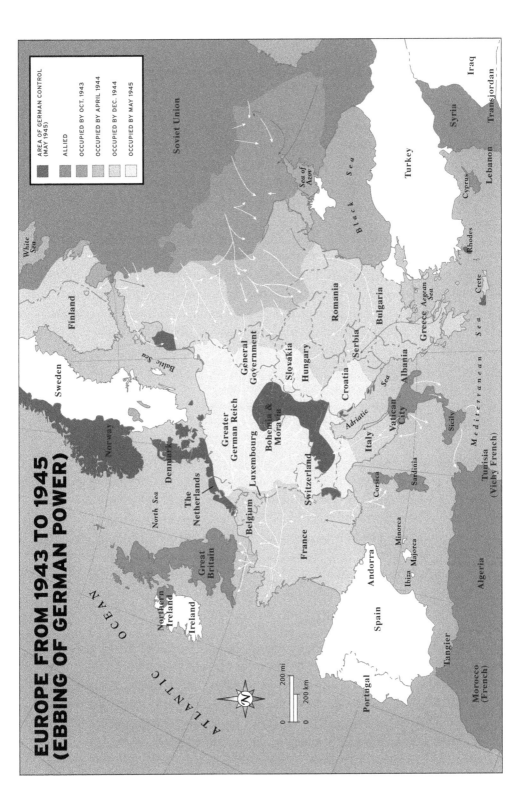

EUROPE FROM 1943 TO 1945 (EBBING OF GERMAN POWER)

AREA OF GERMAN CONTROL (MAY 1945)

- ALLIED
- OCCUPIED BY OCT. 1943
- OCCUPIED BY APRIL 1944
- OCCUPIED BY DEC. 1944
- OCCUPIED BY MAY 1945

ATLANTIC OCEAN

White Sea

Soviet Union

Finland

Sweden

Norway

Denmark

Baltic Sea

North Sea

Great Britain

Northern Ireland

Ireland

The Netherlands

Belgium

Luxembourg

Greater German Reich

General Government

Bohemia & Moravia

Slovakia

Hungary

Switzerland

France

Andorra

Spain

Portugal

Tangier

Morocco (French)

Algeria

Tunisia (Vichy French)

Corsica

Sardinia

Minorca

Ibiza

Majorca

Italy

Vatican City

Sicily

Mediterranean Sea

Adriatic Sea

Croatia

Serbia

Albania

Greece

Romania

Bulgaria

Aegean Sea

Crete

Rhodes

Cyprus

Black Sea

Sea of Azov

Turkey

Syria

Lebanon

Iraq

Transjordan

200 mi

200 km

power in occupied Europe, be they Germans or persons in German service. Further aims were to wash off the shame of the initial defeat and to reawaken patriotic sentiments, to provide vital information to the outside powers fighting Nazism, to assist crash-landed Allied air crews in avoiding capture, and to sabotage war production. Note that helping the persecuted was the goal of only small groups within the various resistance movements. The long-term goal of the resistance was to liberate at least a part of the homeland with its own forces in order to establish a native government before the arrival of the liberating armies. All this was to be done with the use of a clandestine press and radio, political action, and weapons. The resistance movements also made plans to punish those responsible for the original defeat as well as collaborators and, even more important, to bring about a new society. Finally, two barely concealed purposes of the resistance were to bring about a social revolution, or at least a changing of the guard, and to expel or to annihilate some, if not all, of their country's ethnic and religious minorities. Needless to say, all these goals and their execution turned out to be extremely controversial.

Problems varied according to location: there was, for instance, the dilemma of how to resist the German authorities when there were hardly any German soldiers to be seen, such as in the countries allied to Germany. If you hated the German Nazis, were you also morally obligated to fight against your own government, which was assisting the German war effort with men and guns, but might be using the arms deliveries to try to protect the country's freedom of choice and, specifically, its Jewish citizens? And what if the German-friendly government was secretly—and often not so secretly—negotiating with the Western Allies? Was a collaborationist government always an enemy? We will analyze this dilemma especially in the next chapter.

LIFE AND DEATH IN THE RESISTANCE

The first thing to remember is that resistance involved illegal activity, illegal not only in the eyes of the German or other occupation forces but also according to international conventions and the laws of one's country. At least initially, resistance was also unpopular among most of the resisters' compatriots, who rightly dreaded the danger and misery that such activity would bring upon their heads. To resist meant to leave the legal path and to act as a criminal, to the point of using the slang and the code words of the underworld. In order to be able to print and distribute illegal newspapers, one had to steal strictly controlled printing paper and machines and to forge or steal ration cards, banknotes, residence permits, and identity cards. To fight the enemy, the resisters needed to seize arms from military garrisons or from rival resisters. All this required the talents of a burglar, a forger, and a thief. To be in the armed resistance brought the necessity to kill, most often not in open combat but from stealth; thus, the resistance fighter had to be prepared to act as a professional murderer. His or her target was seldom a Gestapo agent or a German soldier; more often the target was a compatriot—a policeman, a factory guard, a railroad engineer, or anyone whom one's superior in the resistance movement suspected of being a traitor, a spy, an obstacle, or a dangerous rival.* The famous Bielski partisans, a Jewish group, which operated in what is now western Belorussia and about whose heroism books were written and films were made, readily admitted having fought Polish and Ukrainian policemen in German service as well as Polish anti-Nazi—but simultaneously anti-Semitic—partisans. Conflicts with German soldiers were rare.

To be in the resistance required distrusting others, hiding, lying, threatening, blackmailing, denouncing, and, if necessary, killing suspects, even if they were your friends. Orders came from higher-ups whom one never met and would not be able to identify but whose emissary had to be blindly trusted. Yet the trust could be tragically misplaced when the emissary turned out to be a police agent.

A resister, especially in an urban setting, could rarely remain long in the same place: he could not sit in a restaurant, cinema, or streetcar without eyeing the door for a quick exit; he had to fear both uniformed policemen and those in mufti who might be from the Gestapo and thus could be much more dangerous. The resister could never be sure that his good friend with whom he had a prearranged meeting in a café had not been "turned around" following unspeakable torture and was now playing the role of Judas. To ring a bell to the apartment of a fellow resister meant to

---

*In the famous and controversial French film *Army of the Shadows* (*L'armée des ombres*) (1969), the director, Jean-Pierre Melville, himself a former *résistant,* pays moving homage to the heroism, devotion, and self-sacrifice of the French fighters against the German occupiers. Yet the Germans play only a small role in the film: the action is among French people, resisters and collaborators. The resisters spend most of their time just trying to survive. The film as well as the novel on which it is based were inspired by genuine events in the World War II French resistance.

court torture and death if the Gestapo was inside. To call first, provided that the person had a working telephone, was no solution either, for the person answering the phone could have had a gun pointed at his head. In an occupied country, every step required a special permit, and every new pair of socks or loaf of bread necessitated a ration card, which could be obtained only through stealing or forgery.

No doubt, there was a touch of glamour and great excitement in all this, but also endless boredom and anxiety when hiding, often in a filthy, cold, terribly small shelter or when waiting endlessly for instructions. And all through this misery, one had to behave "normally," so as not to create suspicion.

The resister had to be able to melt into the population; Gunnar Sønsteby, perhaps the most famous of the legendary Norwegian resisters, changed his name and identity papers several times between 1940 and 1945 while blowing up German army trucks, shooting German soldiers, and providing the British with vital information. What had made this possible was, according to his reminiscences, that he looked inconspicuous, just like any other Norwegian. But this blond, blue-eyed, athletic young man would have appeared fatally conspicuous had he ventured into a non-Nordic country.*

Urban resisters were constantly playing hide-and-seek with the police and fought battles with the enemy or with rivals; resisters in the countryside were often reduced to terrorizing peasants for food or starved and froze in deep forests that made a blanket or a lean-to worth killing for.

In brief, to be in the resistance was a dog's life, and it is a near miracle that so many Europeans chose it voluntarily. Yet it was still better for one's dignity and the nation's honor—if not for the nation's short-term benefit—to try to undertake something against the Nazis and their allies, better, in the eyes of the resisters, than to sit at home and do nothing.

There existed, of course, great situational and geographic differences: an obedient, nonpolitical "Aryan" Western or northern European had little to fear from the German occupiers; a Pole, a Russian, a Serb, or a Greek as well as—after September 1943—an Italian was never immune to arbitrary arrest by the Germans or by the latter's hirelings. Prisons in

---

*For a fine documentary film on and by Gunnar Sønsteby, see *Report from "No. 24"* (produced by the Norwegian Armed Forces, 1994). Number 24 was Sønsteby's code name in the SOE, the famous British organization specializing in "setting Europe ablaze."

Poland were full of people who had been picked up on the street. Some of them had never lifted a finger against the occupiers; others in the same group had fought the Germans with arms. The Gestapo rarely made fine distinctions, and it used the same fiendish methods on a "racially superior Nordic" type it suspected of resistance activity as on a "subhuman" Russian Communist Jew. The results were also similar: only a handful of Communists, Jehovah's Witnesses, priests, and other devotees of a supreme ideology were sometimes able to withstand torture. Only slightly less hard to bear were the humiliations visited on the political prisoners: many high-ranking German army officers who, in 1944, were arrested for conspiring to overthrow Hitler could not bear the humiliation; the former godlike members of the "master race" confessed quickly and relinquished names.

As already indicated, resistance grew gradually from nearly nothing in the first year following the German occupation to a sudden blossoming after the battles of El Alamein and Stalingrad all the way to a final enormous growth in 1944 when it became clear that Germany would soon be defeated. We have also mentioned that resistance could take many forms, from symbolic acts of defiance to large-scale armed combat. By 1944 there were important regions in Europe where the Germans and their allies were in constant danger. Years before the German surrender in May 1945, the anti-Nazi partisans were the law in large parts of German-occupied Russia, Poland, Ukraine, Yugoslavia, Italy, and Greece. In occupied Russia, the partisans often owned the night, and the Germans owned the day; in Yugoslavia, Albania, and Greece, the partisans were in command of the mountains and the forests but not of the valleys and the plains, or they were masters of some small towns but not of the larger cities.

From nearly the first day following the German occupation, army officers, who had avoided capture, met secretly in Poland, Norway, and France to discuss how to wipe out the shame of defeat. Some university students did the same, yet they formed tiny groups until joined by escaped prisoners of war, journalists unwilling to follow the dictates of collaborationist editors, and financially independent young aristocrats for whom it was a matter of noblesse oblige to oppose the vulgar and plebeian German SS. They were joined by a number of eccentric loners. So varied and hard to categorize was the makeup of the resistance movements during the early years of the German occupation.

It does not seem that prewar political beliefs were decisive in one's joining the resistance, except perhaps in the case of longtime Communists, Socialists, and monarchists. In Austria, the Netherlands, and Norway, some monarchists opposed the occupiers from the beginning; in other countries, a few left-wing Socialists and Communists turned on the German occupiers in defiance of Soviet instruction. All in all, there were many strange, nearly unexplainable cases.

THE RESISTANCE PRESS AND RADIO

Gradually, anti-German resistance took more concrete forms. In the literate Western and northern European countries, with a public hungry for uncensored information, clandestine newspapers sprang up with no or only tenuous connections to underground political groups. Alternately, resistance groups set up underground newspapers, as in the case of Combat, perhaps the most famous resistance group in France. The group published a sophisticated yet popular clandestine newspaper of the same name. Characteristically, while the Combat group itself never numbered more than a few hundred activists, their newspaper's print run increased from 10,000 late in 1941 to 250,000 in 1944.

It is still unclear how such a broad-based illegal activity, punishable by torture and death in Gestapo or in French police custody, could take place both in the Unoccupied and Occupied Zones of France. Where did the paper, the ink, and the printing presses come from when all these necessities were strictly controlled? Why were the editorial offices and printing presses so seldom raided by the police? Where did the money for printing come from? No doubt, substantial subsidies arrived clandestinely from Britain; still, little could have been achieved without the anonymous and courageous support of thousands. More help must have also come from some collaborationist French authorities than the resistance was later willing to admit.

Combat was not the only French resistance group assembled around a newspaper; the anarchist Libération and the Communist Francs-tireurs et Partisans groups and papers numbered even more militant members, although not more newspaper copies than *Combat*. The latter's world fame was enhanced by the later Nobel Prize–winning author Albert Camus, who was, during the war, *Combat*'s editor.

The underground papers obtained their information from hearsay as well as reading between the lines of officially authorized papers and BBC broadcasts. Listening to the latter was considered a grave crime, punishable by death in several German-occupied countries. Moreover, the BBC was consistently jammed; still, millions of Europeans were able to hear its programs. In German-allied Hungary, Italy, and Finland, for instance, such "perpetrators" were seldom prosecuted. Even in German-occupied countries, the local police often ignored violations; only repeated denunciations by neighbors and office colleagues forced the police to act against those guilty of the crime of listening to the BBC. Here again is an example of the local authorities often being more tolerant of forbidden activity than the resistance later liked to admit.

Denunciations were the plague that hounded wartime Europe, whether or not occupied by German troops, whether before or after the defeat of Nazi Germany. We will learn more about this in the chapters on postwar justice and retribution.

The BBC had its competitors in the Voice of America, Radio Moscow, and the radio stations of Sweden and Switzerland, but educated people much preferred the measured, unhysterical tone and relatively objective reporting of the BBC. Radio London readily admitted British defeats—and there were plenty to admit in the first three years of the war—while German and Italian (and, let us add, Soviet and occasionally American) war reporting was a mixture of truth, lies, and wishful thinking. In 1943, however, German propaganda minister Joseph Goebbels suddenly revised his broadcasting policy. Having concluded that it would be good propaganda to impress on the German people the mortal threat represented by Bolshevik barbarism and Anglo-American colonialism, he proclaimed a "total war" against the enemy. One form of this new type of warfare was to admit the manpower and material superiority of the enemy and to denounce its allegedly satanic determination to exterminate the German people. Radio releases and newsreels were filled with gruesome reports on civilians burned alive by Allied carpet bombing. Later, German media almost triumphantly published photographic reports on the tortured, raped, and murdered civilians in towns the German troops had temporarily recovered from the Red Army. Convinced that defeat would bring total annihilation, the German people, both soldiers and civilians, resisted the enemy onslaught with an iron determination.

No doubt, local clandestine anti-Nazi radio stations have their place in the resistance story, but the great majority of the so-called local broadcasts emanated from Great Britain, whose editors and broadcasters made it sound as if speaking from next door. One of the most popular of the so-called black programs was a secret military radio station, purportedly operating in Germany, which voiced the grievances of discontented soldiers. In reality, the station broadcast its program from Great Britain.

THE SPECIAL OPERATIONS EXECUTIVE

Among the most controversial yet most effective resistance weapons of World War II was the legendary Special Operations Executive (SOE), which Prime Minister Churchill and Minister of Economics Hugh Dalton had called into being in 1940, whose goal was to "to set Europe ablaze." Unlike the equally legendary British Secret Intelligence Service (SIS, commonly referred to as MI6), which was run by the Foreign Office and whose gentlemanly agents concentrated on discreet information gathering, the SOE was meant to be and indeed became quite conspicuous. Considering that the outfit's cloak-and-dagger operations have become part of universal folklore, it should be enough to focus here on the connections between the SOE and the European resistance movements.

The SOE, whose headquarters were in Great Britain, trained and sent agents to practically every European country with the aim of gathering intelligence, engaging in sabotage, and setting up secret radio stations for transmitting information to Britain. The SOE was also eager to help in creating resistance movements, to smuggle in weapons, and, if possible, to overthrow and replace collaborationist governments. Over the course of the war, the SOE employed or directly controlled some 13,000 persons and supplied another 1 million with money, food, and weapons. Interestingly, there was no equivalent organization on the German side: the German Abwehr and similar organizations—Hollywood movies to the contrary— never seriously attempted to set Great Britain, the United States, or even the Soviet Union "ablaze."

The SOE's specially trained agents were often marvels of courage and tenacity, if not always of perspicacity. Thousands of Europeans were executed for having helped the SOE men and women, and, in turn, hundreds of SOE agents died because of their own or their superiors' negligence. It was said that a secret radio operator had a life expectancy of only a few weeks. Many agents, especially in Western and northern Europe, had dual nationality and were thus equally at home in Britain and in France or the Netherlands. Still, they were too often uncovered and arrested by local Gestapo agents (in France called *la police allemande*) due to a minor mistake in appearance or a lack of absolute familiarity with local dialects and conditions.

Famously, the SOE employed many younger women, who could circulate more easily than men of military age. The SOE also successfully used known homosexuals and aristocrats who had personal contacts in Europe. Yet every move was dangerous, mostly because of prying neighbors; this particular danger diminished only toward the end of the war when the Germans and the local police could no longer protect the denouncer from the wrath of the resisters. Note that the purge of the Nazi collaborators began well before the arrival of the liberators. Clearly, by 1944 it was time for many collaborators to try at least a double game. Many were caught between two fires and could no longer escape their fates.

Despite all the secrecy and careful training, the SOE sometimes made tragic mistakes. This was the case of the secret radio operators in the Netherlands who were caught by the Abwehr, the German army's counterintelligence service, and then "turned around." The term meant forcing the captives to send dictated messages to England. Because headquarters in England overlooked the prearranged warning signal that the operator was in German hands, flight after flight of SOE agents, who were parachuted into the Netherlands, would first be followed and then arrested, tortured, and either killed or also "turned around." The Abwehr called it *Englandspiel,* a play with captured British agents.

The Abwehr included a few brilliant intellectuals who wreaked havoc with some of the best-conceived SOE plans, yet the Abwehr also harbored some of the foremost anti-Hitler conspirators. Thanks to these individuals, some of the captured SOE agents survived the war. The head of the Abwehr, Admiral Wilhelm Canaris, was one of the last anti-Hitler conspirators to be executed just before the end of the war. By then the functions of the Abwehr had long been taken over by the SD (Sicherheitsdienst), the security service of the SS whose cruelty and ruthlessness were matched by its clumsiness.

RESISTANCE IN THE COUNTRIES EXPECTING
BRITISH AND AMERICAN LIBERATION

In the West of Europe, the battle was at first primarily fought with words; only after the beginning of Operation Barbarossa did the Communists enter the fray. They now had orders to weaken the German war machine at all costs. The Communists and their left-wing allies and rivals, such as the anarchists and the Trotskyists, did not hesitate to engage in sabotage and to use weapons, no matter what the consequence for the local population. But resistance became a true mass movement only in early 1943 when Fritz Sauckel, the German minister for labor exploitation, decided that rather than waiting for volunteers from the occupied countries, young West and North Europeans should simply be drafted for labor service in Germany. In France this was called Service de Travail Obligatoire, and although work conditions in Germany were often better than in France, the measure proved unpopular. Droves of young men failed to appear for induction and disappeared from sight, a move supported by the same population that often did not hesitate to denounce a fugitive Jew. As we will see again and again, the public, whether in France or elsewhere, was willing to take risks on behalf of its sons, but not for those judged to be "foreigners."

Some of those who had fled into the high plateaus of southeastern France, called the maquis after the terrain covered with scrub, began to call themselves the maquisards. The name spread rapidly among French resisters, and soon the SOE began parachuting agents, weapons, and radios first into the mountains and then into other parts of France. In the Vercors, a mountain plateau in southern France, some three thousand armed fighters assembled. They were attacked sporadically by Germans and the French fascist *milice* (militia), but only in the spring of 1944 did the fighting become intense. This was after the maquisards of the Vercors had received orders from Britain to attack German military traffic. The purpose was to help the planned Allied invasion in Europe, but it drew a German response of some twenty thousand troops, equipped with modern weapons. Only a small part of this considerable force consisted of Germans or members of the French *milice*; the majority were Ukrainians, Russians, and Caucasians in German uniform.

The conflict on the plateau of Vercors demonstrates persuasively the complexity of the war and especially of guerrilla fighting. In this case, in one camp were young East Europeans who had volunteered for German service mainly so as to avoid death by starvation as prisoners of war in German hands; in the other camp, one found young Frenchmen, many of whom tried to avoid forced labor service in Germany. The two groups should have been fighting together against the Nazis, but life and fate were not as simple and logical as that.

The French maquisards included a good number of refugees from the Spanish Civil War and East Europeans who had escaped from the terrible French internment camps into which they had been thrown as early as 1939. Thus, this was a civil war as well as a clash of ideologies and a conflict among ethnic groups. The battle of the Vercors ended tragically for the maquisards: the majority were killed; those captured were sent to concentration camps, unless executed. The maquisards' casualty rate was three times that of the "Germans," showing that in an open battle, the poorly trained, undisciplined, and insufficiently armed partisans were the great losers. But then it is also true that the battle of the Vercors drew some twenty thousand men in German service away from the Western front.

Now another irony: while the East Europeans in German uniform would never surrender to the French partisans, mostly for fear of being killed, many of the same men eagerly ran over to the Allies following the Normandy invasion. This saved them not only from the wrath of the French partisans but also, they hoped, from the wrath of Stalin. Yet at war's end, the American and British military authorities handed over thousands of the captured East Europeans in German uniform to the Soviet Union, where they were either executed or sent to the Soviet Gulag.

The peculiar nature of underground activity, the varying aliases of its members, and the many arrests forcing leadership changes make it difficult for us to identify the various resistance groups. Not all were real; some existed only in name or in the imagination of their founders. In France division among resistance groups was either sociogeographic, such as urban groups versus the maquisards of the countryside, or ideological, such as Communists and their left-wing allies versus the moderate republicans and conservative monarchists. Because many of the groups jealously guarded their independence, it is almost a miracle that the French resistance, including even the Communists, was willing to recognize the overall leadership of the previously unknown General Charles de Gaulle in London and his secret delegate in France, Jean Moulin.

Moulin had been a fairly important civil servant both in the prewar period and during the early Vichy years; he had engaged in resistance activity while still a high-ranking Vichy civil servant. After a secret visit to London followed by his being parachuted back into France, he convoked several meetings of the national resistance leaders. One of these was to be in June 1943, at a hiding place near Lyon in southern France. By then the German army had occupied the entire country. Tragically, the group of eight had been betrayed; all were arrested, and some, including Moulin, were tortured to death by Gestapo officer Klaus Barbie, whom we will meet again. The circumstances of Moulin's arrest and death have remained controversial and have led to typically endless speculation, especially with regard to the name of the traitor. Similar to other resistance movements, those in the Moulin group who had survived arrest and imprisonment came under suspicion. Young René Hardy was accused of having inadvertently or deliberately led the Gestapo to the meeting place. He protested his innocence, and so did his family after Hardy's early death. He was acquitted in two consecutive postwar judicial proceedings, but the rumor persisted even after the aged Barbie, in 1990, exculpated Hardy by pointing a finger at Raymond Aubrac, another famous resister.

Unlike the proper civil servant Jean Moulin, Raymond Aubrac was born into a family of Jewish shop owners; he had undoubted Communist sympathies. Some historians later accused him of having engaged in the allegedly common Communist practice of betraying dangerous political rivals to the Gestapo. Aubrac vehemently protested his innocence, as did his devoted wife, the no less famous resistance heroine Lucie Aubrac. The latter, a high school teacher of history, had managed to combine teaching, family duties, and a very active engagement in the resistance. One of Lucie's legendary exploits was the freeing of her husband from Gestapo captivity. To this end, she had visited Barbie at Gestapo headquarters while her husband was in jail. At her most elegant and beautiful, she pretended to be the pregnant aristocratic fiancée of Raymond Aubrac. In fact, she was pregnant and now claimed to be eager to wash off the shame of giving birth to a bastard by marrying Raymond. All this was to be done in a hurry, before Raymond would be executed. If not Barbie himself, then one of his younger SS officers fell for this "in extremis" argument, allegedly based on French law, and permission was given for the wedding to take place. When Raymond Aubrac and a group of political prisoners were being driven to another prison, armed resistance fighters, led by Lucie, fell upon the German truck. They shot the driver and five German guards and liberated all the prisoners.

Their situation in France having become impossible, the Aubracs were secretly flown in a British plane to London, where Lucie gave birth to their second child. General de Gaulle was the godfather. Somewhat ironically, the leader of the Communist Vietcong's postwar struggle against French colonialism in Indochina, Ho Chi Minh, later became the godfather of the third Aubrac child. Similar to other former left-wing resisters, Lucie and Raymond supported all colonial liberation movements.

In postwar France, Moulin and the two Aubracs became national icons, even while suspicion of their various activities kept occupying the press. Both Aubracs were politically active for the next many decades and were often described as fellow travelers, nonparty members who nevertheless always supported the Communist movement. Lucie and Raymond each died when nearly one hundred years of age, Lucie in 2007 and Raymond in 2012. Jean Moulin, who in a famous photograph is sporting a hat and a big scarf—which hid a scar from an earlier Gestapo arrest and torture—has remained the great symbol of eternal France, or, as General de Gaulle liked to put it, of *France éternelle.*

As for us, we just have to accept the fact that the war and the occupation produced in France, as well as elsewhere, not only open and shadow armies of resistance but also intrigues, internal struggles, incredible heroism, and unbelievable baseness. Regarding many of these developments, we shall never know the truth.

The story of Lucie Aubrac is as good a place as any to mention that while some women played important roles in the resistance movements, not even a handful of them were in a command position. Remember that in France, women received the right to vote only from the provisional government led by General de Gaulle, in October 1944. Yet European women, who were often exempt from the labor-service obligation, were greatly useful to the movement. They aroused much less suspicion when traveling and when carrying forbidden literature, secret messages, and weapons. Unfortunately, women were often not trusted by resisters, who tended to see them as fallible and venal victims of German temptation. Even though groups of young women were used as couriers and even as fighters, for instance, in the great Warsaw anti-Nazi uprising in 1944, women in the resistance were generally expected to act as nurses and helpers. Only the Soviet Red Army went further by employing, for instance, thousands of women to fly combat aircraft—and not only cargo planes, as was the case in the United States. The Soviet, Yugoslav, and Greek Communist partisan groups included large numbers of armed women. Yet even Communist Party leaderships included only a handful of women.

––––––

The National Council of the Resistance (Conseil National de la Résistance [CNR]), which was the umbrella organization that Jean Moulin had created, proved to be resilient and exercised some influence on the action groups, which went by the name of Free French Forces of the Interior (Forces Françaises de l'Intérieur [FFI]). The CNR and the FFI achieved their moment of glory in the summer of 1944 when they effectively helped the Allies to liberate France. The great political parties of the resistance, namely, the Communists, the moderate Socialists, the radicals, the progressive Catholics, and the Gaullists, formed the first governments of *la France Libre,* or Free France.

Resistance in the occupied countries of Western and northern Europe other than France varied according to the terrain, the country's ethnic makeup, the prewar political system, and the nature of the German occupation. In Belgium, the Netherlands, and the Grand Duchy of Luxembourg, which after World War II constituted the Benelux countries, the terrain was of little use to the resisters, although the Dutch could hide in flooded areas, and Belgium as well as Luxembourg possessed some forests and hills. The crowded cities would have been more useful for the purpose had the superbly efficient national and municipal administrations in all three countries not made it extremely difficult for a person to disappear from sight. The Dutch identity cards, for instance, proved very hard to forge. Moreover, people, especially in smaller towns, knew each other only too well. As political and social identity was traditionally based on religious affiliation,* outsiders were quite conspicuous, which proved especially catastrophic for the Jews.

The Dutch of the Netherlands and the Flemish in Belgium both spoke Dutch; this might have helped in the creation of a united political front against the occupiers, but while the Dutch generally disliked the German occupation, many Flemish, perhaps the majority, welcomed it in the hope that the German presence might allow for Flemish separation from their French-speaking Walloon compatriots.

––––––––––––––––

*Most of the Dutch civic organizations, including the Boy Scouts and soccer teams, were strictly divided into Catholic, Protestant, Socialist, and liberal leagues.

The venerable, independent Grand Duchy of Luxembourg constituted a special case. Even though most of the grand duchy's inhabitants spoke Luxemburgish, a German dialect that most Germans could not understand (the grand duchy's official languages at that time were French and literary High German; since then, Luxemburgish has also become an official language), most people in the grand duchy resented the unprovoked German invasion. This was incidentally a repeat performance from World War I, but the occupiers in 1914 had not tried to indoctrinate and integrate the locals, nor were young Luxembourgers drafted into German military service. This time all of the above ensued, with the result that thousands of young Luxembourgers went into hiding and some even engaged in partisan activity. Meanwhile, the brothers of the resisters served, fought, and died in German uniform. After the war, the reconstituted Luxembourg government successfully negotiated the early release of its sons from Allied and Soviet captivity. The examples of Luxembourg and of the province of Alsace-Lorraine in France prove, incidentally, that linguistic affinities do not necessarily incline the population toward accepting foreign occupation.

Luckily for the Dutch, Belgians, Norwegians, Danes, French, and Czechs, their young men were not drafted into the German army, so their survival rates were much higher than those of the Luxembourgers, the inhabitants of Alsace-Lorraine, and the German-speaking inhabitants of South Tyrol in Italy (which the Third Reich had annexed in 1943). Involuntary labor service in Germany and participation in the anti-Nazi resistance claimed their victims, but their casualty rates were insignificant in comparison with the suffering and deaths brought about by service in the German army during the war.

Resistance in the Netherlands ranged all the way from showing contempt to enemy soldiers* to armed struggle, but, in general, the Dutch resistance's emphasis was on such things as spreading the good word,

---

*A patriotic anecdote that all Netherlanders seemed to have enjoyed telling their visitors after the war was how, when asked for directions, they answered in highly refined German: *"Ich bedauere es äusserst Ihre Sprache überhaupt nicht zu beherrschen"* (I deeply regret not to understand a single word of your language). Another much-remembered resistance act was to glue postal stamps not in the right but in the upper-left corner of the envelope so as to show that only stamps displaying the picture of the exiled queen belonged in the upper-right corner. Reality in the Netherlands was, of course, more complicated than that: judging by the number of Dutch volunteers for the SS and young women consorting with and bearing children of German soldiers, many Dutch were not reluctant to collaborate with the occupiers.

threatening collaborators, helping persecuted Jews, expediting Allied airmen back to England, giving information to SOE radio operators, and conducting strikes and sabotage. The most serious and most dramatic of these events was the clash between armed Jewish groups and Nazi militia in Amsterdam in late February 1941, which led to a violent German intervention and a subsequent protest strike by dockworkers, tramway conductors, and others. It was a unique event in the history of the Holocaust that lasted a few days and resulted in imprisonments as well as the deportation of several hundred Jews to concentration camps, from which only two returned alive. The strike, which had led to the first execution of Dutch resisters, had a serious psychological effect abroad, yet we should have no illusions about its having saved lives. As a result of the combined effort of the Dutch administration and the German-appointed members of the Jewish Council, Jews were duly registered, and beginning in 1941 they were ordered to proceed to assembly points. From there, they were gradually deported to German concentration and death camps.

Within Western and northern Europe, the loss of life among Dutch Jews was proportionally the largest: more than 80 percent. It showed that a relatively low level of anti-Semitism did not necessarily improve Jewish casualty rates; more important in the Netherlands was the law-and-order mentality prevailing in society, the conviction among Dutch Jews that salvation lay in obeying the authorities, bureaucratic zeal, and the determination of the German Nazi Party leadership in charge of the Netherlands to create a *judenfrei* country, a Netherlands free of Jews.

In addition to a student, teacher, and physician strike in November 1941, there was an attempted general strike in the spring of 1943 in response to a German order for released Dutch prisoners of war to report for factory labor in Germany. Very much unlike most other places in the West of Europe, the strike attempt led to nearly two hundred killed. It was on this occasion that the father of the well-known American public intellectual Ian Buruma, unwilling to do labor service in Germany, went into hiding as a university student. After being caught, Buruma's father was deported for forced labor in Germany, where he had to work, under very poor conditions, in a Berlin factory until the end of the war. Yet to show that deportation was not necessarily the same thing for an "Aryan" Dutchman as for a Jew, it is worth mentioning that while the Jewish child Anne Frank was killed at Bergen-Belsen concentration camp, Buruma's father was allowed, among other things, to attend a concert of the Berlin Philharmonic conducted by Wilhelm Furtwängler.[1]

The Dutch resistance had one more great opportunity to show its mettle: the Allied airborne landing at Arnhem in September 1944, when it suddenly seemed that the local resistance would be able to assist General Montgomery's British, Canadian, Polish, and American troops in a final push through the northern Netherlands and deep into Germany. The Allies' and Queen Wilhelmina's call for a general strike in German-occupied areas was a success: the postal and telephone services and especially the railroads stopped working. But the Allied invasion was stopped in the winter of 1944, and although the railway strike continued to paralyze transports, it harmed the Dutch civilians more than it harmed the Germans. The northern part of the Netherlands did not fall to the Allies until the last days of the war; meanwhile, thousands of Dutch people died of starvation.

Divided between its Protestant, Flemish, and Catholic French-speaking Walloon populations, with Brussels as a bilingual capital, Belgium survived the war with somewhat less trouble and suffering than the neighboring Netherlands and Luxembourg. Perhaps because Belgium was ethnically divided—with its French-speaking half less desirable from a Nazi racial point of view—and perhaps because King Leopold III had personally surrendered his troops and not fled to England, Belgium was spared Nazi Party rule, at least until the summer of 1944. The government was in the hands of the military under General Alexander von Falkenhausen, who at first was preoccupied with preparations for the invasion of Great Britain and after Hitler dropped the idea concentrated on the defense of Belgium against an Allied invasion. For this purpose, Falkenhausen needed a tranquil population, a goal that he essentially accomplished.

Falkenhausen as well as his counterparts in France, the related generals Otto and Carl Heinrich von Stülpnagel, were deeply involved in the 1944 anti-Hitler conspiracy, which had not prevented them from taking the sternest measures against the resistance groups and from allowing the Gestapo and the local national police to proceed with the "Final Solution of the Jewish Question." In Belgium these measures resulted in the deaths of half of the Belgian Jews. Pro-German Flemish and the Walloon fascist organizations helped to arrest Jews or handed them over to the Gestapo. The population at large was passive, which was still better than Eastern

Europe, where Jews in hiding were often denounced to the police and where the population generally threw itself on the property of the Jewish deportees.

In defiance of King Leopold's wishes, the Belgian government had fled to England and continued the war from there; the administrative apparatus, however, stayed put and tried to maneuver between German demands and the interests of fellow Belgians. As nearly everywhere else in Europe, society split into three factions: collaborators, a vast majority who were just trying to get by, and a tough nucleus of active resisters. There were always more than enough young men volunteering to fill the ranks of the Flemish and the Walloon SS divisions. Nor did German soldiers lack the affection of Belgian women; meanwhile, Belgian businessmen profited from the needs of the German war industry. Black marketers drove food and clothing prices sky-high, but at least the people in Belgium did not suffer mass starvation. The political views of the resistance movements ranged all the way from a very strong Communist group to a few Rexist fascists who had gone over to the resistance. A no less deep chasm separated the *résistants de la première heure,* those who had opposed the occupation from the first hour, from those who became the *résistants cinque minutes avant minuit,* those who joined the resistance five minutes before midnight.

Problematically for all, the Belgian resisters did not see eye to eye on the future of the country. While the Left demanded that the traitorous King Leopold be made to abdicate after the war, or even that he be arrested, the monarchist anti-Nazi resisters argued that it was thanks to the king, and his personal encounters with the Führer, that thousands of Belgian POWs had been released. There was also the ethnic question: the French-speaking officers, professionals, and intellectuals who dominated the resistance—as they had dominated public life before the war—worked toward social reform or even a socialist revolution; the main concern of the much smaller Flemish resistance was local autonomy and equality in public affairs.

One area in which Walloon and Flemish resistance cooperated was the expediting of thousands of downed Allied pilots back to Great Britain, usually through Spain and Gibraltar. This dangerous activity required the participation of a large number of ordinary citizens, especially farmers, who passed the airmen from house to house or, more accurately, from hayloft to hayloft. Recaptured airmen were generally sent to a stricter prison camp; civilians caught hiding the airmen risked deportation to a concentration camp, where many perished. Since the treatment meted out to the civilian helpers of the pilots was in agreement with The Hague and Geneva Conventions, the civilians became the real victims of that affair, not the Allied pilots.

As a unique feat in the history of the European resistance, a group of Belgian partisans tried to stop the deportation trains leaving with Jews for the East, and one even succeeded, in April 1943, to derail the famous Twentieth Convoy. A few hundred Jews escaped from that train, but most were hunted down, and ultimately only a handful survived the war. The event only confirmed that Jewish survival was a secondary concern, if that, for the resistance movements in Europe.

In Norway everything preconditioned the growth of a powerful resistance movement, yet, in reality, there was less of it than is generally assumed and as was diligently asserted during and after the war by Norway's numerous friends.* To say that the terrain was varied and often impenetrable to the occupiers is an understatement. Some sixty thousand miles of a craggy coastline, including many deep fjords, lent itself ideally for resisters to hide. They could also sail secretly to British-held islands in the North Sea and return with weapons, provisions, and SOE agents. This so-called Shetland Bus, with its nearly constant traffic by Norwegian- and British-manned speedboats (disguised as fishing boats), has achieved world fame.

Then there were the snow-covered mountains and inland forests and hills, with their widely dispersed ski lodges and the narrow trails that in the winter only the hardiest locals could negotiate. The trails led to Sweden, a friendly neutral that Norwegian resisters regularly visited for rest and recuperation. Note also Norway's ethnically nearly homogeneous population, its great democratic and heroic Viking tradition, as well as the daily reminders of the country's recent defeat and humiliation.

Norway's king and government had fled to London but did not resign; thus, unlike the Pétain regime in France, Quisling's self-appointed government in Oslo lacked legitimacy. The Norwegian exiles were well

---

*An assiduous herald of the heroism of Danish and Norwegian resistance to Nazism was the famous comedian and pianist Victor Borge, a Danish Jewish refugee, who settled during the war in the United States. What Borge never mentioned in his public performances on behalf of Denmark and Norway was that, before the war, the Scandinavian immigration laws had allowed only a handful of German and Austrian Jewish refugees to settle in their countries.

provided with British money and powerful radio stations; in exchange, the exile government put the entire Norwegian navy, air force, and huge commercial fleet at the Allies' disposal. What more could one ask for the creation of a powerful resistance movement? Yet most Norwegians remained tranquil throughout the war, and, for a long time, such heroic resisters as Gunnar Sønsteby remained badly isolated. Norwegian collaborators and young Norwegians who volunteered for combat duty on the German side far outnumbered the active resisters. But then, admittedly, it was far easier in occupied Norway or elsewhere in Europe to find a Nazi recruiting station than an underground group and, once located, to persuade the resisters of one's honest intentions. Altogether fifteen thousand Norwegian volunteers served the Germans with arms, nor should it be too cynical to mention that, during the war, in Norway, thirty thousand babies were born from German soldier-fathers and Norwegian mothers.

The main Norwegian resistance organization, called Milorg, was led by army officers in hiding, who saw their main task as preserving the country's unity, to prepare for a takeover at the end of the war, and to prevent a Communist coup d'état. And although there was little chance for the latter, territorial unity was a serious problem. Modern, independent Norway was not yet fifty years old at the time, following the country's secession from Sweden. Different regions of the narrow but endlessly long peninsula of Norway had their own traditions, their own written Norwegian language, and their own dialect. Travel from Kirkenes at the Soviet-Finnish border in the far north to the capital, Oslo, in the far-away south was possible only by air and by boat; the sea voyage could take weeks. Far-away regions regarded the capital, Oslo, as an unwanted tax collector and the source of senseless regulations. Resistance to the German occupation in central and northern Norway took off only after it had become clear that the Germans were even more zealous centralizers than the royal government had been.

Though Milorg soon numbered hundreds of members and toward the end of the war trained a regular army, mainly in Sweden, this resistance organization generally abstained from violent action for fear of massive German retaliation. Attacks on the huge German garrison, at times numbering nearly a half-million men, were rare indeed, as were acts of sabotage.

What the Norwegian resistance was excellent at accomplishing were observing and reporting German troop and naval movements and performing brave and effective commando actions. But all these activities were either under the command of the British army and navy or under the guidance of the SOE.

The most famous commando actions were performed by the combined British and Norwegian naval forces against the Lofoten Islands in northern Norway, especially the action in March 1941. The commandos, which occupied the main islands for a few hours, destroyed all the fisheries, fish-oil processing plants, and arms depots. They also captured the rotor wheels to the German Enigma machine as well as code books that then helped the British to penetrate German military and naval communications. The population of the Lofoten Islands assisted the Allied commandos in every way they could. Also, several hundred volunteers sailed off with the British to join the Free Norwegian Forces. What the chronicles usually fail to mention is that not only did the islanders quietly accept the destruction of their jobs and livelihood, but they were later harshly treated by the German authorities.

Even more famous was the destruction of the German heavy-water installation at Vemork, between Oslo and Bergen, by Norwegian SOE commandos. Heavy water was at that time seen as indispensable for the development of nuclear weapons. Of the five British attempts to destroy the plant, the one by a small group of Norwegians was the most successful. The raiders, all hardened mountain climbers and skiers, stormed the Norsk Hydro Plant via a rock wall. It was a technically perfect operation, but the installation was back in operation within a few weeks. More efficient was the blowing up of a passenger ship that carried heavy water on the way to Germany, but a number of innocent Norwegian passengers were also killed. In any case, today we know that the availability of heavy water did not greatly help the very belated German nuclear energy project.

Norwegians for overseas action were trained in Britain by the SOE; inevitably, then, there were disagreements between the SOE, which wanted to see concrete results even at some cost to both the commandos and the civilians, and the exile government, which tried not to alienate its fellow citizens. The dilemma of costly action versus a wait-and-see position plagued the SOE throughout the war years and typified the dilemma of resistance activity everywhere.

Even though the citizens of Denmark and Norway can understand each other's language, and even though the Germans had invaded the two countries on the same day in April 1940, the two situations differed fundamentally during the war. As we know already, the Danes did not even attempt to resist the German invasion; they surrendered immediately. Nor did their king and government flee abroad; in appreciation, the occupiers allowed the Danes to keep their king, government, parliament, democratic constitution, army, and diplomatic service. Subsequently, Denmark signed the Anti-Comintern Pact, making Denmark an ally of Germany, Italy, and Japan. Danish and German businessmen cooperated in colonizing occupied Soviet Russia.

Norwegians and Danes provided the Waffen SS, the combat arms of the German Nazi SS organization, with roughly a similar number of volunteers, and their women gave birth to a similar number of half-German babies. The two countries also resembled each other in rejecting the ideology of National Socialism; the Norwegian Nazi Nasjonal Samling and the Danish National Socialist Party were popular failures; the occupying power had no choice but to work with decidedly non-Nazi native bureaucracies. But, and this was very important from the point of view of resistance, the two countries differed greatly in terms of geography and terrain. The highest "mountain" in Denmark is less than five hundred feet high; there are no dramatic coastlines, no fjords, no snowy forests, no hidden chalets. The Danish countryside resembles a garden rather than wild nature. During the war, there were no serious food shortages, young men were not drafted into military or labor service, Denmark had little strategic significance, and the SOE did not try to "set it ablaze"—small wonder then that initially no one called for armed (or any other) resistance. What there was of resistance originated from individuals aghast at the spectacle of Danish collaboration with the occupying power. But, gradually, resistance unfolded in that country also, and by 1943 relations between occupier and occupied had become so bad as to cause the Germans to introduce direct rule. But the king and the slightly modified government still remained in place, and with clever maneuvering the country preserved much of its autonomy.

The obvious cooperation between Danes and local German authorities in sabotaging the "Jewish Question" finally led Heinrich Himmler, in the early fall of 1943, to order the deportation of the country's approximately seventy-eight hundred Jews to the death camps. Yet the local German authorities were reluctant to execute the order; moreover, Georg Ferdinand Duckwitz, a commercial attaché at the German legation in Copenhagen, hurried to inform influential Danish personalities, such as the leader of the Social Democrats and various church dignitaries, of Berlin's plan.

Duckwitz even traveled to Stockholm to obtain permission for the secret transfer of Danish Jews to that country. With permission obtained, the exodus was quickly organized, and when the German policemen began  to collect the Jews, most were already gone. This was indeed a magnificent act on the part of the Danes, but it should be seen more as a humanitarian deed than an act of resistance; the latter requires an opponent and involves a great risk for its participants. In this particular case, the local German authorities cooperated with the Danes. Duckwitz had been told about the deportation plans by SS general Werner Best, who was the Reich pleni-potentiary for Denmark; Duckwitz could not have traveled to Stockholm without Best's permission. Duckwitz was later rightfully named "Righ-teous Among the Nations" by the Yad Vashem Museum in Jerusalem. Yet, ironically, his chief, war criminal General Werner Best, whom a Danish court sentenced to death in 1948 but who was later released, deserved the title of righteous even more for this very particular act; after all, Best had taken a great risk by ignoring orders from Berlin.

The transfer of Danish Jews took place in a fleet of fishing boats, and even though it would have been easy for German naval units patrolling the area to stop the exodus, their commanders closed their eyes to the very visi-ble event. Back in Denmark, German policemen had been told to arrest only such Jews who were willing to let them in. At the end, fewer than five hun-dred (mostly elderly) Jews were deported to the so-called model Theresien-stadt concentration camp in Terezín in what is today the Czech Republic. And even there, the Danish Jews enjoyed the protection of their govern-ment, whose representatives were allowed to visit. As a result, the only Dan-ish Jews who passed away during the war died of natural causes. The dark side of this heartwarming story is that in order to be able to offer acceptable quarters to the Danish deportees, Adolf Eichmann's SS transported other Jews from Theresienstadt to Auschwitz, where they were gassed.

Does all this mean that meek submission to the German invasion and occupation, and later an appeal to the occupiers' humanity, might have helped to save Jewish lives in other countries as well?* This is conceivable

---

*One of the persistent popular legends circulating in the Western world is that King Chris-tian X, who surrendered Denmark to the Germans on the day of their invasion, later threat-ened to wear the Star of David on his uniform in case the Jews in his country were obliged to wear one. According to another version of the legend, he actually exhibited the Star of David on his uniform. Actually, no one in Denmark ever had to wear such a thing.

but not very likely. After all, the extermination of the Jews, as a war goal, at least equaled the goal of winning the war. Witness Adolf Eichmann's ability to commandeer as many railroad cars as he wanted for sending nearly a half-million Hungarian Jews to the gas chambers at Auschwitz between May and July 1944, that is, at a time when the German army needed all the existing rolling stock to try to halt the advance of the Soviet troops. Note also that in Nazi eyes, the Russians and the Poles were mere subhumans; the Jews, on the other hand, appeared to them as superhuman, supernatural fiends whose total destruction was an absolute necessity if Germany was to live. Denmark was a unique case: Germanic, peaceful, economically indispensable, strategically unimportant, and with only a few thousand Jews. Moreover, it so happened that unlike the German military commanders and officials in the East, their equivalents in Denmark happened to be less than radical Nazis. And let us not forget that although Hitler wished to incorporate Denmark into the greater German Reich, in the East he wished to colonize the land and leave only useful slaves in place. In Poland, Russia, and similar countries, submissiveness would not have helped matters.

Toward the end of the war, a specially trained squadron of British fighter planes freed Danish political prisoners by destroying Gestapo headquarters in Copenhagen without hitting the floor where the prisoners were held. (Tragically, some pilots mistakenly attacked a neighboring girls' school, causing heavy casualties among students and teachers.)[2] By that time, the Danish underground press had become one of the most successful in Hitler's Europe. Yet, in general, Denmark remained serene and peaceful to the end, to the great benefit of the civilian population—and of the German war industry. Overall, with all one's admiration for the democratic mentality and practices of the Danish people, we must admit that if everybody in German-occupied countries had behaved the way the Danes did, the war would have lasted much longer. How much longer is, of course, difficult to estimate; it all hinges on how we calculate the military value of the European resistance movement. This we will do when discussing the partisans of Eastern and southeastern Europe, where the real resistance struggles and most of the war in Europe took place.

The question remains open as to what kind of resistance profited the national cause and, alternately, the Allied cause in Western and northern Europe. The two issues should be separated. For instance, leaflets, books, and pamphlets, written by outstanding authors and journalists, lifted national morale, but it is hard to measure how this contributed to the Allied war effort. Even the most passionate anti-Nazi patriots had to make a living, and thus the vast majority of people toiled away diligently in factories and offices that contributed to the German war effort. Nor does it seem that sabotage in Norway or France or anywhere else in the West and the North greatly weakened the German armed might. In 1944, however, railway sabotage, especially the deliberate entangling of timetables and the misdirecting of military transports, delayed the German response to the Allied landing in Normandy. The price paid by the resisters was high: many French railway workers were shot in 1944 for sabotage.

Armed struggle did, of course, bring some concrete results: a German soldier shot in the back under the cover of darkness was one less German soldier. But the price for this type of killing was usually horrifying: ten "hostages" executed for every single German soldier killed in Rome in 1944, fifty or one hundred civilians hanged or shot for every German soldier killed by partisans in Serbia. Moreover, the hostages were seldom well-known individuals whose execution might have deterred others from acting against the occupiers; more often, they were bystanders arrested after the event. Often the "hostages" were Jews, Gypsies, Communists, or refugees from the East whose demise the population was not likely to regret. Still, many resistance leaders judged hostage killings too great a price to pay for the life of a German soldier, and so rather than ordering the murder of Germans, they ordered the murder of traitors and collaborators. This in turn opened the Pandora's box of internal conflict or civil war within the fight against the occupiers.

The Allies disliked competition and conflict within the resistance, even though the victory of one group over another may have facilitated the creation of a united front against Germany. Doubting the reliability of the French resistance, the British air command was often reluctant to provide the SOE with airplanes for dropping supplies and agents to local groups. Traditionalist politicians in Britain believed such efforts were useless, even immoral; they also feared that the weapons would end up in German or Communist hands. Churchill himself was suspicious of the resisters for their Communist inclinations; still, he sent SOE agents, military officers, and arms to the Communist Josip Tito in Yugoslavia. He also sent agents to the Communist partisans in Greece, at least until the latter clashed with British troops, in 1944, in liberated Greece. In general, Churchill argued that anyone who was likely to harm the Germans deserved help; at least the partisans' sacrifice would spare the lives of British soldiers.

No matter how we look at it, resistance in Western and northern Europe did not abide by the international agreements on the right of armed civilians to oppose an invader under greatly restricted circumstances—unless one considers German aggression a sufficient reason for any kind of violent resistance. Yet the Germans could not be charged with aggression in the matter of France, which had declared war on Germany on September 1, 1939, and had immediately moved its armies to the German frontier. It is true, however, that Norway, Denmark, the Netherlands, Luxembourg, and Belgium had provided no grounds for a German invasion; on the contrary, they had made great efforts to demonstrate their neutrality in the coming war.

The Hague Convention states that, once enemy occupation has become a fact, the population has to obey the occupation authorities, unless the latter are committing grave illegalities. There is no proof that, in Western and northern Europe, the invading Germans in 1940 committed such grave crimes as rape, robberies, setting fire to undefended towns, or murdering prisoners of war or ordinary civilians. Such things happened in the form of retaliation and only after the start of violent resistance and of SOE activity, both of which provoked retaliation. From that time on, basically from the summer of 1941, both sides piled illegal acts on illegal acts; the Germans, however, had the means to be more ruthless than the resistance. Also, any halfway intelligent West European must have known that the restraint exercised by the German occupation authorities was only temporary and that there could be no doubt regarding their plan to establish hegemony over Europe.

HELPING JEWS

There was one more act of resistance practiced European-wide although by far too few people: the attempt to save Jewish property and lives. The Jews in Europe, as it is so well known today, were condemned to death by Hitler and his associates sometime in 1941, and the first details of the plan's execution were worked out at the Wannsee Conference, in suburban Berlin, in January 1942. We have already discussed the participation or partial participation in the "Final Solution of the Jewish Question" of the governments allied with Nazi Germany. The survival of the Jews was largely in their hands; no government allied with Germany was ever forced to kill or surrender its Jews. The governments of the occupied countries—when there were governments—were in a more difficult situation, but even there the execution of German orders depended largely on the national authorities; witness the case of Denmark, for instance. Where there was no government, as in the Netherlands or Norway, the local authorities could have helped many if not all, had they taken some risks.

Finally, in every single country, including Germany, much also depended on groups and individuals. Those who helped the Jews were in fact practicing a quiet, unspectacular, but highly efficient form of resistance. By occupation or social background, they ranged from German clerics, Italian diplomats, French bishops, Bulgarian metropolitans, and Hungarian police officers to post office clerks, hotel concierges, and taxi drivers, all the way down to the poorest peasants. And although those at the highest levels of society, as well as those living in Western, northern, and southern Europe, risked little in helping Jews, poor people in the East took the biggest risk on themselves and their families. Père Marie-Benoît, a Capuchin monk from France, procured thousands of forged documents and did countless other things for Jews at first in France and then in Italy, yet he was never arrested by either the German, the French, or the Italian police.[3] In fact, the Italian authorities provided his Jewish wards with a safe haven. On the other side, scores of Polish farmers were executed by the Germans, together with their entire families, for sheltering Jews.*

It has been said that about twenty-five people were needed to protect a single Jewish life under German rule; the figure is not an exaggeration. All over Europe, millions were occasionally involved in protecting a Jew or at least in not reporting him or her to the authorities. Still, millions more could have done the same, especially those outside the areas of the most brutal German occupation.

NOTES

1. Ian Buruma, *Year Zero: A History of 1945* (New York: Penguin, 2013), 3–7.

2. See Robin Reilly, *The Sixth Floor: The Danish Resistance Movement and the RAF Raid on Gestapo Headquarters, March 1945* (London: Cassell, 1969).

3. On the life of Père Benoît, see Susan Zuccotti, *Père Marie-Benoît and Jewish Rescue: How a French Priest Together with Jewish Friends Saved Thousands During the Holocaust* (Bloomington: Indiana University Press, 2013).

---

*The Polish Institute for National Remembrance in Warsaw has been able to identify slightly more than seven hundred cases of Poles executed for helping Jews in hiding. In reality, there must have been far more similar Polish martyrs. See Jan Grabowski, *Hunt for the Jews: Betrayal and Murder in German-Occupied Poland* (Bloomington: Indiana University Press, 2013).

CHAPTER SEVEN

Resistance and Civil War in Eastern, Southern, and Southeastern Europe

Western and northern Europe's peculiar relationship between occupier and occupied had only one equivalent in the East, the Protectorate of Bohemia and Moravia, whose capital, Prague, in any case lies to the west of Vienna and Stockholm. As in the West, so in the Protectorate, only a small segment of the population participated in the resistance; armed clashes were few, and people generally obeyed the rules set up by the country's German-controlled national government. Even the arbitrary German destruction of the village of Lidice, in June 1942, to which several hundred innocent villagers fell victim either immediately or later in concentration camps, may be considered, with some indulgence, as an act within international agreements. The Hague and Geneva Conventions had been meant to protect the peaceful population, but in a case such as the assassination of Reinhold Heydrich, the German viceroy of the Protectorate, and the sheltering of the assassins by Czech families and groups, international conventions had set no limits on retaliation. In other words, in case of a rebellion, the occupier was free to act. If many of the perpetrators were nevertheless punished after the war, it was because even a minimal sense of decency and compassion should have told the Germans not to massacre innocent villagers for the actions of a few Czechoslovak soldiers flown in from Great Britain and parachuted over the Czech lands.

In the Protectorate of Bohemia and Moravia, the Germans did not kill without some kind of provocation, nor did they kill with the intention of reducing the size of the population or of committing genocide. The only exception to this policy were the Jews, especially beginning in 1942, whose murder was, as we already know, an all-encompassing German goal.

In Western and northern Europe as well as in the Protectorate of Bohemia and Moravia, resistance in print, political organization, strikes, and even sabotage did not greatly influence the way the Germans conducted the war, but they strengthened national morale and, as we shall see later, had a profound effect on postwar politics. Armed resistance, although minor when compared with what was happening in Poland at that time, did definitely serve the Allied cause. It also provoked the wrath of the occupier and visited great sufferings on uninvolved civilians and resisters alike. Nor was it initially justified by German behavior. But then again, Nazism was such a pernicious ideology and the German occupiers behaved so abominably in other parts of Europe as to justify violent resistance, even when the Germans had no intention of behaving criminally.

A case apart from all others was that of the Italians: they played a double role in the history of World War II, first as Nazi allies and ruthless aggressors and later as persecuted victims and even as heroes of the anti-German resistance. Let us remember that Italy started as Germany's most important political ally in Europe; for many years, Mussolini appeared more as Hitler's mentor and protector than as his minor partner. The Fascist Party in Italy had come to power in 1922, eleven years before Hitler's appointment as Germany's chancellor. The tactics and methods of the Italian fascists in the early 1920s were no less brutal than those, later, of the German SA and SS.* Political murder formed a part of the fascist agenda. In other words, prior to Italy's turnaround in September 1943, the question was not the extent of Italian resistance to the German occupiers but the extent of domestic underground resistance to the Italian fascist regime.

Before 1943 fascist Italy engaged in a series of unprovoked aggressions. In 1935 the Duce's army invaded Abyssinia (today's Ethiopia) without

---

*One of the early Italian fascists' favorite political methods was to force large quantities of castor oil down the throats of antifascist politicians, just before elections. Often adding severe beatings, the fascists incapacitated if not killed their victims.

any justification, and after a horrendous war, during which the air force bombed and gassed many villages, this vast poverty-stricken country was conquered, with King Victor Emmanuel III being declared emperor. In the following year, sixty thousand Italian "volunteers," in reality mostly regular army, navy, and air force personnel, entered the Spanish Civil War on the Nationalist side. In March 1939, Italians invaded Albania, proclaimed it an Italian protectorate, and forced King Zog into exile. In June 1940, Italy attacked France as it was collapsing under the German onslaught, and although repelled by French Alpine troops, it managed to seize a few border areas. Shortly thereafter, a large Italian force invaded Egypt but was soon destroyed by their British adversary: the defeat necessitated a German military intervention on Italy's behalf. In November of the same year, the Italian army attacked Greece, again without the slightest justification, but was beaten back, again requiring German military assistance. In April 1941, Germany, Italy, Hungary, and Bulgaria together conquered and occupied Yugoslavia and Greece. Two months later, Italy joined the gigantic German attack on the Soviet Union, again without any conceivable justification. A year and a half later, a Soviet counterattack demolished the Italian Expeditionary Force on the shores of the Don River. In the summer of 1943, the Western Allies invaded and occupied Sicily; now, at last, the fascist Grand Council forced Mussolini's resignation and ordered his arrest. In September of the same year, the king attempted to surrender his country to the Allies, but a German invasion forced him and his government to flee south; from then on, Italy was split into an Allied- and a German-controlled area. In the latter, Mussolini set up a fascist republic after a German commando raid had freed him from captivity.

In July 1943, the not entirely unmerited tragedy of Italy began. The period also witnessed the rise of the antifascist parties and of the anti-Nazi resistance, upon which we will touch in the next chapter. Here it is worth noting only that the wartime failure of the Italian armies was an indirect blessing for the Allies, who even in the worst of times could point to their triumphs over Italian troops and to the large number of captured Italians. Those, however, who like to make light of "Italian cowardice" ought to consider that when there was finally something worth fighting for, namely, the freeing of Italy from the German yoke, Italian resistance fighters proved to be as brave and efficient as any other in the world. In fact, according to Italian statistics, nearly fifty thousand partisans perished in the fight against the Italian fascists and the German occupiers.

THE EAST EUROPEAN TRAGEDY

Eastern and southeastern Europe during World War II resembled a slaughterhouse into which were driven millions upon millions of soldiers, uniformed or irregular partisans, and partisan-hunting policemen. A vast number of civilians also perished, some because they had sympathized with the German Nazis, others because they were against them, because they were Communists or favored the Communists, or because they were anti-Communists. In addition, millions of ordinary and peaceful civilians were killed because of their alleged race, religious affiliation, place of residence, real or suspected nationality, political beliefs, wealth, or simply for finding themselves at the wrong place at the wrong time.

In this nightmarish world, large disciplined and dedicated partisan divisions fought pitched battles against regular army divisions or rival partisan units, but individuals and small groups also took bloody revenge on their neighbors. Resistance to the Nazis and their allies formed only a part of the generalized struggle and chaos, yet the historical importance of the anti-Nazi resisters is still immense because at the end of the war, they were the ones to come to power everywhere in Eastern (as well as in the rest of) Europe. All this will be amply discussed in the chapter on the victory and the subsequent moral, political crisis of the resistance. What preoccupies us here is how to disentangle the history of the resistance in the huge area extending from the Baltic Sea to the eastern Mediterranean.

By calling it the "bloodlands," American historian Timothy Snyder well describes Eastern Europe during the war,[1] and even though by that name he means "only" what is today Poland, the three Baltic countries, Belorussia, Ukraine, and Russia, the term could well be also applied to East-Central and southeastern Europe. In Sarajevo, Yugoslavia, for example, between 1941 and 1945, people were killed by various enemies for such "crimes" as being a Muslim, Roman Catholic, an Orthodox Christian, Jew, Serb, Croat, person of the Jewish "race" but not necessarily of the Jewish religion, Bosnian, Gypsy, Communist, democrat, member of the Ustasha militia, German soldier, an Italian soldier, Partisan, Chetnik warrior, Croatian soldier, resister, collaborator, or draft dodger.

Except for Poland, all the countries of the region—that is, Estonia, Latvia, Lithuania, Slovakia, Hungary, Romania, Yugoslavia, Bulgaria, Albania, and Greece—had been living in peace during the first year and a half of the war. Yet it was a troubled and perilous peace: the German-Soviet agreement of August 1939 had granted the Soviet Union control not only over the eastern half of Poland but also over the three Baltic countries and parts of Romania. The Soviets established military and naval bases in Estonia, Latvia, and Lithuania, and then, in 1940, local Communists under Soviet control organized make-believe plebiscites, which "approved" the integration of the three countries into the Soviet Union. The Soviet takeovers inaugurated the systematic destruction of the Baltic social, cultural, and economic elites, mainly through deportation into the depths of the Soviet Union, where the majority perished. This, in turn, precipitated the first guerrilla wars of World War II, ironically not against the Germans but against the Soviet occupiers. The Baltic partisans (the first time that such a term was used during World War II), also called "People of the Forest," fought Red rule while hoping for salvation by Hitler's armies.

June 1941 brought Operation Barbarossa, yet even before the arrival of the German tanks, the Baltic partisans and city mobs took bloody revenge on captured Soviet soldiers, suspected Communists, and, above all, Jews, who were held collectively responsible for the cruelties of the Soviet occupation. In reality, as we know today, there were more non-Jews than Jews in Soviet service in the Baltic countries. The anti-Jewish pogroms in Latvia and Lithuania in the summer and fall of 1941 were perhaps the most savage in history.

We have already seen how the three Baltic countries provided the Waffen SS with some of its bravest combat troops. Even today, many people in the Baltic countries claim that their compatriots in the Waffen SS were only defending their country against the "Bolshevik hordes." Of course, in 1942, when the war began to turn against Hitler, anti-German resistance also arose, but those activities did not compare to those of the anti-Soviet partisans. It should be noted here that the United States never recognized the Soviet annexation of the three Baltic countries, which lent the anti-Soviet struggle in the Baltics an aura of legitimacy, greatly shaping present-day Baltic views of their wartime history. The fight in the Baltics against the Soviet occupiers continued long after the end of the war, with the reputed participation of fifty thousand of the so-called Forest Brothers, the last one of whom reputedly surrendered to the Soviet police in 1956. The continued fight against the Soviets in the Baltic states visited untold miseries on the civilian population: at least 10 percent of the population and specifically the educated elite in Estonia, Latvia, and Lithuania were deported to areas deep into the Soviet Union, where many perished. No doubt, the resistance of the Baltic peoples facilitated the transition to independence in the late 1980s, but one can also argue that independence would have come anyway with the simultaneous implosion of the Soviet system.

POLAND: AN EXTRAORDINARY CASE

Polish resistance, first against the German occupiers and later also against the Soviets, was so vast and complex as to defy a satisfactory accounting in so short a tale as ours. Fortunately, the topic boasts a substantial literature; at least in English, however, this literature is rather one-sided and uniformly patriotic. The Poles, if one can generalize about such a large nation, are so steeped in their long history of heroic struggle against foreign invaders, and have such a penchant for painting a romantic, even a messianic, image of themselves, that it is sometimes difficult to detect what actually happened there. If we are to believe the former resisters and the majority of Polish historians, the nation as a whole resisted the Germans from the first day of the war until the last German soldier left the country in the spring of 1945. These historians point out that in order to show their devotion to freedom and to the Western Allies—who in 1939 had failed to help—Poles concentrated on fighting the German oppressors while neglecting the struggle against the Soviet invaders. Only toward the end of the war did some Poles take up arms against the Soviet occupiers and their Polish Communist stooges, for which, again, they received no help from the West.

There is much truth in the above historical interpretation, but it tends to ignore the fact that the majority of the population in Poland, as elsewhere in Europe, were, or at least tried to be, uninvolved bystanders. Poles suffered enormously from being treated as slaves and subhumans, yet many individuals and groups profited from the needs of the German war industry. There were also those who drew benefits from the confiscation of Jewish property and the absence of Jewish businessmen and professionals.

Poles disagree among themselves on the precise nature of the German occupation and on the extent and usefulness of the resistance movement.

It is also an open question as to who the true motors of the resistance were: the traditional Polish social elite—descendants of the great landowning aristocrats and of the szlachta (landed gentry)—or educated people in general and the urban workers. There is also disagreement regarding the respective dedication, popularity, and true role of the main resistance groups: the nationalist, anti-Semitic, and xenophobic but anti-Nazi National Armed Forces, known as the NSZ; the great conservative-liberal, Western-oriented patriotic resistance organization whose political leadership resided in London, claiming to be the Polish government in exile and whose military arm was the Home Army (Armia Krajowa); the peasant-socialist leftist resistance movements; and, finally, the Communist resistance, whose military arm was called the People's Army (Armia Ludowa). The latter's leadership was in Moscow, a tool in the hands of Stalin. Polish historiography said little, until recently, on the Polish resistance movements' strained relations with the ethnic minorities and the latter's underground organizations and not much either on how the Poles in general viewed the Holocaust and what the true relations were between the Polish and the Jewish resistance.

At least until recently, Poles liked to cultivate the self-image of an innocent and fiercely independent nation feloniously attacked by two totalitarian monsters: first, Nazi Germany, which had invaded Poland on September 1, 1939, and, second, the Soviet Union, whose troops entered Polish territory on September 17. The limitless suffering the German occupiers inflicted on the Polish people was symbolized by the German destruction of Warsaw, first in September 1939 and then during and after the great Warsaw uprising between August and October 1944. Thousands upon thousands of Poles were tortured and killed at such places as Pawiak Prison in Warsaw and the Auschwitz I concentration camp.* Polish suffering under Soviet rule was most horribly symbolized by the NKVD massacre of some twenty-two thousand Polish reserve officers and officials, in 1940, at Katyń and similar places in the Soviet Union, and also by the trial

---

*There were actually three major concentration camps in Auschwitz. The oldest, named Auschwitz I, was made up of old converted Habsburg monarchy artillery barracks, where mostly Polish political prisoners suffered. Birkenau was where approximately 1 million Jews were gassed. Monowitz-Buna held prisoners of all nationalities, including even British POWs who labored for German industrialists.

and execution of Polish non-Communist anti-Nazi resisters toward the end of and right after the war.

Poles are correct in saying that there were no important quislings in their country, yet they add only rarely that Poland was the only country in Europe in which the German occupiers never invited collaboration. And although it is absolutely true that Poland was feloniously assaulted by the two superpowers and that the Poles, instead of surrendering, stubbornly resisted the aggressors, only recently did Polish politicians and historians begin to draw a more balanced picture of these events. There was, for instance, the less than fair treatment that interwar Poland had meted out to its ethnic minorities, which at least partly explains the violent hostility of many Lithuanians, Ukrainians, Belarusians, Volksdeutsche (members of the German minority), and Jews toward the Polish state and population. And it is only recently that leading Polish writers have begun to address the issue of popular anti-Semitism during the Holocaust years. Yet it happened all too often that Polish villagers and townspeople grabbed and handed over fugitive Jews to the Polish or the German police. It was a young Polish historian who recently demonstrated in his microhistory of a specific county in southeastern Poland that the majority of Jews in hiding perished as a consequence of betrayal by their Polish neighbors.[2] The common Polish nationalist excuse according to which desperate Polish villagers associated Soviet Communist oppression with Jews, many of whom had joined the Soviet occupation forces, could not possibly apply to a region in central Poland that did not see the Red Army until 1944.[*] The beatings, torture, and lynching of Jews were not a rarity, either; nor was the infamous massacre of the Jews of Jedwabne by their fellow villagers a unique incident.[**] Polish historical memory has only begun to deal with the nefarious activity of the *szmalcownicy*, mostly young men in Warsaw and elsewhere who had made a profession of terrorizing and blackmailing Jews in hiding. When the Jew had nothing left to give, he was denounced

---

[*]Recent archival research by the Berkeley historian Andrew Kornbluth shows that evil practices against the Jews were a common occurrence in many villages and towns within the Polish Generalgouvernement. In most cases, the Germans played no role in the local anti-Jewish excesses.

[**]Jan T. Gross's *Neighbors: The Destruction of the Jewish Community in Jedwabne, Poland* (Princeton, NJ: Princeton University Press, 2001) created a political storm in Poland whose consequences and continued debate have sparked a rich literature.

to the German authorities for a new reward. It is true, however, that Polish underground courts sometimes tried and executed the *szmalcownicy*.

Steadfast opposition to the German occupation was the official policy of the Polish government in exile. Political and military leaders, who had avoided German or Soviet capture, fled to Romania at the end of September 1939, together with a substantial part of the Polish army. Others escaped to Hungary, where they were also warmly received and treated as honored guests. Subsequently, thousands were allowed to leave through the Balkans for the West. The exile Polish government moved to Paris and then to London, followed by an ever-increasing number of able-bodied refugees from whose ranks the British formed entire infantry and armored brigades. Polish refugees also provided the Royal Air Force with some of its best fighter squadrons, and the British navy profited from a fully manned fleet of Polish cruisers, destroyers, submarines, and transports.

The exile government established its Delegatura in Warsaw, complete with military, political, educational, cultural, judicial, and intelligence departments. When and how resolutely to attack the German occupiers was one of the main dilemmas of the resistance. The difficulties were marked by the customary disagreements between cautious commanders and often reckless local leaders. Fortunately for members of the Polish resistance, they could move relatively easily in the country, where they were protected by the traditional prestige of the Polish freedom fighter. What also helped was the noble origin of many resisters, the unpopularity of the German—and Soviet—occupations, and the efficiency of the underground courts in pursuing traitors. Indeed, Poland was one of the few countries in Hitler's Europe where it was just as dangerous to serve the Germans as it was to join the resistance. The Polish resister was the legendary "fish in the water," in the words of Mao Tse-tung regarding the fundamental requirement for a successful resistance. The Polish resister served as a role model for high school students and scouts, both boys and girls, who then served and died as couriers, spies, and nurses in the 1944 Warsaw Uprising.

Perhaps more than any other country, Poland produced some fabled resistance fighters. We will examine only three here in order to illustrate their bravery and dilemmas, and the tragedies of the resistance, in this case especially of the Polish national resistance.

Władysław Bartoszewski, a Catholic journalist and writer, was an early political prisoner at Auschwitz, from which he was released in 1941. He became the most famous member of the Council for Aid to the Jews

(Żegota), founded by Zofia Kossak-Szczucka within the Polish Delegatura in Warsaw as Europe's only underground organization solely dedicated to assisting Jews. Following his participation in the 1944 Warsaw Uprising, Bartoszewski—like so many of his fellow resisters—almost automatically continued his resistance activity once under Soviet rule. Accused of being a spy, he spent several months in prison, but the charges were dropped against him. Meanwhile, he continued his feverish political, journalistic, and cultural activity, traveling around the world and receiving innumerable honors and decorations, among them the recognition by Yad Vashem in Jerusalem as a "Righteous Among the Nations." The Israeli government made him an honorary citizen. Arrested again by the Polish government in early 1981, he was subsequently rehabilitated and, following the fall of communism, served as foreign minister of the so-called Solidarity government. The author of some of the most important books on the Polish resistance movement, Bartoszewski was still serving in a high diplomatic position in 2013, at the age of ninety-one.

A well-known figure in the West for, among other things, having given crucial interviews in Claude Lanzmann's 1985 French documentary film *Shoah*, Jan Karski served during the war as a courier of the Armia Krajowa, the main Polish resistance group. He made several secret trips to France and Great Britain and was once arrested and tortured by the Germans. In 1942 he engaged in his most important clandestine travel, which brought him to Great Britain and from there to the United States. He was carrying documents on German atrocities and on the Jewish death camps, one of which he had visited in disguise. He got as far as the Oval Office in Washington, DC, but neither President Roosevelt nor the latter's advisers wanted to believe him, or if they did, they still could not or would not do anything to help. Karski ended up as a professor of political science at Georgetown University and the author of, among other books, *Story of a Secret State*, a wartime report on the Polish underground, which became a near best seller in the West.[3]

Witold Pilecki, a tragic figure, seemed to have united in him all the major characteristics of the "typical" Polish freedom fighter. As so many other Polish resisters, he was of noble origin. In fact, traditionally, Polish society consisted almost uniquely of noble landowners and serfs—those in the cities were mainly non-Polish speakers—and the numerous nobles considered themselves the only true bearers of Polish nationhood. A landowner by occupation, Pilecki served in the Polish-Soviet War of 1919–1920 and became a reserve army officer. Following the German attack in August 1939, he fought at the head of his unit until complete defeat and then immediately joined the first armed underground organization. In 1940 he persuaded his superiors to let him be arrested with the aim of being imprisoned in Auschwitz concentration camp, which at that time held mainly Polish political prisoners. While there, he set up an underground resistance organization and escaped, in April 1943, carrying documents stolen from the Germans. He then served in the Home Army, distinguishing himself especially during the 1944 Warsaw Uprising. By then, however, he had already made preparations for resisting the Soviet occupation. Arrested in 1947 for sending intelligence reports to the West on Soviet atrocities, he was tried, sentenced, and in May 1948 executed when he was forty-seven. A nonperson in Communist times, he was "rehabilitated" by the post-Communist government and has become a legendary hero in Poland.

It is nearly impossible to calculate the damage the European resistance movements caused to the enemy. Western historians, especially of the career military type, like to believe that the resistance did not seriously weaken the German war machine. Judging by the World War II experiences of Poland, the Soviet Union, and Yugoslavia as well as by the later deadly efficiency of the anti-Soviet guerrillas in Afghanistan and the Vietcong fighting the Americans in Vietnam, such arguments are no longer completely satisfactory. According to official Polish statistics, between January 1941 and June 1944, the non-Communist, non-right-wing Polish resistance damaged 6,930 locomotives, derailed 732 German transports, damaged 19,058 railway wagons, built faults into 92,000 artillery missiles, and more.[4] Even if such precise figures are debatable, there can be no doubt that the German war industry had to spend millions of man-hours to replace machinery destroyed by Polish guerrillas. Nor should we forget the thousands of German soldiers in partisan-infected areas of Poland and the Soviet Union who had to guard transports instead of joining those on the front line.

Three major events defined the fate and the memory of the Polish resistance: the Warsaw ghetto uprising of April–May 1943 and the purported failure of the Polish resistance to aid the doomed Jewish fighters; the great Warsaw Uprising between August and October 1944 and the related questions as to whether the uprising was premature and whether the Red Army had deliberately refrained from helping the Polish fighters; and the Soviet

Image 7.1. German SS soldiers driving Jewish survivors from the burning Warsaw ghetto, probably in May 1943. All were either killed or deported to concentration camps. Source: United States Holocaust Memorial Museum.

mistreatment of the members of the Home Army at the end of the war and the continued fight of the "Brothers," also called the "Cursed Soldiers," against the Soviets and the Polish Communist regime. The fight ended only in 1952, when the group disbanded.

POLISH AND JEWISH RESISTANCE: A DIFFICULT RELATIONSHIP

Parallel to the Polish resistance in which quite a few Jews participated, there was also a Jewish resistance. The Warsaw ghetto revolt and other Jewish ghetto and concentration camp uprisings were carried out by a handful of young men and women, who knew full well that their fates were sealed. Theirs was the defiant struggle of the bravest among the millions of Polish Jews who were under a collective death sentence. The Jewish fighters chose a dignified form of death while also trying to show, against all anti-Semitic slander, that Jews were not cowards. Not surprisingly, both the ghetto leaders and the ghetto inhabitants (the majority had already been transported and gassed at Treblinka) disapproved of the venture. Those still in the ghetto put their hopes in their ID cards, which certified that they were skilled workers serving in the war industry. The fighters themselves were united only in their readiness to die; otherwise, they were divided, even physically within the ghetto, between Zionists and Socialists-Communists. In fact, they perished separately under attack by the well-equipped and ruthless German Waffen SS. The fight could have had only symbolic significance and, truly, the Warsaw Uprising later became one of the foundation stones of the State of Israel and especially of its defense forces.

What role, if any, did the non-Jewish Polish resistance play in the heroic Jewish saga? The Home Army smuggled a few rifles and mostly old pistols into the Warsaw ghetto, and a few units of the Communist-dominated People's Amy (Armia Ludowa) attempted to storm the ghetto. Yet, overall, the help was very small. The Home Army command later claimed that their forces, too, lacked weapons, yet a few more rifles could certainly have been spared while the Polish resistance was not engaged in open battle with the occupation forces. More realistically, the Home Army command saw Jewish resisters as amateurs and as politically alien, even hostile, to the Home Army. Many Poles also reproached the Jews for not having joined them in the struggle during the first year or two of the occupation when Auschwitz and other camps received mostly Polish political prisoners and Jews were not yet systematically murdered.

Poles tended to believe that the Jews were eager collaborators, yet the Polish critics of Jewish behavior overlooked the fact that a person under a death sentence could not uphold the same lofty moral standards as those who could choose between dying and not dying. Working for and thus "collaborating" with the Germans offered the only—mistaken—hope of survival for the members of the Jewish Council, the Jewish ghetto police, and the ordinary Jewish workers.

No doubt, many in the Polish resistance movements and in the general population disliked, even hated, the Jews. As early as February 1940, the young resistance courier Jan Karski reported to the Polish government in exile that "dislike of the Jews created a narrow bridge on which the [German] occupier and a significant part of Polish society could meet."[5] Even Zofia Kossak-Szczucka, who, as we have said, totally dedicated herself during the war to helping Jews, freely confessed to anti-Jewish feelings. As a humanitarian, she risked her life daily for the Jews and spent time in prison and in a concentration camp, yet she advocated the expulsion of Jews after the war. Her Catholic prejudice against the Jews as "Christ killers" was combined with the conviction that Poland should belong exclusively to Polish speakers, to the Polish people. Many in the Polish resistance shared the same feelings about the Jewish, German, Ukrainian, Belorussian, and Lithuanian minorities.

It would be good to be able to talk of the solidarity of the resistance movements under German occupation, but of this there exists precious little evidence. Ethnic, political, regional, and professional groups were keen on protecting their own, and aside from the Communists, who obeyed the orders of Stalin and not their own conscience, only such genuinely internationalist and cosmopolitan groups as the Trotskyists and other dissident Communists, the high aristocracy, and a few religious communities such as Jehovah's Witnesses were able to cross ethnic boundaries.

Czesław Miłosz, the winner of the 1980 Nobel Prize for Literature, as well as other Polish writers have described how, during the Warsaw ghetto uprising, music played and children rode a carousel in a playground next to the ghetto wall. Meanwhile, from the other side of the wall, people could be heard screaming as they jumped from burning buildings onto the pavement. Nor did anyone seem to notice the surviving ghetto inhabitants, mostly women and children, as they were being driven through the gates of the ghetto with hands raised in terror. The story symbolizes the profound gap between the diverse ethnic groups and, especially, between Jews and non-Jews in Hitler's Europe. But it also shows how successful the Nazis were in creating a new, hierarchical society in Poland, in which the Reich Germans were on top, the local German Volksdeutsche came second, followed by the badly oppressed Poles, who were still privileged in comparison with the Jewish pariahs.

The great Polish Warsaw Uprising in the late summer and early fall of 1944 involved tens of thousands of fighters and hundreds of thousands of victims and had grave worldwide political consequences whose effects are still felt. To free one's own country from German occupation before the arrival of the Allied or Soviet liberators had been many European resisters' dream. As we know, it was achieved only in some Balkan countries. In their case, however, we must note that, in late 1944, when self-liberation occurred in Greece, Yugoslavia, and Albania, the German army was already fleeing from the Balkans. Thus, the main question for the resistance in the Balkans was which group among them would be taking the

Germans' place. Everywhere else in Eastern Europe, the German army fought on with bitter determination.

Poland's successful self-liberation would have helped other countries to establish genuine postwar independence. For Poles, the matter had become even more urgent by the German discovery, in 1943, of the 1940 Katyń massacre, about which the London exile government dared publicly to complain. This then gave the Soviets the excuse to break diplomatic relations with the Polish exile government in London and to treat its local representatives as enemies.*

Back in 1941, following Operation Barbarossa, the Soviet Union recognized the legitimacy of the Polish exile government in London; Poland sent an ambassador to Moscow, and an independent Polish army, later called the Anders Army (named after its commander), was allowed to organize in the Soviet Union. Composed mostly of Poles found in Soviet POW and concentration camps, the Anders Army was allowed to leave the Soviet Union and would soon be fighting on the Allied side, mostly in Italy. Following this brief and not at all easy honeymoon in Polish-Soviet relations, things went quickly from bad to worse. After the Katyń scandal, the Soviets created a Polish antifascist committee, later called Lublin Committee, which they strictly controlled and to which they added a Polish army recruited from prisoners of war and equipped as well as supervised by the Red Army command. Thus, by 1944, non-Communist Poles again had two official major enemies, Nazi Germany and the Soviets.

To be able to greet the Red Army's arrival in Warsaw with a reconstituted national administration and a substantial armed force would greatly facilitate, so the Poles hoped, the re-creation of a free Poland. The opportunity for self-liberation presented itself in the summer of 1944 after the Red Army's gigantic campaign, called Operation Bagration, which had virtually annihilated the German central front, called Armeegruppe Mitte. Having captured hundreds of thousands of German soldiers, the Red Army's central front, numbering several million men as well as tens of

---

*One of the early troubles between Poles and Soviets was that when the Anders Army was being set up in the Soviet Union, thousands of Polish officers known to be prisoners of war were nowhere to be found. When questioned, the Soviet interlocutors explained, not very convincingly, that the officers must have escaped to Manchuria. In fact, they were long dead, having been murdered by the Soviets at Katyń.

thousands of guns, tanks, and planes, advanced steadily toward Warsaw. Meanwhile, Soviet radio broadcasts repeatedly called on the Polish people to rise up against "the Hitlerite fascist bandits."

Although not yet quite ready for action, General Tadeusz Bór-Komorowski, the commander of the Warsaw Home Army, ordered the uprising to begin on August 1, 1944, while the first Red Army troops were settling down on the opposite side of the Vistula River, less than a mile from the center of Warsaw. The first days of the uprising brought nothing but successes for the Polish fighters. Equipped with captured German weapons and arms hidden in 1939, often dressed in remnants of the German uniform, the insurrectionists seized large parts of the city. Yet a solid, contiguous front was never established, and losses were enormous under steady bombardment, even from the air. The German command sent in some of the most brutal soldiers of any army, such as the Dirlewanger Regiment, made up of common criminals (the commander, Dr. Oskar Dirlewanger, was himself a convicted rapist), and the Russian soldiers of the SS Kaminski Brigade. Meanwhile, no Soviet help was forthcoming; Moscow publicly condemned the uprising as a mad adventure and denounced the Home Army fighters as fascists. True, the Soviet troops needed a rest after many weeks of wild fighting, but nothing explains the Soviet Union's refusal to allow Allied war planes, for example, to land and refuel at its airfields. As a result, British and American planes flying in from southern Italian airfields were able to drop only a minimal amount of supplies to the Warsaw fighters.* Early in October, the Warsaw garrison surrendered; surprisingly, its thirty thousand fighters were treated as POWs, which meant that most of them survived the war. Not so the civilian population, tens of thousands of whom, mostly women and children, were killed by the thugs of the German army. The Polish capital itself was razed to the ground.

Was the Warsaw Uprising of any use to Poland and the Polish people? Some politicians and historians question the value of such a "suicidal enterprise" that cost nearly a quarter-million lives and wiped out a capital city; others argue that the sacrifice was not in vain. Communist-run Poland and the Polish people would not have been able successfully to defy

_____

*Soviet rejection of Allied supply runs to Warsaw was one of the important psychological causes of the later Cold War. Another major Allied grievance, discussed at the Yalta Conference in February 1945, was that British and US pilots, who had crash-landed in Soviet-held territory, were often treated as spies and imprisoned.

the Soviet Union as early as 1956, and then again in the 1970s and 1980s, without the self-respect gained and the worldwide admiration inspired by the uprising and the Polish resistance. Admittedly, however, thousands upon thousands of people in Warsaw would not have been killed if their city had not played a heroic role.

RESISTANCE IN THE GERMAN-OCCUPIED
PARTS OF THE SOVIET UNION

Operation Barbarossa and the German invasion of the Soviet Union were events whose extent and brutality surpassed all other tragic events in Europe, except perhaps the Holocaust, which, of course, was closely connected to the invasion of the Soviet Union. One might even argue that without the German army setting foot into Soviet territory, the systematic attempt to kill all the Jews of Europe is unlikely to have taken place. The millions of East European Jews suddenly in German hands and the frustration Germans felt for not being able to dispose quickly of the Soviet enemy were the major reasons the Nazis decided on the "Final Solution of the Jewish Question."

Anti-Nazi resistance in the occupied parts of the Soviet Union and the invaders' hunt for resisters took place on an enormous scale and involved the greatest brutality on all sides. "All sides" is the proper term here because, aside from Germans and Soviet citizens (the latter consisting of hundreds of different ethnic groups), nearly all the nations of Europe were involved in the fight. Remember that not only did Italy, Hungary, Romania, Finland, Croatia, and Slovakia send troops to the "anti-Bolshevik" front, but neutral Spain dispatched an entire army corps of forty thousand men, and thousands of volunteers came from Norway, Denmark, the Netherlands, Belgium, France, and even Switzerland and Sweden. The non-Germans were either at the front or voluntarily or involuntarily fighting against the Soviet partisans. In the conflict, partisan hunters and partisans committed the gravest atrocities.

Resistance is actually not the right word to explain what took place in the Soviet Union, for clandestine newspapers, underground political parties, and individual attacks on enemy targets, which characterized resistance in the West, were not primary preoccupations in German-occupied parts of the Soviet Union. Instead, resisters there formed armed units, the larger ones under Soviet officers parachuted in or smuggled across the lines. The Soviet partisans originated from among the hundreds of thousands of soldiers left behind during the precipitous withdrawal in 1941 and who preferred the forests to German POW camps. Others wanted revenge for their murdered families or for their villages put to the torch. Moreover, Stalin had ordered all people to resist the invaders with absolute determination; chances were that those who had failed to heed the order would be punished following liberation. Finally, many became partisans simply because it was better to be armed than to try to get by in a world where unarmed civilians could be anyone's target.

Of course, most of the time, the partisans were doing no fighting; it was hard enough to stay alive in the frozen forests, the enormous mosquito-infested Pripet Marshes, or the ruins of cities. Partisans extorted food from the peasants, and peasants murdered the partisans, as they had back in the Thirty Years' War. Neighboring partisan groups were often a threat. Ukrainian partisans killed Jewish and Polish partisans, Polish partisans killed Ukrainian partisans, Communists shot "reactionaries" and Trotskyists, anarchists disposed of "nationalists," while nationalists felt free to kill almost anybody who was not of their nationality. Yet many other units were highly disciplined, with their own administrations, radio stations, kindergartens and schools, hospitals, security services, and counterintelligence units. Moscow treated Soviet partisans as members of the Red Army; they had to take their orders from the center, and their commanders were flown out periodically to report on the situation.

Guerrilla war in the East was waged on a very large scale. In France during the war, resisters lost thousands of their comrades killed in battle, in prison, or in concentration camps; in turn, French resisters killed hundreds of German soldiers and executed a considerably larger number of suspected collaborators and traitors. In the Soviet Union, partisan casualties numbered in the hundreds of thousands, as did the victims of partisan activity.

One of the darkest sides of the partisan war was the brutalization of the German, Hungarian, Romanian, Finnish, and other occupiers. The invading soldiers, from army commanders down to privates, had been instructed to be ruthless and been assured of no legal consequences for executing suspects. After all, Jews, Gypsies, and Russians were considered subhuman enemies of the Aryan race. We know, from Omer Bartov's excellent study, that the German army executed fifteen thousand of its own soldiers, most of them on the Russian front, for desertion (during the war, the United States executed a single GI, Private Edward "Eddie" Slovik, for desertion), cowardice, dereliction of duty, political agitation, theft of government property, rape, and other offenses,[6] but the German army executed not a single German soldier for shooting Jews, Gypsies, Communist commissars, and suspected partisans. Yet, as we have seen, the German military code, valid even under the Nazis, strictly forbade the murder of innocents. It occurred to only a small minority of German officers and officials to try to win over the local population by showing some toleration and clemency. Had the army as a whole tried to do so, the Germans might have won the Eastern war. Instead, the campaign in Russia was marked by corpses dangling from trees or from balconies, villages burned down, towns blown up with dynamite, deportations, and torture. Only rape was untypical of German behavior, the exact opposite of Red Army practices.

Tragically, even those German officers who were prepared to sacrifice their lives in the plot of 1944 to get rid of the Hitler regime did not hesitate to order atrocities against the local populations, nor did they try to save Jews. At this point, it is worth emphasizing again that, during the war, the Jews of Eastern Europe, numbering about 5 million, were not all killed in gas chambers; in the first year and a half of the Barbarossa campaign, at least 1 million Eastern Jews were shot, mainly by members of the military police battalions made up of middle-aged reservists. Other members of the German armed forces—infantrymen, artillerists, aircrew, sailors— also lent a helping hand, or at least engaged in what must be called Holocaust tourism, watching and apparently mostly enjoying the show. Some were scandalized, but there is nothing to prove that any one of the millions of German soldiers or their officers ever tried to interfere with the systematic massacres.

Soviet partisans did not think much of the Western type of intellectual, "bourgeois" resistance, and after the war they proclaimed loudly that they, the Communists, had been the only true, uncompromising resisters. This was a vast exaggeration, but there can be no doubt that in Eastern and southeastern Europe, the Communists outnumbered all others both in the smallish resistance movements operating in Hungary and Romania and in the very large guerrilla wars in Yugoslavia, Bulgaria, Albania, and Greece. Yet the final political outcome, as we shall see, depended less on the extent of the Communist presence in the resistance and much more on great-power politics.

Image 7.2. Civil war in Yugoslavia: Slovenian quisling Home Guards (Domobranci) poster from 1944 warns against "Brother [fighting] Brother," in this case partisans shooting peasants, setting fire to villages, and freely engaging in sex. Source: Bundesarchiv, Plak 003-056-008 / designer: DOM [Dombrowski, Ernst Ritter v.].

RESISTANCE AND CHAOS IN THE BALKANS

During the war, Germany and its allies Italy, Hungary, Bulgaria, Croatia, and the semiautonomous state of Albania occupied the entire Balkan Peninsula. Moreover, even Greece and Serbia (the latter the official successor to Yugoslavia) were allowed their own collaborationist governments and national police and thus were, in many respects, Germany's allies. Yet, in reality, after the triumphs of 1941, the occupiers effectively controlled less and less territory. More and more, the Balkans were dominated by various guerrilla groups: Communists, republicans, monarchists, and ethnic minorities in Greece; nationalist Chetniks and Josip Broz Tito's Communists in Croatia, Serbia, and other parts of the former Yugoslavia.

The guerrillas were combating not only the occupation powers but also, just as often, each other. Meanwhile, Germans and Italians were far from being in agreement on every issue. After September 1943, when Italy attempted but failed to surrender to the Allies, the Germans treated the Italian occupation forces in the Balkans not as friends but as hated and

Image 7.3. The Serbian Communist partisan Stjepan Filipović exhorting the crowd just before his hanging. This famous photograph often appears in history books with the erroneous caption that the Germans are doing the hanging. In reality, nearly all those in uniform surrounding Filipović are soldiers of the collaborationist Serbian government under General Milan Nedić. Source: United States Holocaust Memorial Museum.

despised enemies. Italian troops were disarmed, and those who disobeyed or resisted were killed. Captured Italian soldiers were sent to concentration camps. By the beginning of 1944, the German army was solely responsible for the entire Balkans. This situation did not last long, because following Romania's change of sides on August 23, 1944, the Germans began a precipitous retreat. Meanwhile, civil wars erupted or continued until, finally, Tito's Communists, the Soviets, and the British established order, took power over the Balkans, and divided the area among the victors.

Guerrilla war in the Balkans has been described in many books and films. German Alpine troops, mostly recruited in the Austrian provinces, stormed one lofty mountain after the other, but by the time they got to the plateaus, the guerrillas had evaporated. So the Germans burned down villages and killed their inhabitants. The partisans did not have it easy, either, for they had to drag their sick and wounded with them, and often they were starving. Famous newsreel pictures exist of young Yugoslav Communist partisans, dressed in tattered uniforms, treading the snow, their feet wrapped in rags. At first, no help was forthcoming to the partisans; the Soviets did not or could not offer much assistance, but then the Western intelligence agencies as well as Churchill's SOE intervened. In Serbia the British, and later the Americans, at first dropped arms and advisers to Draža Mihailović, a Yugoslav army officer whom the exile Yugoslav government in London had made minister of war. But Mihailović's Chetniks were an individualistic, disorganized, and occasionally very brutal bunch who pursued the dream of a greater Serbia and not of a restored Yugoslavia. Moreover, when confronted with the more disciplined and "internationalist" (that is, all-Yugoslav) Communists whom they hated, individual Chetnik leaders sometimes made common cause with the Germans and the Italians. Accordingly, Churchill and his parachuted advisers, such as William Deakin and Fitzroy Maclean, as well as Churchill's son, Randolph, decided to support Tito and his Communists. Developments were not very different in Macedonia and Greece, and so a strange situation arose wherein the British and the Americans gave arms and medicine to Communists for which the latter were anything but grateful. Ultimately, however, Churchill's gamble paid off, because Greece and reconstituted Yugoslavia, now under Tito, never entered the Soviet bloc.

THE GORGOPOTAMOS SAGA

The basic principle of the Special Operations Executive was to give aid to the most determined enemy of the Germans, irrespective of the guerrilla group's political ideology. This allowed for one of the organization's rare genuine triumphs, the bringing down of the Gorgopotamos viaduct on the crucial Thessaloniki-Athens railway line in central Greece. The story unfolded in November 1942, at a relatively early stage of SOE activity there. Reading about it today, one feels that it was a sort of honeymoon period between the British agents and the various Greek guerrilla groups. Of many different ideological persuasions, they all worked together for a great Allied cause. The leader of the republican and anti-Communist guerrilla group the National Republican Greek League, called EDES, under Colonel Napoleon Zervas, happily shared the task of approaching the viaduct with the Greek People's Liberation Army, or ELAS, the fighting arm of the Communist resistance organization the National Liberation Front, or EAM, under Aris Velouchiotis. Both groups accepted the leadership of the twelve British soldiers whom the SOE had parachuted into Greece. The British team included combat engineers, radio operators, and interpreters; the names of their commanders, Lieutenant Colonel Edmund "Eddie" Myers and Major Chris "Monty" Woodhouse DSO, Fifth Baron of Terrington, read like excerpts from the social register. The three combined teams totaled 150 men against 80 Italian and 4 German guards. While the Greeks attacked the garrison from both sides, the British placed the explosives, bringing down a large part of the bridge. Only four guerrillas were wounded; history keeps no record of the losses among the Italians and Germans. Later, however, in an act of revenge, the Germans executed 16 local Greeks.

Lieutenant Colonel Myers and Major Woodhouse subsequently remained in Greece and accomplished further great deeds. Myers was eventually recalled to England for having particularly favored the Communist guerrillas, and his place was taken by Major Woodhouse, a later conservative cabinet member and the author of many excellent books on Greece. As for ELAS and EDES, they were soon at war with one another.

The aim of this so-called Harling Operation had been to prevent German supplies from reaching Greek harbors, from which they were regularly transported to General Rommel's troops in Libya. The SOE's goal was achieved, except that, meanwhile, General Montgomery's Eighth British Army had destroyed the Italian-German line at El Alamein and the supplies would not have reached Rommel in any case. All this was, then, a clean and morally justifiable operation with few civilian casualties and great damage to the enemy.

Finally, let us raise the question of resistance in countries allied to Germany by looking at two examples, Slovakia and Transylvania, the latter a much-disputed province in Romania.

SLOVAKIA AND TRANSYLVANIA

Our first concern here is the Slovak resisters who, at the end of August 1944, began a national uprising against German troops in Slovakia and the collaborationist government of Monsignor Jozef Tiso. The Communist resisters, a highly active group within the uprising, wished to help the Soviet Union in its struggle against Hitler; they also hoped to seize power in Slovakia. But the Slovak army officers who rebelled against Tiso simultaneously with the Communists hated not only the Nazis but also the Communists and the Soviet Union, and many were also very much opposed to capitalism and the Jews. The reason the officers rebelled was a desire to free their country from the deadly German embrace before the arrival of the Soviet Red Army. Despite their vast differences, Communists and army officers fought desperate battles together against the German SS and those Slovak troops who had remained loyal to the government of Tiso. Of course, in the long run, their mutual enmities could not have been reconciled.

Other problems also gnawed at the heart of the Slovak resistance movement: the Slovak Protestants generally did not agree with the Slovak Catholics on the future of Czechoslovakia, and pro-Czech resisters confronted such anti-Nazi resisters who favored an independent Slovakia. As a result, the latter sometimes found themselves on the same platform with Tiso, the resistance movement's greatest enemy but an advocate of absolute Slovak independence.

Those who opposed the Germans and their allies were rarely without rivals and competitors. The goals, methods, and personnel of the resistance movements overlapped, became entangled, and frequently led to wars within the war against the German, Italian, Hungarian, Romanian, or Bulgarian occupiers. We have already seen the differences between the incredibly complicated Eastern European and the relatively simple Western and northern European situation.

In northern and Western Europe, resisters fought the Germans and the local traitors in expectation of the arrival of the Allied liberators, but the situation was much more complicated in the broad range of countries from Estonia to Greece and from the Czech lands deep into Russia. Let us imagine ourselves, for instance, in the old and picturesque Transylvanian city that its medieval German-speaking inhabitants called Klausenburg. Its official Hungarian name was Kolozsvár but, after 1918, bore the official Romanian name of Cluj, although today its name is Cluj-Napoca. It had been the capital of the Principality of Transylvania, created in the eleventh century by the kings of Hungary, and it became an autonomous principality in the sixteenth century under Ottoman-Turkish suzerainty. Later, it functioned as a grand duchy under Austrian Habsburg rule and, in 1867, was again reintegrated into Hungary. Following World War

I, Transylvania was annexed by Romania, but in 1940, as we know, Nazi Germany ordered it divided between Romania and Hungary. Five years later, at the end of World War II, the victorious Soviets reunited Transylvania under Romanian rule, where it remains today.

The year 1940 at Cluj/Kolozsvár brought foreign occupation to the Romanian minority and liberation to the city's Hungarian majority. But liberation became a tragic irony for the mostly Hungarian-speaking Jews, inasmuch as the government immediately subjected them to Hungary's anti-Semitic laws. Because the Jews at first celebrated the arrival of the Hungarian troops, many Romanians saw them as traitors; this, however, did not endear them to the Hungarians, who suspected the Jews of being on much too friendly terms with the Romanians. Meanwhile, both Romanians and Hungarians abominated the Jews as "Christ killers." In 1944 the Hungarian authorities deported the Jews of the city—and the country—to Auschwitz, where the great majority were gassed. Later in the same year, Soviet troops liberated Cluj and handed it back to Romania, but then, because of the Romanians' mistreatment of the Hungarian inhabitants, the Soviet military reassumed control over the city. With the return of the city to Romania in the same year, the people of Cluj now had to suffer from the vagaries of various Stalinist and National Communist administrations. Note that during the entire war, the only anti-Nazi resistance movement in Transylvania worthy of its name consisted neither of ethnic Hungarians nor of ethnic Romanians but was made up mostly of Jews from the underground Communist Party. When caught by either the Romanian or the Hungarian authorities, the Communist resisters were tortured and executed. Meanwhile, Romanians and Hungarians accused each other of being "soft on communism."

To illustrate the dilemmas of European resistance movements a step further, let us now examine three specific cases of partisan attack and the occupiers' reprisal, as well as the tragedy of civilians caught in the clashes.

NOTES

1. Timothy Snyder, *Bloodlands: Europe Between Hitler and Stalin* (New York: Basic Books, 2010).

2. See Jan Grabowski, *Hunt for the Jews: Betrayal and Murder in German-Occupied Poland* (Bloomington: Indiana University Press, 2013).

3. Jan Karski, *Story of a Secret State* (Boston: Houghton Mifflin, 1944).

4. Bohdan Kwiatkowski, *Sabotaż i Dywersja* (London: Bellona, 1949), 1:21, as cited in Marek Ney-Krwawicz, *The Polish Underground State and the Home Army (1939–45)*, translated by Antoni Bohdanowicz (London: PUMST, 2001); http://www.polishresistance-ak.org/2%20Article.htm, an article on the pages of the London Branch of the Polish Home Army Ex-Servicemen Association.

5. Cited in Grabowski, *Hunt for the Jews*, 56.

6. Omer Bartov, *Hitler's Army: Soldiers, Nazis, and War in the Third Reich* (Oxford and New York: Oxford University Press, 1991), 6.

CHAPTER EIGHT

Freedom Fighters or Terrorists?

Case Studies of Resistance and Reprisal

We are concerned here with three separate armed resistance actions, one in Italy, one in France, and one in what was then Hungary but is now Serbia. This selection is based on the consideration that the fairly well-known resistance actions and reprisals in Italy and France offer the possibility for further readings to those interested, while the third terrible event is almost unknown in the West and should cast a light on the entanglement of anti-fascist resistance with ethnic and political conflict. The three actions were the bombing attack, in March 1944, by Communist partisans on German military policemen at via Rasella in Rome and the retaliatory execution by the SS of 335 Italian citizens in the Ardeatine Cave; the concerted attacks by French maquisards on German troops during the Normandy invasion, in June 1944, and the massacre that SS soldiers perpetrated in reprisal at Oradour-sur-Glane in west-central France; and the sporadic firings by Serbian partisans, late in 1941, on Hungarian soldiers who, in alliance with Germany, had occupied the Bachka region in northern Yugoslavia. In re-taliation, Hungarian army and gendarmerie units massacred at least 3,000 civilians.[1] There were, of course, thousands of similar partisan attacks and similar German—and non-German—reprisals during World War II. In addition to the two cases involving Germans, the Hungarian example shows that not only Germans but Germany's allies also suffered what they called terrorist attacks and, in exchange, engaged in counterterror.

Note that while proportionally few Jews participated in parti-san activities, reprisals hit the Jewish community the hardest. The SS

Einsatzgruppen in Russia, in 1941, which shot about 1 million Jews, the vast majority children, women, and old people, charged them with "banditry" and other "terrorist" acts. In our three cases, a large number of Jews were killed regardless of their being totally innocent of the partisan attacks.

It is also worth noting that in the two cases involving the German SS, their own authorities did not try the culprits for shooting or burning alive hundreds of innocent people, while in the third case, that of Hungary, in a nearly unique development during World War II, the military commanders of the massacres were tried and sentenced by their own military courts during the war. It is true, however, that the foremost defendants were able—or were allowed—to escape to Nazi Germany. In a supreme irony, while those who had committed mass murder at Oradour went practically unpunished in France after the war, the innocent Hungarian population in postwar northern Yugoslavia suffered mass murder and deportation by the Titoist authorities.

THE VIA RASELLA AND THE ARDEATINE CAVE

As we know already, following the Allied landing in Sicily, in July 1943, Mussolini's followers forced him to resign; soon thereafter, he was arrested. Although the king and the new prime minister, Marshal Pietro Badoglio, officially continued the war, secret negotiations with the Allies led to an armistice on September 3, 1943. The king and his government then fled to the Allies in southern Italy, leaving their armies and administrations without leadership and instructions.

In brilliant countermeasures, the often minuscule, but determined, German military forces disarmed the vast Italian army on the Italian peninsula and in the Balkans, Greece, and France. In addition, German paratroopers freed Mussolini, who then decided to form the so-called Salò Republic in northern Italy—a puppet regime that was nevertheless not completely unpopular. There followed a terrible civil war between Italian partisans, many of them Communists, and the forces of Mussolini's fascist republic. Even though the Kingdom of Italy declared war on Germany, the attempt to liberate the country in a few easy steps had failed badly: Rome was freed only on June 4, 1944, and northern Italy a few days before Germany's surrender in May 1945. The Allies had missed one great opportunity after another. The best one followed the Anzio landing in January 1944, when there were no German troops between Anzio and Rome and individual US officers were able to drive to the Eternal City in their jeeps. But the US and British tanks had not been ordered forward and in any case were caught in a vast bottleneck near the shore.

In Rome there was considerable anti-German resistance activity by three groupings: the conservative monarchists (Badoglio), the moderates (Christian Socialists, Social Democrats), and the Communists and allied Socialists. The monarchists supported restoring the prewar regime minus the fascists, moderates wanted democracy, and the Communists and left-wing Socialists hoped for a social revolution. However, all accepted a common goal, which was to prove national innocence, or at least to atone for Italian crimes committed in Abyssinia and the Balkans. The main force driving the resistance was the Communists, their risk taking fostered by the Allies, who, following their troubled landing at Anzio, put pressure on the partisans to attack the German army.

The first major partisan attack was planned and executed by Communists who had noted that a German military police company was marching through central Rome, specifically through the narrow little via Rasella, every day and always at the same time. Strangely, when reaching via Rasella, the column also sang the same song. The military policemen were draftees from the South Tyrol, a German-speaking region in Italy whose inhabitants had been Austrian citizens until 1918, were Italian citizens between the two wars, and now were German citizens. (Today, South Tyrolians are Italian citizens who are enjoying a good deal of autonomy.) Note that there were very few Germans in Rome at that time: the Gestapo and the SS in general had only token forces there; the German military police consisted of two companies, totaling 400 men.

On March 23, 1944, the partisans, disguised as sanitation workers, hid a bomb in a rubbish cart that, when exploded, killed 33 German military policemen and wounded hundreds. Several soldiers were blinded for life. In the ensuing chaos, bewildered German soldiers fired into the neighboring buildings, killing and wounding some civilians.* Note that all 16 partisans escaped unharmed, and none was ever caught.

The German dilemma was, what to do now? Three options were considered. Hitler suggested massive retaliation and the destruction of the area where the attack had occurred: Generalfeldmarschall Albert Kesselring,

---

*The main Italian actors in the drama were the partisan organization Gappisti, which was associated with the Communist Azione (Patriotic Action Group).

commander in chief in the southern theater of war, recommended that 10 Italians be executed for every German soldier who had died. German diplomats in Rome favored no retribution, mainly because of the weakness of the German garrison in the city.

Kesselring's suggestion was adopted: 10 Italians would be executed for every dead German soldier. Lieutenant Colonel Herbert Kappler, who was the SS security chief in Rome, at first expected to have to execute only those who were already in prison and under a death sentence. Yet only 4 such Italians were found; therefore, the target groups had to be enlarged to include other political prisoners, common criminals, bystanders from via Rasella, Italian POWs (including a general), and 78 Jews—the latter with the argument that all Jews were under virtual death sentence in any case. The public in Rome tended to condemn the partisan attack; Pope Pius XII was particularly outraged by what he perceived as an attack on the Holy City, in preparation for a Communist takeover. But at least the pope tried to help some individuals selected by the SS for execution; unfortunately, for everyone released through his good offices, another innocent person was arrested. In the end, 335 Italians were killed in the Ardeatine Caves (Fosse) outside Rome by untrained, unprepared, and finally drunken SS men, under gruesome circumstances.

The German retaliation had not been unsuccessful; Roman resistance was weakened for the duration. Since then, the question has been raised many times whether the German action was legal. Hostage taking (and hence hostage shooting) as well as reprisals had been recognized as perfectly legal by The Hague Conventions and also, somewhat surprisingly, by one of the American-led Nuremberg Tribunals in 1948. (See the case of the southeastern European field of military operation, Field Marshal Wilhelm List.) Kappler was sentenced to life in prison by an Italian court in 1948, but in 1977 his wife smuggled the then-terminally ill and very thin Kappler out of jail in a large suitcase. Some guards assisted her, whether wittingly or unwittingly. She took him to Germany, where he soon died.

His deputy Captain Erich Priebke had a more adventurous life that became public knowledge in October 2013 when he died in Rome at the age of one hundred.[2] Undoubtedly, he had been the oldest surviving German war criminal. Having escaped to Argentina after the war, Priebke became a butcher, living under his own name and using a revalidated German passport to visit Italy, among other places. In 1995 he was extradited, to his and other people's great surprise, to Italy, where he was tried by a military court.

[Handwritten margin note, marked ②]: How did the suggestion change turned into more killings?.

[Handwritten margin note, marked ③]: There should be quotation at oh dll

Image 8.1. SS Lieutenant Colonel Herbert Kappler, the head of the German police in Rome, facing his Italian judges after the war. In 1977 his wife smuggled him out of jail in a large suitcase and took him back to Germany. Source: Bundesarchiv, Bild 183-M0521–500 / photo: o.Ang.

That court, however, released him with the argument that he had acted under orders. A great outcry, especially by Italian Jewish organizations, led to his being rearrested. He was tried again by a military court and was finally sentenced to life imprisonment, but because of his advanced age was put under house arrest. It could not have been a very harsh imprisonment, for Priebke was regularly allowed to leave the house under the supervision of two policemen. He himself never felt guilty of any crime, not even for the killing of 5 extra victims. The deaths of 33 German soldiers required 330 Italians to be executed, but because of a clerical error, 335 were produced at the cave. Fearing that, if released, the 5 would talk about what they had seen, Priebke had them shot as well. This was not quite a valid argument, because Priebke, who had been ordered to execute only Italian citizens, released a prisoner who turned out to be a German military deserter.

The Priebke case raises troubling dilemmas concerning guerrilla attacks. The German military policemen had been draftees; they had not chosen their unit, nor is there proof of any of them having previously committed a war crime. Nor was it the policemen's choice to be at first Austrians, then Italians, and then Germans; citizenships were imposed on them by political changes.

The vast majority of the victims of the massacre had nothing to do with the Italian resistance. The partisans must have known that there would be terrible revenge. Priebke and Kappler had been torturing innocent victims at Gestapo headquarters, but these acts were unconnected with the Ardeatine Cave massacre. Priebke was guilty of having ordered the killing of the 5 supernumeraries; one wonders, however, how many military commanders would have acted differently in his place.

Even if hostage taking was legal (today it is no longer), it is unclear why the victims of the Ardeatine Cave massacre are often called hostages. Traditionally, the latter were selected from among respectable citizens in an occupied town in order to prevent attacks on the occupiers. This atrocity, however, was an act of revenge. Moreover, even the postwar Nuremberg court did not attempt to resolve the question of how many hostages could be "legally" shot for every soldier killed: 5 for 1, 10 for 1, or perhaps 100 for 1? During World War I, generally only a few hostages were executed for every German soldier the guerrillas had killed. During World War II, the Germans executed a minimum of 10 persons for each German soldier killed; in Serbia they hanged or shot 50 civilians for every German soldier and 100 for every German officer killed.

The Ardeatine Cave massacre remains morally indefensible, but the dilemmas that an army of occupation faces do not lend themselves to easy solutions. The fact is that the German army executed thousands upon thousands in retaliation for the killing of its soldiers in Russia, the Baltic countries, Poland, and the Balkans. We know that compared with this dark record, the practices of the Allied armies and even of the Soviet Red Army were very mild indeed.

From an Italian patriotic point of view, via Rasella was not a futile exercise. It strengthened the image of Italians as victims, not as perpetrators. This propaganda line was consistently and successfully exploited by Italian diplomacy, literature, and film, such as Roberto Rossellini's famous 1945 movie *Rome, Open City* and many other war films.

Even today, Right and Left in Italy debate whether the partisans involved in the bomb attack should have surrendered to the German authorities, thereby possibly preventing the massacre of 335. Yet it is most likely that had they voluntarily stepped forward, the retaliation would still have gone on; in any case, an appeal for their surrender had never been launched.

The partisan couple whose bomb had killed the German policemen, Carla Capponi (Elena) and Rosario Bentivegna (Paolo), were celebrated as heroes in postwar Italy; they eventually became Communist parliamentary deputies. When criticized for their action, the two usually replied that without the risk of innocents getting killed in the action, no armed resistance could ever have taken place. The radical thesis that "one cannot make an omelet without first breaking an egg" is what generally separated Communist from non-Communist resisters. Those who chose less lethal avenues for action were then subjected to the charge of inefficiency, even cowardice.

THE ORADOUR TRAGEDY

This Oradour-sur-Glane incident both resembles and is quite different from the terrible events in Rome. There is, for instance, the similar ethnic setup: the German policemen in Rome had been Italian citizens in the interwar years; the German killers at Oradour had been mainly French citizens before the Nazi conquest of Alsace-Lorraine in 1940.

Oradour, a village in west-central France, is in the historic province of Limousin. In 1940 it became a part of Vichy France, which means that it saw no German soldiers until November 1942, when the latter occupied the rest of France. The region was poor, neglected by the central government, with many adherents of the French Communist Party. All this would play a crucial role in the later confrontation between Alsace, where most of the SS soldiers had come from, and Le Limousin, many of whose inhabitants these soldiers had massacred.

On June 10, 1944, four days after the first Allied landings in Normandy, a company (120 men) of the SS Panzer Division "Das Reich" passed through the region on the way to the front. By then, the division had been subjected to guerrilla attacks, including the torture and killing of some 40 captured German soldiers in the village of Tulle, not far from Oradour. For that outrage, the division had already taken revenge by torturing and killing 97 Frenchmen in Tulle.

Acting on the rumor that a Waffen SS officer was being held captive by the maquisard guerrilla fighters and confusing one village with another, the SS company under Major Adolf Diekmann entered Oradour and within a few hours killed, mostly by burning them alive, every inhabitant to a total of 642, including even the smallest of children. One woman managed to escape from the burning church, and a few villagers happened to be away at that time, including some POWs in Germany.

During the massacre, the company seemed to have acted according to a previous plan; thus, theirs was not an outbreak of fury by soldiers who were being harassed and expected to be killed sooner or later. (In fact, the majority of the SS killers at Oradour, including their commander, fell in battle a few weeks later.) Official French history states that there had been no previous attacks at Oradour on occupiers and that, therefore, the victims were all innocent: the massacre was a misplaced retribution for guerrilla attacks at Tulle and elsewhere.

It is still unclear from whom the order to kill originated. In 1951 a French court sentenced the commander of the division, General Heinz Lammerding, to death in absentia for the killings at Oradour and Tulle, among other places. However, the British authorities refused to extradite Lammerding from their zone, and German judicial proceedings were closed against him because of the French proceedings. A highly successful engineer in West Germany, Lammerding died much later in his bed.

Other German perpetrators, writing later from the safe haven of West Germany, argued that the partisan attacks at Tulle and Oradour had been in violation of The Hague and Geneva Conventions as well as of the 1940 armistice agreement. They all forbade civilian attacks on the military, not to speak of the torture and killing of captive soldiers. Some Germans argued that the SS officer the company was looking for had been burned alive, although where this allegedly happened is not clear. Others said that the village church blew up with the women and children not because it had been set on fire by the soldiers but because partisans had been hiding ammunition there. In brief, in the eyes of the apologists, only the murder of the men in the barns was a true crime for which Major Diekmann would certainly have been prosecuted by the German authorities.

But even if all this were true, German defenders of the culprits still overlook that clause of The Hague Convention that states that whereas the execution of guerrillas is justified, the torture and killing of their family members and of innocent bystanders are war crimes. This was confirmed by the so-called International Military Tribunal, consisting of US,

British, French, and Soviet judges, which met in the ruined German city of Nuremberg in 1945–1946 to try the major German war criminals. In one of its major decisions, the tribunal established the principle of crimes against humanity, a crime whose accountability would never lapse.

Note that the Allied landing in Normandy was generally interpreted by the resistance in France as a call for immediate guerrilla action; however, the slowness of the Allied advance allowed the Germans to crush these uprisings. German revenge, as at Ascq and Tulle, was inevitably aimed at civilians and particularly at Jews, for whom few cared.[3]

Tragedy was followed by a tragicomedy at the Bordeaux trial in 1953, during which some survivors of the SS company were tried. It turned out that fourteen of the twenty-one defendants had once been French citizens; in court they all claimed to have been forcibly drafted into the SS. These were the famous *malgré nous,* persons who had served against their wishes. Almost as a whole, people in Alsace bemoaned the tragic fate of the poor boys who had to kill so as not to be killed by their own superiors. But such an explanation would have been rejected at Nuremberg, which categorically repudiated the alibi of superior orders. Moreover, as Christopher Browning and others have amply shown, no policeman or soldier was ever punished in the German army or the Waffen SS for refusing to shoot unarmed victims. We shall see in the case of Novi Sad that in all three affairs, the defendants used the argument, successfully in France and Italy, unsuccessfully in Hungary and Yugoslavia, of having been reluctant killers forced to obey superior orders.

At Bordeaux not only were the *malgré nous* virtually acquitted, but the single Alsatian who had admitted having volunteered for the SS was also treated mildly. Within five years all the killers, whether French or German, were free. The conclusion is inescapable that at Bordeaux, politics took precedence over morality and legality. The loyalty of Alsace-Lorraine to France was more important to the French government than that of a southern French province that had no choice but to remain loyal and whose inhabitants had been voting Communist. At the cost of justice, the unity of France was preserved, and the French people were reassured that, rather than having been accomplices, they had been victims of Nazi oppression. Simultaneously, the newfound warm relations between France and West Germany were preserved. All were winners, except the families of the Oradour victims. No doubt, had the trial taken place in 1945–1946, the SS men would have been hanged.

REVENGE AND ETHNIC CLEANSING AT NOVI SAD

In January 1942, following some widely scattered and not very effective attacks by Serbian guerrillas, Hungarian soldiers and gendarmes in
what was then southern Hungary murdered nearly four thousand civilians, the absolute majority being Serbian speakers. But there were among
the victims also a thousand Jews, some Gypsies, twenty-one non-Jewish
Hungarians, and a few others. This event became one of the great trau-
mas of World War II Hungarian and Yugoslav history, with one important redeeming feature for the Hungarians: those who had commanded
the massacres were tried twice, in some cases even thrice: first in a royal
Hungarian military court, then in the courts of the postwar antifascist
Hungarian republic, and, finally, in the court of Communist Yugoslavia.
Justice was severe: at least a dozen defendants were put to death either in
Hungary or in Yugoslavia.

More even than at Oradour and Rome, at Novi Sad ethnicity played a
crucial role, for the killers were Hungarians and the victims were mainly
non-Hungarians. Yet ethnicity could not have been everything, because
while most Serbs were killed simply for being Serbs, there were also some
Hungarian victims suspected of Communist sympathies. In an irony of
ironies, nearly all the Jewish victims were Hungarian speakers. In that
region, Jews were in their majority Hungarian patriots; it did them no
good—they were killed for being Jews.

The city of Novi Sad, in Hungarian Újvidék, had been a part of historic
Hungary for many hundreds of years, but at the end of World War I it
fell to the newly constituted South Slav Kingdom, later called Yugoslavia,
together with the rest of the so-called Bachka region. There was never any
doubt regarding Hungary's revisionist territorial ambitions in Yugoslavia,
Romania, and Czechoslovakia: the three countries together had grabbed
two-thirds of historical Hungary's territory and population. But it needed
Hitler's rise to power and German support of Hungary's revisionist claims
for it to receive parts of the lost lands, one after the other, with the Bachka
being last on the list. In fact, the Bachka was the only region within the
reannexed lands where Hungarian speakers formed a minority. Thus, the
Hungarian military occupation in the spring of 1941 was not a triumphant
march among a jubilant population but one racked by fear and mutual
hatreds. Similar to the Germans in Belgium in 1914, the invading Hungarian soldiers were, in the words of one of their commanders, seized by

"mass hysteria," firing at unseen enemies who more than once turned out to be fellow Hungarian soldiers. Following some scattered Serbian guerrilla attacks, causing one or two deaths, the high command in Budapest demanded retribution, mainly with the aim of forcing as many Serbs as possible across the Serbian border. But, as Hungarian historians assert, there was another, more subtle, reason: unwilling to send even more soldiers to the Russian front, the Hungarian high command used the excuse of its forces being needed to deter South Slav partisan attacks. The main advocate of this tactic was the chief of general staff, General Ferenc Szombathelyi, whom the Germans later confined to a concentration camp and the Yugoslavs later executed.

At the orders of Budapest, local military commanders, who were all radical rightist sympathizers, went into action, in January 1942, at Novi Sad and at dozens of other places. Theoretically on the lookout for Communist bandits, the military shot innocent civilians. This was no genocide, for even after the massacre there remained at least 150,000 Serbs in the region. The Hungarians' aim was to redress the ethnic balance that had been altered by the interwar Yugoslav government's policy of bringing South Slav settlers to the rich Bachka region. Alternatively, the Hungarian commanders simply wanted to show who was master in what had again become a part of southern Hungary. The result was a series of terrible atrocities.

But why kill the Jews? In Rome and around Oradour, few cared about what would happen to the Jews; in Hungary the commanders and many of their officers and men hated the Jews, who served as convenient and defenseless scapegoats for all of Hungary's recent misfortunes: defeat in World War I, the so-called Red Terror in 1919, the country's dismemberment, the economic collapse, and the allegedly nefarious influence of corrupt, "Judaized" Budapest on the countryside.*

There followed a series of protests by a handful of deputies in the Hungarian parliament; uniquely in Eastern Europe, Hungary still had a working multiparty legislature that shielded its members from prosecution. In the following year, a new cabinet under Prime Minister Miklós Kállay opened secret contacts with the Western Allies in order to discuss

---

*The events at Novi Sad have been most successfully re-created in András Kovács's 1966 movie *Hideg Napok* (Cold Days) with, as the most terrible scene, the shooting of the victims into holes drilled in the ice on the Danube River.

(5) How could one group be blamed for all of this? Doesn't make sense.

surrender. But the negotiations led nowhere because of Hungarian insistence that only British and US but no Soviet troops come to Hungary, a strategic and political impossibility.

In another sign of Hungarian goodwill toward Nazism's enemies, fifteen army and gendarmerie officers, among them two generals, were court-martialed for war crimes committed during the antipartisan action at Novi Sad and elsewhere. The defendants were allowed to remain free on their word of honor as officers and gentlemen, which did not prevent the four highest ranking among them to flee to Germany. There, they were immediately admitted into the Waffen SS with the same rank they had held in Hungary. The Hungarian military court sentenced some of the defendants to death in absentia; others received heavy jail sentences, but then, on March 19, 1944, German troops occupied Hungary. The fugitive officers returned to Hungary only to flee again, at the end of 1944, because of the arrival of the Red Army. Before they fled, the four made sure of the torture and execution of General János Kiss, who had been their judge in the royal military court. Arrested by the Americans, the four were returned to democratic Hungary, where they were retried and sentenced to death, only to be extradited to Tito's Yugoslavia for another trial. They were tried and executed there, in 1946, together with General Ferenc Szombathelyi, the former inmate of the Germans at the concentration camp at Mauthausen.

There was a tragic follow-up to this bloody affair—something that would have been inconceivable either in Italy or in France—namely, the postwar persecution of the Hungarian population in the Bachka region. After all, Italy and France, too, could have expelled or killed their German-speaking minorities; instead, the inhabitants of the South Tyrol and of Alsace-Lorraine became privileged minorities. Although Yugoslav source materials are largely unavailable, it seems that, during the period of postwar revenge, Tito's partisans murdered tens of thousands of Hungarian speakers in the Bachka region (estimates vary between ten and fifty thousand) and expelled tens of thousands more. Thus, the final victims of this tragic affair were Hungarian civilians whom the Hungarian military occupation forces had thought they were protecting, back in 1941, by murdering masses of Serbian and Jewish Hungarian civilians.

We have seen that the sole beneficiary of the via Rasella incident was official Italy, which after the war succeeded in projecting the image of itself as an innocent victim of German aggression, thereby making the world forget about the grave Italian atrocities in Abyssinia, Libya, and the

Balkans. Similarly, the only beneficiary of the Oradour massacre was official France, which, in order to satisfy the inhabitants of Alsace-Lorraine, two wealthy and important provinces, let justice go by the board and allowed the murderers at Oradour to remain virtually unpunished. Finally, the sole beneficiary of the Novi Sad tragedy was the Yugoslav Communist government, which, in an act of brazen ethnic cleansing, wiped out thousands of local Hungarians in order to systematically replace them with South Slav colonists imported from poverty-stricken southern Yugoslavia.

In sum, then, World War II armed resistance was both ethical and unethical; it was ethical because it combated the Nazis, and it was unethical because of the havoc and suffering it caused. From a military point of view, only a few resistance groups, such as those in Yugoslavia, Russia, and Poland, became powerful enough to cause serious trouble to the German army. Yet it is also true, as we shall see, that the wartime resistance movements exercised a profound influence on postwar democratic developments.

Finally, it must be said that extreme violence on the part of an occupying power is not an absolute necessity when threatened by guerrillas. The occupier can at least try to respect the laws of war and thereby win friends among the population. That such a thing is possible was shown by the Germans in Western and northern Europe during the first years of the war and often even later. It was also proved by the Allies in Germany in 1945–1946 when, despite some violent guerrilla activity, they showed great restraint toward the civilian population.

NOTES

1. For the events at Oradour, see, among others, Sarah Farmer, *Martyred Village: Commemorating the 1944 Massacre at Oradour-sur-Glane* (Berkeley: University of California Press, 1999). On the via Rasella tragedy, see Alessandro Portelli, *The Order Has Been Carried Out: History, Memory, and Meaning of a Nazi Massacre in Rome* (New York: Macmillan, 2003). The Újvidék/Novi Sad events are described and analyzed by Enikő A. Sajti in *Hungarians in the Voivodina, 1918–1947,* translated by Brian McLean (Boulder, CO: distributed by Columbia University Press, 2003).

2. See the *New York Times,* October 12 and 15, 2013.

3. This type of event is shatteringly analyzed by the Franco-Bulgarian philosopher Tzvetan Todorov in *A French Tragedy: Scenes of Civil War, Summer 1944,* translated by Mary Byrd Kelly (Hanover, NH: Dartmouth College, 1996).

CHAPTER NINE

The End of the War, the Apparent Triumph of the Resistance Movements, and the First Retributions

Let us draw a picture of Europe in the last months of the war with a focus on the collaborators and the resisters—in other words, those who tried to delay the German defeat and with it their own demise and those who rushed to hasten the end of Hitler's empire and with it their coming to power. Needless to say, in the spring of 1945, unlike during the first years of the war, the resisters outnumbered the collaborators.

In June 1944, in what became the most celebrated event of modern Western history, British, American, Canadian, Free French, and Polish divisions landed in France. Although the problem of supplying the troops across the often stormy Channel and determined German counterattacks delayed the breakout from the Normandy peninsula, by August General Dwight Eisenhower's armies were racing across Western Europe. By the fall, they had taken the capitals of Italy, France, Belgium, and Luxembourg; they even conquered a small corner of Nazi Germany, where, incidentally, the first acts of German collaboration with and resistance to the Anglo-American forces occurred. But then supplies, especially fuel, became a huge problem, and the Allied commanders could not agree on who should lead the final thrust into the heart of Nazi Germany. While the troops settled down for a long winter's wait, the Germans launched a ferocious counterattack in the Ardennes Forest, near the Belgian border, which threatened to push the Allies back into the sea. At last, the armored Waffen SS divisions were stopped by a great American effort, German fuel shortages, and a gigantic Soviet offensive that forced Hitler to withdraw his best-armored and Waffen SS infantry divisions from the Western front.

The final Allied offensive, which began in March 1945, met with varying degrees of opposition: some Germans were prepared to defend their county to the last bullet; others fought the Allies only so as to protect the backs of their comrades on the Eastern front; again others, probably the majority, could hardly wait to surrender to the Western Allies—anything to avoid falling into Soviet captivity. But the attempt to surrender was made very risky by, among others, the German military police's practice of executing any soldier found not with his unit. As a characteristic act of Nazi madness, in besieged Berlin hundreds or more were hanged for alleged cowardice, among them children and old men drafted into service just before the total collapse. Following the general surrender, in May 1945, but before having been captured by the Allies, some German military courts still meted out death sentences to soldiers accused of cowardice and desertion. In at least one case, a captive German unit borrowed rifles from its British guards to execute some fellow soldiers accused of desertion prior to the general surrender.

THE END IN GERMANY

German behavior in the last months of the war was influenced by such things as the Allies' insistence on unconditional surrender, the soldiers' dread of Soviet revenge, and the population's fear of the liberated concentration camp inmates. German civilians also had to reckon with the presence of millions of foreign prisoners and involuntary workers in Germany. Hitler's desire to destroy the German people who, as he said repeatedly, had proved themselves unworthy of him did not help matters, either. And even if Hitler's order of national self-destruction was generally ignored, there were enough fanatics to create an atmosphere of hysteria. In Austria, for instance, at the orders of the local *Gauleiter* (district leader), a group of SA militiamen stormed the prison at Stein in Lower Austria, just before the arrival of the Soviet army, and shot 229 political prisoners, claiming that they would otherwise be instrumental in the postwar reconstruction of Austria. The prison director and 5 guards were killed for refusing to participate in the massacre. In the eyes of these Nazis, there was to be no life in Germany and Austria without the Führer.[1]

Just before the end, German cities and factories were devastated by huge Allied bombing raids and by fighter planes strafing anything and anyone that moved. The northern Netherlands, Denmark, Norway, and northern Italy were liberated only early in May, more or less simultaneously with the German army's final surrender.

During the last year of the war, resistance movements were active everywhere; moreover, they received the influx of those joining, to use a then widespread contemptuous expression, "five minutes before midnight." Many among the newcomers had been ardent collaborators: the Paris police, for instance, had for years readily lent the Germans a helping hand, especially in hunting down Jews. Yet in August 1944, the police in Paris fired enthusiastically on German soldiers trying to flee north across the city. Some policemen also participated in the orgy of revenge and retribution that marked Paris and the rest of Western Europe in the following months. Liberation from the German yoke brought not only general rejoicing but also an often brutal hunt for real or alleged collaborators. Particularly rough treatment was reserved for such women who had engaged in *collaboration horizontale*—sexual relations with German soldiers. Some observers asserted that those who were most aggressive in shaving the heads of female collaborators or in hanging "traitors" had dirtied their hands during the occupation and now tried to get rid of eyewitnesses. Yet even though many real or alleged collaborators were lynched or executed by individual action or by orders of arbitrarily constituted so-called kangaroo courts, the major resistance groups generally maintained order. Somewhat surprisingly, Stalin did not exploit the general devastation and the lack of functioning administrations: by continuing the Popular Front policy of the war years, the Communist Parties from Norway to Italy did not even attempt to grab power. Only in Greece, as stated, did the popular Communist guerrillas endeavor to seize power. However, the freshly landed British troops were quick to crush them with the force of arms, and the Soviet Union did not protest this action. The former collaborationists had either joined the resistance, gone into hiding, or fled with the Germans and were now waiting to be arrested. During General de Gaulle's solemn entry into Paris on August 26, 1944, some shots fell from the rooftops, creating pandemonium, but it is still not known whether the marksmen were truly former collaborators, as it was assumed at that time. As a general rule, the collaborators did not try to resist the entry of the Allies. A good example for such a relatively tranquil takeover was provided by Norway, in which, in May, the underground Milorg Army accepted the peaceful surrender of more than three hundred thousand German soldiers. Simultaneously, many Norwegian collaborators also surrendered to the new authorities. Lucky were the countries of Norway and Denmark, where virtually nothing had been destroyed, where few people had been killed, and from which the equally lucky German occupiers were soon sent home. Not so fortunate were the German POWs in France and Belgium, who would spend the next few years toiling in the mines. Even less fortunate were such German soldiers who, even though they had surrendered to the Western Allies, were handed over to the Red Army because their units had been on the Eastern front, and thus, "legally," they belonged in Soviet captivity. There they went together with thousands of East Europeans who, because of the extension of Soviet boundaries, were now legally Soviet citizens. It made no difference whether the individual Eastern European in question had voluntarily or involuntarily served the Germans.

Why would they do this?

③ The German soldiers who had surrendered to the US Army in the millions were kept in giant so-called cages in Germany in which many perished under the primitive outdoor conditions. Interestingly, however, there is no evidence of any mutiny among the German prisoners, whether in the remarkable comfort of the POW camps in Canada and the United States or in the rain-soaked, shelterless fields of the cages.

④ *Ironic*

Those who fared the worst were the German and German-allied soldiers who had fallen directly into Soviet captivity. They died by the hundreds of thousands, less often as victims of Soviet revenge and more often because the Soviet civilians themselves had nothing to eat. During the 1946 famine in Russia, civilians lined up in front of POW camps in the hope of obtaining some food. Of the roughly ninety thousand Germans who had surrendered at Stalingrad in January 1943, only about five thousand ever made it home.

At the approach of the enemy armies, some Nazi leaders, especially Joseph Goebbels, tried to train a number of so-called Werwolves, young people who would wage a partisan war behind enemy lines. But such incidents turned out to be rare, and it now seems that "Operation Werwolf" was mostly propaganda and myth. Yet it was an effective myth: both the Soviets and the Western Allies took the matter seriously. For instance, great excitement was caused by the rumor of a so-called Alpine Redoubt, a series of bunkers and hiding places the Nazis had allegedly erected in

Bavaria and Austria and from which fanatical Werwolf youth were expected to sally forth. In reality, there never was an Alpine Redoubt; still, it is said that because of this rumor, General Eisenhower diverted the triumphant American thrust toward Berlin in a southerly direction. According to other sources, however, Eisenhower refused to send his troops to Berlin simply so as to avoid conflict with the Soviet army, which, according to earlier agreements, was to take control of the Berlin region.

Not only was there no Nazi Alpine Redoubt, but there was also very little German anti-Allied guerrilla activity. The single major act of German anti-Allied resistance occurred at Aachen, in southwestern Germany, which the US troops had occupied in September 1944 and where the "collaborationist" German mayor was assassinated by some young men loyal to the Führer. This and similar resistance acts were punished by execution; in some places, but especially in the Soviet-occupied zone, massive punitive actions brought the burning down of localities and the arrest, even the shooting, of entire groups. Historian Perry Biddiscombe estimates that three to five thousand people died in connection with anti-Allied German resistance activity, most of them teenagers executed by the Soviets and the Western Allies, generally for imaginary partisan activity.[2] Overall, the Germans proved to be ideal collaborators: submissive, peaceful, hardworking, and well educated. Loneliness, hunger, or love drove many German women into the arms of US, British, French, or Soviet soldiers, as many of their men were now dead or in captivity.

THE LEGACY OF THE GERMAN RESISTANCE

German collaboration with the victors did not mean, however, that the German people in general would have forgiven those who had resisted Hitler, especially in the form of the July 20, 1944, attempt to assassinate him. One hesitates a little whether to include German resistance in a book on collaboration with and resistance to foreign, especially German, occupations during the Second World War: after all, the Germans (and Austrians) did not collaborate with Hitler; they were, with some honorable exceptions, Hitler's own nation, and they simply executed his will as he executed the German people's will. But then the July 20 conspiracy was the only resistance movement in Europe that had the means and actually came close to putting a sudden end to the Nazi regime and thus also to the war. The next question is whether the attempt on Hitler's life was a

[handwritten margin note: (So many) The German did not choose Hitlers ways.]

[handwritten margin circled: 5]

genuine resistance act or, as many historians see it, a desperate measure
on the part of some of Nazi Germany's highest-ranking soldiers and administrators to save their own skin and to save Germany from total ruin.
Actually, the true German resisters were Communists, Social Democrats,
and many democratically or religiously motivated individuals who often
gave their lives in the struggle. But their ranks had been so greatly reduced
by the Gestapo and by public hostility as to make them totally ineffective.
The July 20 conspiracy was an entirely different matter.

Unlike the Communist or Socialist workers or some anti-Nazi youth
in the big cities, the July 20 conspirators included some field marshals,
dozens of generals, at least one admiral, members of the army's general
staff, hundreds of other career and reserve officers, high-ranking members of the SS and the SA, the mayors of some large cities, and important diplomats. Many of these men had originally been ardent Nazis; a
few, like the famous Colonel Claus Count von Stauffenberg, had developed genuine democratic ideas. Some, such as former chief of the general
staff General Ludwig Beck, had tried to overthrow the Führer as early as
1938; others had joined recently, and many more sat on the fence, knowing
about the conspiracy but doing nothing against it. The list included such
great personalities as the philosophical anti-Nazi Helmuth James Count
von Moltke, lawyer Hans von Dohnányi, and theologian Pastor Dietrich
Bonhoeffer. Most of the conspirators came from the aristocracy; they felt
responsible for upholding their brave family traditions and honor of the
fatherland. Only a few among them transcended national feelings, such
as Stauffenberg, who was convinced that by assassinating the Führer, he
would help humanity to rid itself of evil.

By the summer of 1944, many of the highest-ranking military commanders were involved in the coup preparation or, at least, knew about it
and failed to report it to the Gestapo. Field Marshals Gerd von Rundstedt,
Günther von Kluge, and Erwin Rommel, for instance, who together commanded the entire Western front against the Allied forces, had been informed by their underlings of the anti-Hitler plans and were now waiting
to see the outcome. Try to imagine, if you will, General George S. Patton
(commander of the US Third Army), General Omar Bradley (commander
of the Allied Twelfth Army Group), and General Dwight Eisenhower
(supreme commander of the Allied forces in Europe) having all been ap-
proached separately by their immediate underlings with the request that
they join the conspiracy to assassinate their commander in chief, President

Franklin Roosevelt. All three would give noncommittal answers, referring to their soldierly oath, but none would call in the military police to arrest the conspirators. Moreover, they would allow their chiefs of staff and others to continue in office. Almost uniquely in the history of resistance movements, many of the conspirators were fighting unswervingly at the front while planning to assassinate their commander in chief.

Throughout the war years, individual attempts were made, or at least planned, to take the life of Hitler, but all failed. Finally, matters were taken in hand, if one can use this expression in connection with Colonel Count Claus Stauffenberg, who had lost seven fingers and his left eye in General Erwin Rommel's North African campaign. Had he had the use of all his fingers and both eyes, there is little doubt that he would have been able to light the fuses of both bombs he was carrying in a briefcase at Hitler's headquarters in East Prussia. He had had access to that secret location on account of his position as chief of staff of the German home army. The single bomb that went off only slightly wounded Hitler, whose most devoted underlings then succeeded in quashing the coup d'état attempt.

Stauffenberg was shot at the orders of a fellow conspirator who was trying to cover up his own tracks; the same man caused General Beck to commit suicide. In the following months, thousands of Hitler's important enemies and critics were tortured, shot, hanged, or thrown into concentration camps. Some were executed just a few days before the arrival of the Allied troops. Those killed included Field Marshal Erwin von Witzleben and Admiral Wilhelm Canaris; others, such as Field Marshal Rommel, were allowed to commit suicide.

After the war, in the Soviet occupation zone, the Communist martyrs of the resistance were idolized; others, especially the July 20 conspirators, were ridiculed as reckless fools or as unrepentant fascists. The Communists accused them of wanting to preserve capitalist, militarist, and imperialist Germany but without Hitler. In the British, American, and French occupation zones, some of the few surviving resisters were given minor posts, especially in the soon-to-be-built democratic Federal Army, but as far as the general population was concerned, the German resisters had been traitors. It took many decades for the West German government and the younger generations of Germans to recognize that the likes of Stauffenberg and Moltke had been, with all their shortcomings, the best of Germans.

By the end of the war, some 11 million foreign citizens had been assembled in Germany, whether as paid volunteers, paid but forcibly imported workers, unpaid slave laborers, refugees, or concentration camp prisoners. In some of the camps, prisoners had organized into resistance groups, planning to oppose SS attempts at a wholesale massacre just before the Allies' arrival. In fact, there were only very few such attempts, and most guards simply melted away into the retreating German army. In consequence, immediate revenge, whatever there was of it, concentrated on the most brutal *Kapos*—inmates who had collaborated with the SS in torturing and killing their fellow prisoners.

THE END IN THE EAST

As always, everything was quite different in the Eastern theater of operations, where, besides millions of soldiers, masses of collaborators and resisters faced each other. Their methods and goals were far more complex than of those in the West and in Italy, where, basically, the question was whether to welcome or to fear the Allied armies. In the East and in southeastern Europe, liberation as a goal was intertwined with such goals as the establishment or the reestablishment of national independence, the defense or the expansion of the country's political boundaries, administrative centralization, the introduction of some form of revolutionary socialism, and the expulsion or even annihilation of the ethnic minorities. All through the war, Ukrainian nationalists, for example, struggled for political independence and the elimination of the Polish and the Jewish minorities; in these endeavors, the German and the Soviet occupation forces often acted as useful instruments. The two major, mutually hostile, occupation armies knowingly or unknowingly assisted in making Ukraine a country of Ukrainians (and Russians). As an ironic addition, the German occupation gave justification to the expulsion, at the end of the war, of the entire native German population. Almost identical developments characterized Czechoslovakia, Hungary, and the Baltic countries. The Hungarians, for instance, who in 1944 had handed over nearly 500,000 Hungarian Jews to Germany for slaughter, a year later, under a new democratic government and with the permission of the victorious Allies, expelled nearly 300,000 of their German fellow citizens. Something very similar happened in the rest of Eastern and southeastern Europe.

As for the nature of the popular revenge, *les tondues* (the shorn) were not in fashion in Eastern Europe; women's heads were only rarely shaved for "sexual collaboration" with the enemy. In fact, female collaborators were treated no better and no worse than the men. In countries that had been allied with Nazi Germany, public sentiment was generally on the side of the former collaborators; in countries formerly occupied and oppressed by the Germans, the postliberation targets were all the former collaborators, whether male or female. Even more, the targets of popular wrath were the local Germans. And there was some good reason for such hatred because, during the war, the Volksdeutsche, the local Germans, had formed a privileged class, something between the Reichsdeutsche demigods—soldiers, administrators, and businessmen from Germany—and the non-Germans. Indeed, the postwar killing and expulsion of the German speakers formed an important part of the general ethnic cleansing sweeping Eastern Europe. It can be taken for granted that the ethnic Germans would have been expelled even if they had not worked for the occupiers and had not pledged loyalty to the Führer. At best, they would have been treated less brutally.

Although the statistical data on the fate of the Germans in Eastern Europe are as unreliable as are all other statistics in Eastern Europe for that period, German experts maintain that, during and after the war, up to 13 million German civilians fled or were driven from a region between northern Estonia to southern Yugoslavia and the Bulgarian border. Of them, maybe 2 million died on the road or were killed by partisans; by Soviet, Polish, and Czechoslovak soldiers; by enraged civilians; and by bandits. Truly, Hitler had achieved the secret hope of millions of East Europeans: the "cleansing" of their countries of Jews and Germans.

We have already seen that much more blood was shed in Eastern Europe than in Western Europe. In Eastern Europe, the retreating Germans burned everything in sight, killed or drove away the livestock, and blew up entire city blocks as well as the bridges and the rail lines. As for the triumphant Red Army, although it is true that its soldiers looted and raped with abandon, it is less clear whether these crimes were truly revenge for atrocities committed by the Germans and their allies. Certainly, Soviet soldiers treated the conquered German population with particular brutality, but this may have been, at least in part, because of the fierce German military resistance in the area. The Soviet soldiers, who theoretically represented

[handwritten margin note: ⑧ never thought about it like this.]

the much-heralded New Soviet Man, behaved in the old tradition of soldiers: in places where many of their comrades had fallen, they looted and
raped much more savagely than in areas and cities where there had been
no bitter fighting.

During the war, both Romania and Hungary had been the Soviet
Union's enemies; Hungarian and Romanian soldiers had committed terrible atrocities against the Soviet populations. Yet in August 1944, Romania not only surrendered but also turned against the Germans: as a result,
Bucharest fell to the Red Army without firing a shot. Nor did the Red
Army soldiers misbehave in the city. In Budapest, German and Hungarian
troops fought on from December 1944 to February 1945, with horrendous
losses on both sides. Consequently, Soviet troops often behaved abominably. Add to this the traditional warrior concept prevailing among some
ethnic minorities in Soviet Asia, namely, that rape and looting were the
just rewards of victorious soldiers. It is the same conviction, incidentally,
that seems to have driven Morocco's so-called Goumier regiments, who
served within the Free French forces in Italy. For the Goumier soldiers,
Italian women were a well-merited booty.

One of the worst parts of the Soviet presence, aside from drunk soldiers
raping women and sometimes shooting their husbands, was the deportation of entire populations. Not only had the Volga Germans, Poles, Tartars,
the Chechen-Ingush, and other peoples been moved from their European
homelands to Siberia, where thousands perished, but at the end of the war
German civilians, mostly women, were deported from Romania, for instance, to help in the reconstruction of the Soviet Union. In Hungary the
Soviet army picked up and deported thousands of civilians to make up for
the vastly exaggerated number of German and Hungarian soldiers whom
the Soviet commanders fraudulently claimed to have captured.

All of this was not general knowledge at that time because of Soviet
censorship and the inevitable Soviet-friendly policies of the new East European governments. While the Soviet occupation authorities quickly
imposed Communist Party control on Romania and Bulgaria, Stalin for
various reasons allowed the reestablishment of a multiple-party system in
Poland, Czechoslovakia, and Hungary. Still, even in those countries, the
police, especially the political police, were in Communist and Soviet hands
from the beginning. In brief, the division of Europe was an accomplished
fact before the Yalta Conference in February 1945 and the Potsdam Conference in June 1945 put a stamp of approval on this situation. Great-power

cooperation was still the slogan of the day, with the coordination and synthesizing of the planned retribution one of its great symbols. The renewal of the economy and of society was seen everywhere as closely related to the need for European-wide cleansing of traitors and war criminals. The latter took place under the aegis of the trials of the major Nazi war criminals at Nuremberg in 1945–1946, which at least in theory served as a model for the other trials taking place in individual national settings.

NOTES

1. See Gerhard Jagschitz and Wolfgang Neugebauer, eds., *Stein, 6. April 1945* (Vienna: Bundesministerium für Justiz, 1995).

2. Perry Biddiscombe, *Werwolf! The History of the National Socialist Guerrilla Movement, 1944–1946* (Toronto: University of Toronto Press, 1998), 276.

CHAPTER TEN

Purging Hitler's Europe

The great war-crimes trials of 1945–1946 held in Nuremberg, Germany, marked the ultimate triumph of a worldwide coalition over one of history's most evil regimes. No less important, the trials were expected to serve as a precedent for holding the leaders of sovereign states individually and collectively responsible for their actions. For these two reasons, the proceedings of the Nuremberg Tribunal tended to overshadow the nearly simultaneous political, administrative, and judicial purges that took place in the rest of post–World War II Europe, from Norway to Greece and from France to the Soviet Union. Yet the main Nuremberg trial involved only twenty-three defendants, and even if combined with the dozen so-called Nuremberg follow-up trials, it affected only about two hundred persons. Meanwhile, judicial retribution and political purges held elsewhere in Europe, such as the trial of Marshal Philippe Pétain in France and the firing, at least in theory, of all the Dutch teachers who had belonged to the Dutch Nazi Party, amounted to one of the greatest social and demographic upheavals in history.

Those tried at Nuremberg were important German leaders, without, however, the chief culprits of Adolf Hitler, Heinrich Himmler, and Joseph Goebbels, who were dead by that time. The non-Germans brought to trial and executed outside of Germany for such crimes as treason, collaboration with the enemy, and crimes against humanity included an even more amazing number of important personalities. The heads of state or prime ministers who were executed after the war included those of Italy, France, Norway, Slovakia, Hungary, Romania, Bulgaria, and Serbia. In postwar

Image 10.1. Hungarian fascist Arrow Cross leader Ferenc Szálasi takes the salute of German commandos who had brought him to power through a coup d'état on October 15, 1944. Behind Szálasi is a Hungarian general. Source: Bundesarchiv, Bild 101I-680–8284A-37A / photo: Faupel.

democratic Hungary, one former head of state and four former prime ministers were either hanged or shot; the record, however, was held by Bulgaria, where, on February 2, 1945, the ruling Communists executed the last prime minister as well as twenty-four cabinet members and sixty-eight parliamentary deputies for treason and crimes against the people. Yet, as we already know, Bulgaria had never entered the war against the Soviet Union, and its declaration of war against Great Britain and the United States had been a formality. Moreover, no Bulgarian Jew was killed or handed over to the Germans during the war.

The list of non-German Europeans executed for treason, collaboration, and war crimes included thousands of generals, police chiefs, city mayors, politicians, and journalists. In addition, hundreds of thousands were thrown in jail or internment camps, and millions were affected by some other punitive measure. If we now consider that those affected by the East European transfers and expulsions belonged, more often than not, to national minorities that had also often formed their countries' social and economic elites, then it becomes clear that, at least in Eastern Europe, the postwar political purges were closely combined with ethnic cleansing and class warfare. A simultaneous examination of the enormous extent and profound depth of these purges and of the Nuremberg International Military Tribunal's proceedings should allow us to gain some insight into this crucial period in European history. Yet we must note that neither the Nuremberg Tribunal nor the European courts recognized the unique historical significance of the Holocaust, or Shoah; instead, they tended to underplay the tragedy of the "Final Solution of the Jewish Question" while overplaying what the courts saw as the innocence, suffering, and heroism of the various European nations. Indeed, it was not until the trial of the chief administrator of the Holocaust, Lieutenant Colonel Adolf Eichmann, in Jerusalem in 1961–1962, that the Jewish Holocaust gained the supreme judicial attention it deserved. Note that similar to other German Nazi mass murderers, Eichmann had escaped to South America at the end of the war, and he could be tried only after having been kidnapped by the Mossad, the Israeli intelligence agency, from Argentina in 1960.

But why were so few tried at Nuremberg? The answer is that the victorious powers agreed to punish only those who best represented the crimes of entire groups and institutions, such as the Reich Chancellery or the leadership of the Nazi Party, the SS, the SA, the armed forces general staff, the war industry, lawyers, judges, and the medical profession. The prosecution of the other German war criminals was left to the Germans, but this never really happened in the American-, British-, and French-occupied parts of Germany. Yet it was in those occupation zones that most German war criminals settled after the war. The reason for this was the Cold War, during which the West Germans turned into valuable allies of the Western great powers and the East Germans turned into the allies of the Soviet Union.

We must also face the fact that while in many European countries the new regimes, made up of former resisters, wished to purge and to change society, the German people had no such wish. As for the Western Allies, they soon ran out of enthusiasm for a societal shake-up, whereas in Soviet-occupied East Germany, the undemocratic, even totalitarian-minded, Nazi leaders were replaced by undemocratic, even totalitarian-minded, Communists.

THE ROAD TO NUREMBERG AND TO
THE NATIONAL COURT TRIALS

Historical precedents existed for the trial of individuals charged with crimes committed as occupiers, but these precedents were hardly satisfactory. For centuries, as we already know, attempts had been made to codify the laws of war.[1] The Geneva and Hague Conventions, for instance, categorically prohibited the killing of surrendering soldiers and ordered that prisoners of war receive the medical care, pay, and food normally given to one's own troops. International conventions also regulated relations between the occupied and the occupiers.

Some of these agreements were violated in World War I. The German shelling of Louvain Cathedral, for instance, was a clear violation of the 1907 Hague Convention, which had been signed by forty nations, but the same agreement did not prohibit the taking and even killing of hostages. Nor was the sinking of the American passenger ship *Lusitania* in 1915 by a German submarine illegal under international law, for only hospital ships were protected. The zeppelin attacks on London were strictly speaking legal because London was not an undefended city. Finally, The Hague Convention could not be applied to the World War I Turkish massacre of the Armenians because, according to international law, the massacre was a domestic affair.

Notwithstanding such legal loopholes, Western public opinion after World War I wanted to see the German leaders punished for their alleged crimes. Article 227 of the Versailles Treaty stipulated that five judges from the United States, Britain, France, Italy, and Japan try the kaiser for "a supreme offence against international morality and the sanctity of treaties." Articles 228 and 229 required that the German government deliver up its own citizens for trial on war-crime charges by tribunals set up by the victorious powers.

Little came of the attempt to punish German war crimes after World War I. The kaiser had fled to the Netherlands at the end of the war, and to everybody's relief the Dutch refused to surrender him to the victorious powers. Similarly, the idea of an international court of justice for German war criminals was soon abandoned; instead, a list of 854 people to be tried in court was presented to the new German republic. Again, there was great indignation in Germany, but the Supreme Court in Leipzig finally sentenced 13 German soldiers and sailors to relatively short prison terms. The accused were found guilty of crimes such as beating British prisoners of war, shooting wounded French soldiers, and, in the case of two U-boat officers, sinking a hospital ship as well as deliberately destroying two of the hospital ship's three lifeboats. In the absence of the U-boat commander, the Leipzig court tried two of his underlings and in its verdict rejected their excuse that they had only been obeying orders.[2]

Needless to say, a number of British, French, and American soldiers and sailors could have been accused of exactly the same crimes. Still, the Leipzig trials, especially the one affecting some U-boat officers, created a precedent that would have allowed the Allies, had they cared to do so, to demand again in 1945 that the Germans prosecute their own criminals.

As we know from Chapter 1, new treaties and conventions to mitigate the cruelty of warfare, particularly for civilians and military prisoners, and even to outlaw war were signed in the interwar years. Unfortunately, only a few of these agreements were respected during World War II, and if they were, then not in the East—only in the West.

Well before the end of the war, the Allies began to discuss what to do with the German leadership. At first, Prime Minister Churchill proposed that the principal Nazis be dealt with by a political decision of the Allied powers, to which Stalin countered that fifty thousand German general staff officers be summarily shot (there had never been that many), but the Americans, who were the dominating force at Nuremberg, wanted a real trial that would show the triumph of legal fair play over terrorist methods.[3]

The London Agreement of August 8, 1945, established the Nuremberg Tribunal and outlined its jurisdiction. It also drew up the famous four counts of crimes for which a select number of German leaders would be tried:

1. Planning, preparing, initiating, or waging wars of aggression.
2. Participating in a common plan to accomplish any of the foregoing. (The first two categories were referred to as "crimes against peace.")
3. War crimes, a broad category including murder, ill treatment, and deportation of civilians in occupied territory to slave labor in Germany; crimes against prisoners of war; killing of hostages; the plunder or wanton destruction of cities, towns, and villages; and devastation not justified by military necessity.
4. Crimes against humanity, a new idea, applying to inhuman acts committed against civilians before or during the war on political, racial, or religious grounds.[4]

These crimes were to fall within the jurisdiction of the tribunal, "whether or not in violation of the domestic law of the country where perpetrated." The third count was meant to deal with crimes committed by the Nazis in occupied territory or against the slave laborers they imported from Eastern Europe. The fourth count concerned crimes committed in Germany as well as racial, religious, or other persecution in general.[5]

JUSTICE AND INJUSTICE AT NUREMBERG

With the hindsight of seven decades, it is difficult to understand how so many flaws and contradictions could have been built into the indictment of the major war criminals at Nuremberg, and even more so into the proceedings. For example, one of the indictments rightly charged the Germans with aggression against Poland in September 1939, but it failed to mention that the attack could not have taken place without the preceding Nazi-Soviet Non-Aggression Pact and its secret clause regarding the partition of Poland. On September 17, 1939, as we know, Soviet troops invaded Poland, which was already succumbing to German aggression. The Nazi-Soviet Pact was in preparation for a war of aggression, yet its breach by the Germans in 1941 was cited confidently at Nuremberg in order to indict the Germans for their unprovoked attack on the Soviet Union. Absurdly, the indictment ignored the unprovoked Soviet attacks on Poland and Finland in 1939, Bulgaria in 1944, and Japan in 1945.

The Germans were initially charged with the massacre of 925 Polish officers in the Katyń forest, even though the Western prosecutors were fairly certain by that time that the massacre had been the work of the Soviet political police. Later, at the insistence of the chief Soviet prosecutor, Roman A. Rudenko, the number of Polish victims at Katyń was increased from 925 to 11,000 (in reality, there were more than 20,000). But because the Soviets did not produce a shred of evidence against the defendants in the matter of Katyń, and because some American officials at home angrily protested such a parody of justice, Katyń was quietly dropped from the charges. It was not mentioned in the final verdict. Some forty-five years after Nuremberg, one of the last gestures of the collapsing Soviet system was to admit that it was Stalin who, in 1940, had ordered the horrifying Katyń massacre.[6]

Taking and killing hostages figured prominently among the crimes imputed to the Germans, yet this practice had not been outlawed before

Nuremberg and was again declared legal in 1948 at one of the Nuremberg follow-up trials,* on the grounds that hostage taking at least limited the number of potential civilian victims in case of guerrilla attacks on occupation forces. Without hostages, the military's thirst for revenge might threaten the entire population. The Nuremberg court simply skirted the issue of how many hostages could be executed for the murder of each occupation soldier when it stated that there ought not to be "too many" hostages or "too many" executions.

Resistance fighters regularly operated in disguise and killed their German captives; the German military tortured and executed captured partisans even if they had been "recognizable at a distance." The Allies made extensive use of resistance fighters during World War II; at Nuremberg as well as elsewhere, they condemned the Germans for repressive measures taken against partisans and their suspected helpers.

Despite such moral and legal problems with resistance activity, the Nuremberg court took the view that because of the extreme brutality of the Nazi system, violent opposition to the German occupiers had been inevitable and necessary. This made anti-Nazi resistance a justified act; it also made collaboration with the Nazis a crime.

JUSTICE AND INJUSTICE IN THE NATIONAL COURTS OF JUSTICE

The major Nuremberg war-crimes trials presented an unforgettable spectacle of superb organization, great dignity, and, frankly, often intolerable boredom. Documentary film evidence and a number of often excellent feature films testify to the sparkling uniforms of the American military police, the hordes of uniformed stenographers and translators, the grave judges, the rather forlorn German defense lawyers, and the strange group of defendants, most of them subdued, in shabby civilian clothes or in uniforms without insignia. Against this single great courthouse in a single courtroom in Nuremberg, we must imagine the thousands of war-crimes trials set up by various governments from Oslo in Norway to Athens in Greece and from Bordeaux in France to Helsinki in Finland. Many but not all were inspired by the Nuremberg example. Some of these trials were located in splendid old judicial buildings, others in shacks set up in ruined cities. Oftentimes,

---

*The trial concerned the southeastern European field of military operation where Field Marshal Wilhelm List had been commander.

the courtrooms were unheated. In Budapest, for example, even at the trial of former prime ministers, the presiding judge, jurors, lawyers, defendants, and spectators all sat in their overcoats, protected by scarves, hats, and gloves. During the pauses in the proceedings, judges and war criminals ate the same soup often doled out by the Soviet occupation army.

Perhaps the splendor of the Nuremberg court, financed mostly by the American taxpayers, and the poverty of the other court proceedings can explain the enormous differences between the existing literature on these two events. The documents of the main as well as of the follow-up trials at Nuremberg together form seventy volumes, encompassing a total of 126,897 pages.[7] Another invaluable primary source is the interviews that several psychiatrists conducted independently of one another with the defendants and with many witnesses.[8] Then there are all the historical and legal studies on the subject, of which we should hold up for special praise Brigadier General Telford Taylor's *The Anatomy of the Nuremberg Trials*. It appeared in 1992 and has as its peculiarity that Taylor had been a US prosecutor at the main trial as well as the chief prosecutor at the twelve follow-up trials. The latter were, incidentally, international in name only; in reality, Americans alone sat in judgment over members of the murderous SS Einsatzgruppen, high Nazi Party functionaries, medical doctors, judges, generals, industrialists, and SS commanders. Although there is much rich historical literature on the Nuremberg trials, comparative studies of the many court trials in Europe barely exist. Yet the court trials and other punitive proceedings in countries other than Germany involved millions of people. Moreover, their nature and character differed from those at Nuremberg, where the victors sat in judgment over the defeated. In the national courts, the judges dealt mainly with fellow nationals accused of collaboration, treason, and war crimes. It is all the more surprising, then, that there are no comprehensive works on the subject and that the best essay collection exists only in German. There are a good number of studies on retribution and the purges within individual countries, but the production is very uneven: several books and articles treat the postwar purges in France, Norway, Denmark, the Netherlands, Hungary, Czechoslovakia, and Greece, but similar studies on Yugoslavia and the Soviet Union, for instance, are few and almost inevitably biased. Most valuable, primarily from the point of view of later generations, are the documentary collections, such as those of the trials in France of Marshal Philippe Pétain and Prime Minister Pierre Laval.

Image 10.2. Women collaborators are marched down the street by members of the French resistance and other long-standing or newfangled opponents of the Nazi occupation. Source: Corbis.

During the first postwar years when the former resisters were still unwilling to make their peace with the men of the prewar regime and with wartime collaborators, strongly partisan reports appeared on the trials of such political leaders as Vidkun Quisling in Norway, Pétain and Laval in France, Marshal Ion Antonescu in Romania, Draža Mihailoviç in Yugoslavia, and Ferenc Szálasi in Hungary. But even in that period, there were marked differences between such countries as France, where the debate in the press, no matter how prejudiced, was often carried out on a high intellectual level, and most other countries, where the press mainly heaped insults on the defendants. Finally, in the Soviet Union and the Communist press in general, the accused were proclaimed guilty before they could have opened their mouths in court.

Studies with genuine scholarly ambition did not appear until much later. New approaches to the subject originated mainly from France, where

intellectuals had played a major role in both resistance and collaboration and where the debate over French wartime behavior and the postwar épurations has become a veritable national pastime. In reply to the
Gaullists' celebration of the moral purity and unanimity of the French
wartime resistance, apologists of the Vichy regime launched the figure of
one hundred thousand victims of lynch justice at the end of the war.[9] (Today, we know that the number of real or alleged collaborators shot, beaten
to death, or summarily executed did not exceed ten thousand, still a diz-
zying figure.) The appearance of such apologetic writings was made possible by the Cold War, which allowed former fascists to claim that they had
been but early defenders of Western civilization against the Soviet Bolshevik menace.

But what, indeed, is one to think, for instance, of the French politicians' claim that, during the war, their nation had been overwhelmingly
opposed both to the German occupiers and to the traitors at Vichy? They
knew only too well that, in 1944, the people of Paris received two visiting statesmen with seemingly the same enthusiasm: Marshal Pétain, who
came on April 28, and General de Gaulle, who arrived under the protection of the US Army on August 26. Looking at contemporary newsreels,
one gets the impression of the same elegant motorized policemen escort-
ing the two visitors, the same pretty *Parisiennes* throwing flowers, and the
same delirious crowds singing "La Marseillaise."

For an example of postwar purges, we might turn to American historian
Benjamin Frommer's monograph on retribution in Czechoslovakia. It
shows, among other things, that the new democratic Czech regime proceeded with the utmost severity not only against the German and Hungarian minority populations, which had been declared collectively guilty
of treason, but also against collaborationists of Czech nationality. Most
of the cases involved not important political and business leaders but ordinary people who had denounced their neighbors during the German
occupation and who were now sometimes denounced by the same neighbors. More often than not, the goal of the denunciation was to acquire
the home, the job, or the shop of the victim. Ironically, the Czech courts
experienced difficulties similar to those of the earlier Nazi courts in trying
defendants in ethnically mixed marriages or those who were the children
of mixed marriages. And while the Nazi courts did not quite know how to

define a Jew, the courts of democratic Czechoslovakia had similar trouble in deciding who was a German. This was all the more important as a German defendant was likely to be expelled from the country, whereas a Czech often landed in jail.[10]

Some of the best balanced accounts have originated from the pens of American and British historians, who have the advantage of their countries not having been occupied by the Nazis during the war. These writers are justly critical of the European collaboration with the Nazi occupiers; the only trouble is that they tend to ignore the extent of British collaboration in the German-occupied Channel Islands and the readiness of American civilian internees to work for the Japanese in the Philippines during the war.[11]

Interestingly, while the Nuremberg trials are generally held to have shown the way to the national courts during the purges, retribution in many parts of Europe began well before the Nuremberg judges convened in November 1945. We have already noted that in Poland, for example, underground courts functioned throughout the war, trying and sentencing traitors in as legalistic circumstances as possible. In the Soviet Union, Yugoslavia, and elsewhere, partisan courts operated throughout the war. In France, on the other hand, judicial retribution began at the moment of liberation in 1944.

In Budapest the main people's court held its first session at the end of January 1945, while Soviet and Romanian troops, on the one side, and German and Hungarian troops, on the other, were clashing in the city. On this occasion, two former guards from a forced-labor company were accused of having participated in the torture and killing of 124 Hungarian Jewish and Communist forced laborers during the anti-Soviet campaign in Ukraine. The two guards were sentenced to death and immediately hanged in a public square. These proceedings showed that the Hungarian people's courts, just like many other tribunals in Europe, assumed a revolutionary role: they wished not only to punish traitors and war criminals but also to purge and renew society. The countries formerly within Hitler's Europe did not wait for the precedent shown by the Nuremberg International Military Tribunal to engage in retribution. In any case, the armistice agreements concluded individually between the Allied powers and the former allies of Germany had ordered Austria as well as Finland, Hungary, Romania, Bulgaria, and Italy to prosecute war criminals irrespective of their nationality. As it later turned out, Nuremberg proved to be an occasional obstacle to prosecution in national courts. The tribunal allowed some of the major German war criminals to appear in East European courts only as witnesses; in consequence, such a monstrous murderer of Jews as the German diplomat Dr. Edmund Veesenmayer had to be returned from Hungary to Nuremberg in 1947. Freed four years later, he became a successful businessman in West Germany.

The international military tribunal was neither a catalyst nor even a model for the purge trials in Europe. We find, however, many references in court proceedings to specific aspects of the Nuremberg trial as well as statements indicating that the judges in the national courts were acting in the same manner as the great Allies at Nuremberg. Even more often, judges used the Nuremberg example to foster orderly court proceedings. In Budapest, on December 18, 1945, at the trial of the three men chiefly responsible for the deportation of the Hungarian Jews to Auschwitz, court president Péter Jankó admonished the audience to be on its best behavior, stating that "the world's attention is on us; we should make sure that the foreign press write about us that here prevailed the same cool and detached atmosphere as that which prevails at the Nuremberg trial."[12] In reality, there reigned anything but a cool and detached atmosphere at this trial, the judge's remarks having been provoked by spectators calling the three defendants murderers and scum. Of course, it was easier to keep cool at Nuremberg, where there was no audience but only judges, prosecutors, lawyers, interpreters, stenographers, journalists, defendants, and guards in the courtroom.

European audiences were difficult to control, made up as they often were of survivors of the Holocaust and selected left-wing followers of the new governing political parties. The trial of Pierre Laval in France, for instance, was repeatedly interrupted by shouting in which even the lay judges participated. As with the Nuremberg follow-up trials, interest in the proceedings gradually dwindled, and so did the severity of the sentences.

The Nuremberg court represented a revolutionary innovation, with the judges and prosecutors sitting in judgment in the name of the four great victorious powers. Most other European courts of the time were also revolutionary in that they were new creations, often called people's courts, and ruled on events that, before the war, had not legally risen to the level of criminal actions. Quite naturally, the people's courts proceeded on the basis of European and not Anglo-American common law, meaning that the judge examined, exhorted, admonished, and scolded the defendants, with the prosecution and the defense playing a secondary role. The tone of the proceedings varied enormously, but in every people's court the system was basically the same: in Denmark two jurors delegated by the parties of the resistance movement assisted the single professional judge; in France there was one professional judge for four representatives of the parties originating from the *Résistance;* in Hungary the five antifascist parties, plus the association of the trade unions, delegated to every major trial all the so-called people's judges as well as the public or "political" prosecutors and the so-called people's prosecutors. Public prosecutors were usually intellectuals; people's prosecutors were workers and peasants. Lawyers for the defense were selected from a list approved by the coalition of antifascist parties.

Nuremberg imported its judges from the victorious great powers; the national governments had to face the problem that many trained and experienced judges, if not the majority, had collaborated with the enemy or had at least faithfully served the defunct and despised wartime and prewar regimes. In Austria, in 1945, there was scarcely a sitting judge who had not belonged to the Nazi Party. As a result, judges who were untrained or politically tainted (or both) had to be engaged.

The traditionalist and nationalist training of the judges often clashed with the revolutionary goals of the resistance movements that had created the people's courts. In Poland, where the Communists had come to power almost immediately, judges inherited from prewar times tended to mete out inexcusably mild sentences to those who had denounced Jewish fugitives or had even killed Jews. As historian Andrew Kornbluth has demonstrated, courts in Poland punished traitors harshly but were gentle with those guilty of anti-Jewish crimes, especially if the defendants could claim some resistance merits.[13] We also learn from the 1946 pogrom at Kielce and in some other Polish towns that the Polish public tended to associate Jews with communism and consequently boycotted such Poles who had saved Jews during the war. Not only in Poland but also in other East European countries with a good number of Jewish survivors, many in the public perceived the murder of a Jewish Communist as an act of national resistance.

Even in Western Europe, there were many with good reason to worry that the Jewish survivors would claim their stolen belongings. All this should remind us how difficult it often was to distinguish between former resisters and former collaborators.

The Nuremberg court could mete out only death sentences and imprisonment; the people's courts had an array of measures at their disposal. Punishment of the guilty included death sentences, imprisonment, hard labor, condemnation to national disgrace, the loss of civic rights, fines as well as such administrative measures as expulsion, police supervision, loss of the right to travel or to live in certain desirable places, dismissal, and the loss of pension rights.

Amazingly, the harshest sentences were pronounced in Norway, Denmark, and the Netherlands, countries that exist in Western lore as examples of heroic resistance to the German occupiers and as the brave saviors of Jews. The courts in these countries knew better, however, and thus in Norway more than 90,000 people were tried after the war, nearly 4 percent of the population.* This would be equivalent to roughly 12 million persons of the present-day US population of 300 million being tried for treason and similar crimes. Because most of those tried were adult males, a very high proportion of Norwegian men were tried for collaboration with the enemy. Nearly similar proportions existed in Denmark, while in the Netherlands 150,000 people were detained after the war under the suspicion of collaboration and treason; about 60,000 of them were subsequently convicted, 152 were condemned to death, and 40 were actually executed. That not all the guilty were caught at that time is attested by the scandals of the 1970s when it turned out that a number of war criminals, among them a Jewish con man who had denounced his fellow Jews to the Gestapo, had never been punished.[14]

Norwegian courts dealt harshly with women who had had sexual relations with German soldiers. Worse even, the new laws denied citizenship to their children; thousands of these "half-breeds" accordingly spent their lives as virtual nonpersons.

The long-term discrimination in Norway against the children of German soldiers was actually an exception; all the Western countries made great efforts to rehabilitate the condemned collaborators, in part so as to relieve overcrowding in the prisons, in part to increase the workforce. In the Netherlands, for instance, the institution of Voluntary Monitors was created whose task was to supervise and to reeducate the released convicts. Because this amounted to frequent house visits, one wonders who suffered

---

*More precisely, 92,805 Norwegian citizens were tried after the war in Norwegian courts for treason; of them 30 were executed and 17,000 were sent to prison.

more, the collaborators who were subjected to frequent preaching on the value of democracy or the volunteers who had to sermonize their wards.[15]

Obviously, the great majority of those tried in the people's courts and similar institutions were not generals or government ministers. In Hungary 300,000 persons, or about 3 percent of the total population, suffered some kind of punishment, such as loss of employment or pension, interdiction to live in the capital, loss of civil rights, or imprisonment. At the other end of the spectrum was capital punishment: in Hungary between 1945 and 1948, 146 persons were executed for treason, war crimes, and "crimes against the people." One can assume that they were all major war criminals and traitors. Later, there were even more executions, but their statistics defy categorization because they took place in the period of extreme Stalinist terror, when those executed as "fascists," "former Gestapo agents," "Titoist henchmen," or "American spies" were often democrats or even loyal Communists. Of the 300,000 Hungarians punished after the war, about two-thirds were ethnic Germans whom the democratic Hungarian government expelled for real or alleged treason.[16]

In Austria people's courts initiated proceedings against 137,000 persons, a figure that does not include the many hundreds of thousands of civil servants, including teachers, postmen, railway workers, and others who were dismissed from their jobs because they had been members of the Nazi Party. Needless to say, these judgments and decisions were quashed within a few years, and so, ultimately, the proportion of Nazi killers punished in Austria was even lower than in Germany. And because in Austria almost everybody who was anybody had belonged to the Nazi Party, after the war the democratic parties now governing the republic, especially the Social Democrats, had no choice but to lure former Nazi Party members into their ranks. This they did with abandon, and so it came that in the 1970s, the Social Democratic chancellor Bruno Kreisky, who was of Jewish origin, took several confessed former Nazis into his cabinet.

In France, as we have already said, nearly 10,000 real or alleged collaborators were lynched during the last months of the war, or at the moment of liberation, and about the same number were summarily shot in Italy. Thereafter, however, the courts were relatively mild in their judgments in France and even milder in Italy.

Both the former collaborators and the former resisters primarily blamed the Germans for the tragedy of their nation and for the genocide of the Jews. The courts listed crimes against the Jews under the category of "crimes against the people," even if the crimes against the Jews had been committed mainly by the people themselves. Few courts admitted that it was their country's own administration that had handed over the Jews to the Germans, often with the silent approval or even active participation of the citizenry.

In France the prosecutors tended to single out actors, actresses, cabaret singers, journalists, writers, poets, and philosophers. In Western and northern Europe, women accused of having consorted with the German soldiers were a special target for retribution. But once their shorn hair had grown back, the women were generally reaccepted into society. In Soviet-dominated Eastern Europe, the main targets were the old nobility and the former officers and officials, especially if their members belonged to an ethnic minority. The harshest treatment was reserved for the ethnic minorities. In several decrees promulgated in 1945, the Beneš government, first in London and then at home, declared the German and Hungarian minorities, constituting nearly 30 percent of the prewar Czechoslovak population, collectively guilty of treason. Members of the two ethnic groups were officially denationalized and, with the exception of the proven antifascist fighters, were to be expelled from the country.

The three main charges at Nuremberg were crimes against peace, war crimes, and crimes against humanity; in the people's courts, the same charges could be found, although often under different names. Field Marshal Ion Antonescu in Romania was condemned for having waged aggressive war against the Soviet Union; the similarly aggressive behavior of the Soviet Union between 1939 and 1941 was quietly ignored both at Nuremberg and in the Romanian courts.

Just as at Nuremberg, in the national or people's courts there occurred, inevitably, many awkward situations and illogical proceedings. For example, pre–World War II members of the fascist Nasjonal Samling in Norway were judged more harshly than those who had joined the party during World War II. Considering that the party had been perfectly legal in the prewar years, it is strange that the courts considered commitment to a cause a greater crime than opportunism. In Hungary presiding judge Ákos Major scolded former prime minister László Bárdossy for trying to reannex Hungarian territories lost after World War I, yet, according to Major's memoirs, he himself agreed with Bárdossy that Hungary had had justified territorial ambitions and that Bárdossy's pro-German policy was a "historical necessity."[17] These considerations did not prevent Judge Major from sentencing Bárdossy to death. Such examples of illogical proceedings could be listed ad infinitum. In view of the political chaos and the ideological confusion in Europe as well as the beginning of the Cold War, it is a miracle that justice was served at all. Yet justice was indeed served.

The Nuremberg military tribunal tried and sentenced not only individuals but also institutions, such as the SS and the Nazi Party leadership; the people's court in Hungary declared the Arrow Cross regime that had seized power on October 15, 1944, as well as the country's gendarmerie collectively guilty. The preceding regime under Regent Miklós Horthy was not considered automatically guilty, even though it had been the Horthy regime and not the Arrow Cross that deported nearly a half-million Hungarian Jews to Auschwitz. Collective guilt meant that a former German SS leader or a Hungarian gendarme was considered guilty unless proven otherwise. In reality, such judgments and rules were only selectively enforced.

Just as at Nuremberg, in most people's courts the defendants pleaded innocent, their usual defense being that they had remained at their posts during the occupation to prevent someone more radical from taking over. Marshal Pétain's defenders argued that he had acted as the shield of France, whereas General de Gaulle had been the country's sword during the war. The court did not buy the argument and condemned Pétain to death; General de Gaulle, however, who was then president of the republic, commuted the sentence to life imprisonment, during the course of which Pétain died.

In general, the defendants intimated that the nation owed them thanks for having shouldered such a thankless assignment. Only a few stubborn fanatics, such as ferociously anti-Semitic French writer and journalist Robert Brasillach and the Hungarian self-appointed führer, Ferenc Szálasi, proudly proclaimed their fascist beliefs in court. What is important is that, except for the trials held in the Soviet Union, these were not show trials. Whereas in the Soviet Union real or alleged traitors invariably confessed to their crimes and asked for exemplary punishments, even in Yugoslavia the defendants were allowed to claim innocence. All this made little practical difference in Yugoslavia, where thousands of suspected collaborators as well as members of the Albanian, German, and Hungarian minorities were routinely killed after the war, but at least not even the Yugoslav Communist courts could be accused of having set up show trials. Even the most cowardly defense lawyer in that country or elsewhere in Europe brought up some mitigating circumstances for his client; only in Soviet courts did the public defender heap further abuse on the victim.

It is another question whether the sentence of the main defendants was the outcome of a genuine debate among the professional and the lay judges or the result of a governmental decision. There is no doubt, for instance, that the execution of Vichy prime minister Laval was decided by General de Gaulle and the French government. All in all, it is impossible to generalize about the courts and the judges involved in the great European retribution.

The American goal at Nuremberg was to outlaw aggression and to make clear that thenceforward all those committing aggression, be they heads of state or commanding generals, would be ruthlessly prosecuted. The main goal of the people's courts was to bring about a great catharsis and to create a more progressive, social, or even socialist Europe. Yet within a few years, the Cold War changed everything.

Many negative things have been said and written about the post–World War II national purges, and many of these criticisms are not without foundation. However, the fact remains that never before had the peoples of Europe attempted, on such a large scale, to deal with the political criminals in their midst. Nor had there ever been such a continent-wide soul-searching; those who were punished for good reason far outnumbered those who had been innocent.

NOTES

1. See Telford Taylor, *The Anatomy of the Nuremberg Trials* (New York: Alfred A. Knopf, 1992), 6–11; and W. Michael Reisman and Chris T. Antoniou, eds., *The Laws of War: A Comprehensive Collection of Primary Documents on International Law Governing Armed Conflict* (New York: Vintage Books, 1994).

2. Taylor, *Anatomy of the Nuremberg Trials,* 17–18.

3. Churchill's and Stalin's proposals are discussed in ibid., 29–30.

4. See Eugene Davidson, *The Trial of the Germans: An Account of the Twenty-Two Defendants Before the International Military Tribunal in Nuremberg* (New York: Collier Books, 1966), 19–20.

5. Judith N. Shklar, *Legalism* (Cambridge, MA: Harvard University Press, 1964), 174.

6. Taylor, *Anatomy of the Nuremberg Trials,* 466–471. The most recent documentation is *Katyń, Documents of Genocide: Documents and Materials from the Soviet Archives Turned over to Poland on October 14, 1992,* selected and edited by Wojciech Materski (Warsaw: Institute of Political Studies, Polish Academy of Sciences, 1993).

7. The Nuremberg documents are most easily accessible in the form of *The Nuremberg War Crimes Trials Online [Electronic Resource],* compiled by James Joseph Sanchez et al., Anthony Hursh, Bdexx developer (Seattle: Aristarchus Knowledge Industries, 1995).

8. G. M. Gilbert, *Nuremberg Diary* (New York: Farrar, Straus, and Giroux, 1947); Leon Goldensohn, *The Nuremberg Interviews,* edited by Robert Gellately (New York: Alfred A. Knopf, 2004).

9. On this issue, see the precise calculations of Peter Novick in *The Resistance Versus Vichy: The Purge of Collaborators in Liberated France* (New York: Columbia University Press, 1968), 202–208.

10. Benjamin Frommer, *National Cleansing: Retribution Against Nazi Collaborators in Postwar Czechoslovakia* (Cambridge: Cambridge University Press, 2005).

11. British collaboration with the German occupiers on Jersey, Guernsey, and the other Channel Islands during World War II is discussed in, among others, Madeleine Bunting, *The Model Occupation: The Channel Islands Under German Rule, 1940–1945* (New York: HarperCollins, 1995). American collaboration in the main Philippines internment camp under Japanese rule at Santo Thomas is analyzed by James Ward in "Legitimate Collaboration: The Administration of Santo Tomás Internment Camp and Its Histories, 1942–2003," *Pacific Historical Review* 77, no. 2 (2008): 159–201.

12. László Karsai and Judit Molnár, *Az Endre-Baky-Jaross Per* (Budapest: Cserépfalvi, 1994), 101.

13. See Andrew Kornbluth, "'There Are Many Cains Among Us': Polish Justice and the Holocaust," in *Holocaust: Studies and Sources* (Warsaw: Polish Center for Holocaust Research, 2013), 9:157–172.

14. See Gerhard Hirschfeld, *Nazi Rule and Dutch Collaboration: The Netherlands Under German Occupation, 1940–1945* (Oxford: Oxford University Press, 1988).

15. L. Huyse, "How Government in Belgium, France, and the Netherlands Organized the Return into Society of Wartime Collaborators," paper presented at the Conference on the Legacy of World War II in Europe, New York University, April 24–27, 1997.

16. See László Karsai, "The People's Courts and Revolutionary Justice in Hungary, 1945–46," in *The Politics of Retribution: World War II and Aftermath,* edited by István Deák, Jan. T. Gross, and Tony Judt (Princeton, NJ: Princeton University Press, 2000), 233–251.

17. Ákos Major, *Népbíráskodás—forradalmi törvényesség: Egy népbíró visszaemlékezései* [People's justice—revolutionary legality: The reminiscences of a people's judge], edited by Tibor Zinner (Budapest: Minerva, 1988), 203.

CHAPTER ELEVEN

The Long Aftermath of Collaboration, Resistance, and Retribution

World War II was not yet over when world leaders began to realize that it would be extremely difficult to maintain harmonious relations among the "policemen of the world," as President Roosevelt imagined the future role of the United States, the Soviet Union, Great Britain, and China. Despite an initial genuine will to cooperate, mutual suspicion between the Western powers and the Soviet Union was already eating away at the alliance at the Yalta Conference in February 1945. Two of the major bones of contention were the governmental system and future of Germany and the independence, domestic politics, and future geographic location of Poland. Besides, there was the problem of the United States possessing the atomic bomb and the Soviet Union not yet possessing it. In the end, the West abandoned Poland and the rest of Eastern Europe to Stalin; in exchange, the Soviets let the United States dominate Japan and the Western world.

The German question proved to be insoluble, and in 1949 the country was officially divided into a Western-oriented Federal and a Soviet-oriented German Democratic Republic. By then, West and East had been arming against one another. Recognizing that German manpower, talent, and industry had become indispensable, the new West German chancellor, Konrad Adenauer, offered unconditional German assistance in what was now increasingly called the Cold War in exchange for American support in building West German multiparty parliament prosperity and

NATO COUNTRIES   NEUTRAL

SOVIET UNION AND ITS ALLIES

0   500 mi

0   500 km

EUROPE AFTER WORLD WAR II

Iceland

Norwegian Sea

Sweden

Finland

Helsinki   • Leningrad

North
Atlantic
Ocean

North Sea

Norway

Denmark

Baltic
Sea

Soviet Union   • Moscow

United
Kingdom

Ireland

Netherlands

East
Berlin

Warsaw

London

East
Germany   Poland

• Kiev

Brussels   Bonn

Belgium

Prague

Paris

Luxembourg   West
Germany

Czechoslovakia

• Budapest

France   Switzerland

Austria   Hungary   Romania

Bucharest

Belgrade   •

Black Sea

Yugoslavia

Bulgaria

Portugal

Spain

Italy

Albania

Turkey

Madrid

Greece

Athens

Mediterranean Sea

Morocco   Algeria   Tunisia

political independence. To this deal, Adenauer added a further, unofficial, condition: virtual amnesty to all German war criminals. ① Interesting bc of how bold + conversational that request was + not smart

THE COLD WAR AND THE SUSPENSION OF RETRIBUTIONS

Actually, the gradual releasing of German mass murderers and other Nazi criminals well preceded the creation of the German Federal Republic. The trials at Nuremberg were not even over when the American and British military commanders already amnestied some of the worst Nazi criminals. As a result, aside from the seventy-odd Nazis executed under orders of the Nuremberg Tribunals and other American-dominated courts during the first years after the war, all other Germans tried and sentenced by the Allies in West Germany were released. Their properties were restituted, and they were given good jobs or pensions.

A typical case was that of former SS commander Otto Winkelmann, who had been a higher SS leader and police general in Hungary in 1944 and who, as Himmler's supreme representative there, bore a major responsibility, together with Dr. Edmund Veesenmayer, for the deportation and death of nearly a half-million Jews. Captured by the Americans at the end of the war, Winkelmann was handed over to the Hungarians so as to be a witness at the trial of the major Hungarian war criminals, most of whom were subsequently hanged. The Hungarians would surely have hanged Winkelmann, too, had they not been obliged to send him back to the Americans. He was never prosecuted and lived for several more decades in West Germany, enjoying the generous pension of a "police general."

In theory, the Nuremberg trials should have been followed by the Germans trying their other war criminals, but the West German courts, mostly presided over by former Nazis, were reluctant to act. When they rarely did, they claimed lack of evidence or, in extreme cases, meted out symbolic punishment. In any case, the West German authorities made sure that the prisoners would soon be released, mostly on grounds of ill health. Because all the Western Allies agreed to appease and to support the Federal Republic, by the end of 1956 there were just a handful of Nazi war criminals in German, British, French, or American prisons. Among them were three major German war criminals, sentenced by the Nuremberg International Military Tribunal to Spandau prison in the British zone of Berlin, living under four-power supervision. The last of these convicts, the disputably innocent Rudolf Hess, hanged himself in 1987, at the age of ninety-three. As he had been the last remaining prisoner in that vast jail, supervised by hundreds of Soviet, American, British, and French military and other personnel, with his death, one of the last bits of World War II four-power cooperation in Germany came to an end.

In the erroneous belief that former Nazi policemen possessed a profound familiarity with Soviet politics, geography, and even the Russian soul, the American intelligence services protected some of the worst war criminals or allowed Far Right underground organizations and the Vatican to smuggle them to Argentina.

Nazi criminals fared less well if caught in the East. Moreover, the Western Allies had handed over a few Nazis to Poland and Czechoslovakia, where they were tried and hanged. All in all, however, we can state with confidence that in contrast to non-Germans, many German war criminals literally got away with murder. In this connection, let us remind ourselves that the murderers were not all from the SS; on the contrary, the majority had been ordinary Wehrmacht soldiers and non-Nazi, middle-aged German policemen. They were guilty of torturing prisoners, killing villagers, and shooting an untold number of Jews.

Another example of American willingness to forgive valuable Nazis their often heinous crimes was the secret importation, after the war, of about one thousand German scientists for the purpose of creating the American rocket industry. The basis for this was the Germans' V2 rocket with which they had bombarded Great Britain toward the end of the war. No one seemed to care that the head of the project, Wernher von Braun, and many other of these scientists had unhesitatingly used concentration camp prisoners to build the mostly underground Peenemünde and other rocket bases in Germany. It seems that in the Dora-Mittelbau concentration camp alone, twenty thousand inmates had perished in the process.

While meditating over this deeply discouraging story, we must admit, however, that the former SS murderers not only turned into peaceful and hardworking citizens of the German Federal Republic, but managed to act as good democrats in the new Germany, which itself had become a model democracy.

The political purges in Western and southern Europe were thorough, but they did not change society fundamentally: within a few years, former collaborators, former bystanders, and former resisters worked together in the capitalist and social welfare society sustained with American assistance. In Eastern Europe, drastic social, economic, and ideological change was brought about not by the former resisters but by Soviet power and by local Communists. Yet by far, not all Communists had been in the domestic underground or in concentration camps; many were coming back from exile in the Soviet Union or from places such as Mexico.

No sooner did the Soviet troops arrive in Eastern Europe than the NKVD began to arrest non-Communist resisters and even some Communists suspected of being "Trotzkyites" (followers of the dissident Soviet Communist leader Leon Trotsky) or anarchists. These victims of Soviet "justice" landed in the same jails and internment camps with the Nazi war criminals. Beginning in 1949, they were joined by hundreds if not thousands of loyal Communists who had been arrested at the orders of Stalin or their own paranoid Communist comrades. Indeed, toward the end of Stalin's life, it was more dangerous in Czechoslovakia, for instance, to be a former Communist member of the resistance than to be a former fascist and collaborationist. In the infamous Slánský trial, eleven Communist leaders, ten of them of Jewish origin, were hanged at the orders of the Czechoslovak Communist government in Prague in 1952. All were officially "rehabilitated" a few years later by the same Communist regime.

In Hungary the people's courts in 1949 sentenced to death and executed László Rajk, the former resistance fighter and after the war an extremely zealous Communist minister of the interior. In a show trial, Rajk was accused of being, and publicly confessed to having been, an agent for the Gestapo, for Tito's Yugoslavia, as well as for the CIC (Counterintelligence Corps) and the CIA (Central Intelligence Agency). One of his torturers was his closest friend and party comrade János Kádár. But this did not save Kádár, because soon he, too, was arrested and spent several years in prison. He later emerged as Hungary's long-term and surprisingly popular Communist dictator.

The decisive event in the Cold War had come in September 1947, when the Soviet delegation, at a meeting of the world's Communist Parties at Szkarlska Poręba in Poland, ordered a "sharpening of the class struggle." It meant that the Communist Parties everywhere would have to put an end to their Popular Front policy; in the capitalist countries, they would leave the coalition governments they had formed with "bourgeois parties"; in the Soviet-occupied countries, they would get rid of the non-Communists within the governments. Thus, France and Italy in one camp, Czechoslovakia and Hungary in the other camp, took simultaneous steps, although in the opposite directions. Communist and non-Communist former an-ti-Nazi resisters were now in mutually hostile camps.[1]

Besides such fundamental issues as German unification, the American Marshall Plan, and nuclear weapons, the main question separating the Communists and their left-wing Socialist allies from the other former re-sisters was decolonization.* Britain, France, Belgium, and the Netherlands expected that their world empires would be restored to them after the war, but both the Soviet Union and the United States thought otherwise, and so did the colonial peoples who had seen the colonists defeated, humiliated, and imprisoned, mainly by the Japanese, during the war. Soon the Nether-lands, Great Britain, and France were sending troops abroad to restore the power of the *métropole* and to protect fellow Europeans who sometimes, as in Algeria, made up a substantial part of the local population. In these wars, the Communists and many other former resistance intellectuals sup-ported the colonial rebellions, while the non-Communist former resisters and many political leaders argued for the preservation of at least some kind of relationship with the colonies. The crisis became particularly acute in the Algerian war of the late 1950s, when the French government, made up mostly of former resisters, tolerated, nay ordered, the taking of Arab hostages, the burning of villages, and the torturing of prisoners. In ex-change, the Algerian Muslim rebels threw bombs into cafés crowded with *pieds-noirs,* Europeans living in Algeria. This and similar acts inaugurated a new age in the history of resistance: deliberate terrorist acts aimed at noninvolved civilians regardless of whether there were fellow ethnics or persons of the same religious persuasion among the victims. The goal of the Muslim "freedom fighters" (a comparatively new expression, not much used during World War II) was to force everybody to choose sides and si-multaneously to cause the flight from Algeria of those of European origin.

The roles had changed: Maurice Papon, a former police chief in Vichy France who had been responsible for the deportation of thousands of Jews, as police prefect of Paris in 1961 had some two hundred unarmed Mus-lim demonstrators murdered by the police and the bodies thrown into the Seine River. Meanwhile, his supreme protector, General and now President de Gaulle, was experiencing a change of heart and decided to surrender

---

*Jennifer L. Foray's monograph *Visions of Empire in the Nazi-Occupied Netherlands* (Cam-bridge: Cambridge University Press, 2012) deals specifically with the question of how resist-ers of different political views planned the future of the Dutch world empire.

Algeria to the rebels. Subsequently, Algerian independence brought the massacre of hundreds of thousands of pro-French Muslims and the flight of a million *pieds-noirs* from Algeria. Perceiving de Gaulle as a traitor, exasperated French army officers, many of them former anti-Nazi resistance fighters, led a revolt against him. Yet several attempts on the general's life failed, and the rebellion was suppressed.

RENEWED ATTEMPTS AT REPRISALS

World events, and especially the Cold War, diverted public attention from the punishment of war criminals at least until 1960, when the Israeli secret police captured and abducted Adolf Eichmann from Argentina. He was tried, sentenced, and hanged in Jerusalem two years later. The Eichmann trial inspired a whole series of new proceedings, among them the so-called Auschwitz trial (1963–1965) in Frankfurt, West Germany.* No less significant were the creation and showing, in 1972, of Marcel Ophüls's devastatingly honest film *The Sorrow and the Pity,* which demonstrated the hitherto unimaginable extent of French collaboration with the German occupiers in a midsize French city. Yet only in the late 1970s began a very gradual reexamination of the issue of European collaboration and resistance as well as the responsibility of the European nations for the Shoah. This, then, led to the trial or retrial, as late as the 1990s, of a few such individuals who had evaded prosecution. The charge against these men was invariably crimes against humanity, the only crime that, by the decision of the United Nations, would not lose its legal standing.

(handwritten marginnote: ③ War criminals needed the attention.)

The very belated wave of prosecutions was particularly visible in France, where four famous cases surfaced, those of Klaus Barbie, Paul Touvier, René Bousquet, and Maurice Papon. Among the four, Klaus Barbie alone was not French but a German; he had made a career in the SS and was, during the occupation of France, called the "Butcher of Lyon." If half of what is said about this quiet and unobtrusive man was true, then he amply deserved this name: he had ordered captured resistance fighters

---

*The trial of some of the SS men involved in mass murder at Auschwitz was remarkable because instead of dragging his feet, as most West German prosecutors had been in the habit of doing, public prosecutor Fritz Bauer was zealous in getting the defendants convicted. See Rebecca Wittmann, *Beyond Justice: The Auschwitz Trial* (Cambridge, MA: Harvard University Press, 2005).

to be skinned alive and perpetrated various other horrors. This monster among monsters was able, at the end of the war, to take up service with the British military counterintelligence and then changed to the CIC, the American military intelligence organization. All this occurred under the British-American illusion that Barbie would be able to teach them things about the new enemy, the Communists and the Soviet Union. True, Barbie had killed many people suspected of communism, but this had not made him an expert on the Soviet Union.

Barbie also helped the British and the Americans to spy on each other. When, however, the French threatened to reveal the Barbie connection, the Americans avoided embarrassment by letting the Nazi "rat line" and a Croatian Catholic priest expedite him to Juan Perón's Argentina. Barbie later moved to Bolivia, where he allegedly helped in the murder of Che Guevara, but in view of the obscurity surrounding secret services, nothing about this is definitive. Extradited to France in 1983 by a different Bolivian government, Barbie was tried for crimes against humanity, including the deportation to the East of French Jewish children. He was defended by the radical lawyer Jacques Vergès, who quite successfully turned the case into an indictment of French crimes committed in Indochina and Algeria. Barbie was nevertheless sentenced to life imprisonment in 1987 and died in a French jail four years later, at the age of seventy-eight. His case showed, as if further proof was needed, that the Cold War had begun immediately after if not during the war and that the Western, especially the American, intelligence services were the easy dupes of any clever Nazi mass murderer who could persuade them that he possessed some magic knowledge of Soviet communism.

The case of Paul Touvier, a torturer and killer, who had started as someone close to being a common criminal, became the first Frenchman to be condemned, in 1994, for crimes against humanity. As a commander of the collaborationist Milice, he had been a disciple of Klaus Barbie and had earned the nickname the "Hangman of Lyon." Following liberation, he went into hiding while being condemned to death in absentia. Hiding in his case did not amount to much because this good son of the Catholic Church was quite openly sheltered by high-ranking members of the clergy. Moreover, in 1971, he was amnestied by President Georges Pompidou and was able to recover the property he had mostly stolen from deported Jews. Protected and sheltered this time by a Catholic bishop, Touvier was finally arrested in 1989 and sentenced to life in prison, where he died two years later.

While in court, Touvier claimed to have been successful in greatly reducing the number of Frenchmen to be executed in retaliation for the assassination of a pro-Nazi Vichy French minister of information. Thus, Touvier, too, claimed to have been engaged in some sort of resistance activity.

While the collaborationist Touvier only pretended to help resisters in trouble, the collaborationist René Bousquet did actually engage in some resistance activities, at least toward the end of the war. Bousquet had been in the vanguard of the many who served two masters and were appreciated both by the Nazis and by the enemies of the Nazis. Pursuing a characteristic French administrative career, reserved for the best of the best, Bousquet almost automatically advanced to the position of a prefect following the armistice in 1940; this occurred in spite of his Socialist family background and his own Socialist inclinations. Again, he was not alone: Pierre Laval and the radical fascist writer Marcel Déat had long been Socialists, and Jacques Doriot, the most militant fascist at the time of the German occupation, had once been a Communist leader. In 1942 Bousquet became general secretary of the French police, working closely with the German SS commander Carl Oberg, who was in charge of the German police in France. Bousquet was personally responsible for the Rafle du Vel' d'Hiv (the Roundup at the Vélodrome d'Hiver, the winter bicycle stadium) in 1942 and for the deportation of some thirteen thousand Jews, mostly women and children, to the death camps. He was instrumental in lifting the exemption from deportation of small children and their parents. Not without reason did Heinrich Himmler call Bousquet "a precious collaborator."

In December 1943, Bousquet resigned from his post and later even claimed to have been dragged by the Germans into Bavarian exile. After the war, the French High Court of Justice condemned him to five years of "national degradation," a largely symbolic punishment, which was immediately lifted in view of his merits in the resistance. Later, the Legion of Honor was restored to him, which he had earned before the war for saving the victims of a great flood. Again later, he became an intimate of President François Mitterrand, who himself had been both a collaborator and a resister—so when, in 1991, he was finally accused of crimes against humanity, he did not lack friends. But the possible outcome of his trial remains a matter of speculation, for in 1993 he was shot dead by a lone avenger of the Vichy criminals. Bousquet was right when he claimed that he could

not possibly have become an efficient resister had he not maintained contacts in the highest collaborationist circles, but somehow his good deeds,
as those of Maurice Papon, never matched the gravity of the crimes he, as
collaborator, had committed. The husband-and-wife team of Serge and
Beate Klarsfeld, one a French Jew, the other a Christian German, had been
certainly right in relentlessly pursuing Bousquet and others of his ilk. In
fact, the two seem to have brought more murderers of Jews to justice than
the entire French judicial and administrative apparatus.

We have met Maurice Papon already as the quintessential survivor,
who was also the quintessentially ruthless police chief ready to have anyone killed whether guilty of a crime or not. Following the Eichmann trial
in 1961, German American philosopher Hannah Arendt created a sen-
sation with her book *The Banality of Evil* (1963) in which she described
Eichmann as an indifferent bureaucrat who would have been as ready to
administer the distribution of milk among infants as he was to deliver
millions to the gas chamber. Critics later pointed to Eichmann's cruelty
and his very fanatical hatred of Jews as negating Arendt's claim that anyone in Eichmann's place might have been able to do the same thing. In
fact, Papon seems to fit the image of the indifferent bureaucrat better than
Eichmann, for he might truly have acted without any passion.

Like so many talented French youngsters, Papon had chosen an administrative and political career. This, in France, lent a person greater
prestige and power than perhaps any other career. Having studied in
the right *grande école,* he made a quick career, easily shifting from left to
right in his political allegiance. His transition in 1940 into the Vichy administrative system was as smooth as his transition in 1944 to the new
regime formed by resistance leaders. Then, as a senior police official of
the Vichy regime in Bordeaux, he sent sixteen hundred Jews, including
many children, to French concentration camps from which they would be
transported to German death camps. He was also instrumental in getting
rid of Jews in the economy. While a senior official in the postwar regime,
he was awarded the Legion of Honor, mostly on the basis of his having
protected a resistance leader. Whether both the resistance leader and de
Gaulle knew about Papon's wartime misdeeds against the Jews can only
be surmised, although it would have been easy for them to learn the truth.
In 1961, as police prefect of Paris, a post of immeasurable power, Papon
ordered the massacre of unarmed Muslim demonstrators; a few months
later, he ordered the killing of a dozen demonstrating Communists. No

one was punished for these misdeeds, and the French government from de Gaulle down consistently lied about the events. When finally retired from civil service, de Gaulle helped Papon to a most lucrative industrial assignment, also of course financed by the French state. Evidence about Papon's wartime behavior surfaced, at last, thanks to the Klarsfelds; there followed fourteen years of judicial entanglement and, at last, a long, drawn-out trial. Given ten years in prison in 1997, he was released three years later for being incapacitated. He died in 2007 at the age of ninety-six.

The end of communism in the early 1990s led to no such purges as had characterized the post–World War II period. Although in the former East Germany and Czechoslovakia many people were fired from their jobs, especially from their academic posts, in other countries formerly under Communist rule almost no one was dismissed. The especially tyrannical Romanian Communist dictator Nicolae Ceauşescu and his wife, Elena, were executed but, overall, except in Romania, fewer than a dozen people were jailed for political crimes committed in Communist times. Not even the mass shooting of civilian demonstrators in Poland on repeated occasions between 1953 and the 1970s led to more than a handful of trials. The reasons for this were that, unlike Nazism, Communism had not collapsed in a period of war, there were no masses of dead and no devastation, and the Stalinist period, during which most of the Communist crimes had been committed, was followed by long years of less and less harsh party rule. Unlike the Nazis and the World War II criminals, most perpetrators of Stalinist crimes were no longer available for prosecution and trial following the collapse of communism in 1989–1990.

Yet there are also some astonishing new developments. As I write these lines, in 2014, Romanian prosecutors have charged the former commander of a Communist-era prison with genocide for cruelties committed some sixty years ago. Not to be left behind, a Hungarian court in May 2014 sentenced Béla Biszku, a former secretary of the Hungarian Communist Party Central Committee, to five and a half years in prison for having ordered the shooting of demonstrators during the 1956 anti-Soviet revolution. Meanwhile, German prosecutors have opened investigations against thirty surviving guards from the Nazi Auschwitz-Birkenau concentration and death camp. The youngest of the suspects is eighty-seven years old. The charge against them will be that they served as sentries in a camp where about 1 million human beings were killed. It is not even necessary for the prosecution to prove that the accused participated in the killings; all that the prosecutors are intending to prove, with the help of three-dimensional virtual models of the camps, is that the accused would have been able to see the killings from his or her post. (Note that a former female guard is among those being investigated.) Most of the accused were not German citizens when the crimes were committed.[2]

And now another surprise: after many years of a cover-up, German prosecutors in Cologne are charging an eighty-eight-year-old former Waffen SS soldier of murder committed in 1944, at Oradour-sur-Glane. Early reports do not say whether Werner C.—his last name is not made public, in keeping with German privacy laws—is known to have committed a specific murder or is being charged simply because he belonged to Captain Diekman's company that massacred the villagers. Yet because Werner C. was eighteen years old at that time, one inevitably wonders about the extent of his guilt, at least in comparison with that of his elders. Indeed, the cannon fodder of World War II, especially in the German army, were the teenagers, without rank, privileges, or the right to protest against being put in harm's way. The victimization and the crimes committed by children are a tragic chapter of war.

There are attempts today to rehabilitate such historic figures as Mussolini, Laval, Quisling, Antonescu, Bárdossy, Szálasi, Tiso, and the Croatian leader Ante Pavelić, but none of these movements is dynamic and popular enough to force the issue. All the condemned wartime heads of state continue to stand condemned. The post–World War II purges do not present an important political subject in Europe today.

Even though few doubted that Eichmann deserved to be hanged, the legality of Israel's procedure was occasionally called into question at that time. Yet today, we are accustomed to agents of a country arresting its own citizens on foreign soil or a country insisting that another country arrest and try a person who had committed no crimes in the host country. In addition, we now have functioning and active international courts that consciously imitate the example of the Nuremberg Tribunal.

———

What did Nuremberg and the postwar purges accomplish? No doubt, one of the international military court's major achievements was to introduce the concept of individual responsibility into international justice. US insistence on a fair trial, no matter how heinous the Nazi crimes, was another outstanding success, even if, in reality, the proceedings at Nuremberg were not always fair. As for the national courts, they punished many of the guilty, and they virtually outlawed fascism and Nazism, neither of which has made a comeback. The trials also made clear that no one could hide behind the defense of superior orders or that of the absolute rights of the sovereign state. On the negative side, the purges played a crucial role in the acceleration of the ethnic cleansing that has been plaguing Eastern Europe for the last one hundred or more years. War ruins have generally disappeared from the face of Europe; the guilty have been forgiven, but what can never be reversed is the extermination, deportation, or flight of millions of Jews, Germans, Poles, Ukrainians, and Hungarians whom the majority ethnic groups no longer tolerated. In this respect, the postwar purges were only one egregious stage in the process of ridding Eastern Europe of its most valuable minorities. It is a process that has set back the region economically, culturally, and morally by many decades.

The great irony of history is that whereas Eastern Europe paid a heavy price for its political purges and its ethnic cleansing, Germany, which hardly had any purges and received millions of German and other refugees, soon became a model democracy and the motor of the postwar European economy.*

NOTES

1. On the Szklarska Poręba conference, see, among others, Charles Gati, *Hungary and the Soviet Bloc* (Durham, NC: Duke University Press, 1986), 108–123.

2. See the *New York Times*, January 9, May 5, and June 19, 2014.

---

*On the shameful inadequacy of the prosecution of Nazi mass murderers in West Germany, see, among others, Jeoffrey Herf, *Divided Memory: The Nazi Past in the Two Germanys* (Cambridge, MA: Harvard University Press, 1997), 267–333. Remarkably, the West German courts, generally presided over by judges who had themselves been Nazi Party members, were reluctant to condemn even such German doctors and nurses who had murdered thousands upon thousands of mentally and physically handicapped fellow Germans.

Epilogue

One might ask, referring to the title of this book, how well Europe on trial passed the test of the troubled times. The answer is, unfortunately, that Europe did badly. The list of failures is very long indeed, beginning earlier with the suicidal madness of World War I and followed by all the land grabbing and the ethnic miniwars. Although coaxed by President Wilson to engage in ethnic self-determination and international cooperation, within a few years most European countries replaced their parliamentary governments with strongman rule. Populist nationalism showed intolerance toward the minority populations. Moreover, when an extreme form of aggressive nationalism arose, first in Italy and then in Germany, the Europeans refused to synchronize their defensive measures; they preferred submission to resistance. By the late spring of 1941, all the countries of Europe, except for Poland and Great Britain as well as a handful of strategically unimportant neutrals, were on the side of Nazi Germany either as official allies or as defeated countries led by collaborationist administrations. Even the Soviet Union, traditionally "Hitler fascism's" most vociferous enemy, between September 1939 and the spring of 1941 proved itself the Third Reich's most valuable friend. The unprovoked—and ultimately suicidal—German attack on the Soviet Union, in June 1941, did not shake the general European expectation of the Nazis' ultimate victory. Only after the Battle of Stalingrad did the Europeans begin to wonder whether Hitler might not, after all, lose the war. Thereafter, the European resistance movements attempted to compensate for the general defeatism of the earlier years. Still, except in the Balkans, liberation was brought about not by the peoples themselves but by Soviet, American, British, and Commonwealth troops. It was mainly in Eastern and southeastern Europe that resistance often played a strategic role, but there resistance to the German occupier was nearly always closely combined with civil war and ethnic cleansing.

The worst part of it all was the European-wide crisis in compassion and humanity. Not only were most Europeans indifferent to the fate of their Jewish, Roma, sectarian, and homosexual neighbors, but millions among them participated in manhunts or at least profited from the disappearances and deaths of the victims. There were many who risked their lives for the persecuted, especially among aristocrats, intellectuals, nuns, priests, policemen, and such individuals who did not like to fit into "normal" society. Yet the true—or at least the truer—representatives of the Europeans remained the Norwegian policemen who readily handed over their Jewish compatriots to the Gestapo, the Dutch bureaucrats who diligently prepared precise "Jew lists" for the Nazi occupiers, and the Hungarian medical doctors and midwives who unhesitatingly answered the call of the authorities to appear at the railroad stations, naturally for the promise of overtime pay, to search for hidden jewelry in the orifices of Jewish women awaiting deportation. Nor should we forget the state-owned railroad companies, which delivered Jewish and other deportees to the East European concentration and death camps by charging group-tourist fees for the prisoners crammed into cattle wagons. One wonders how many—if any—railroad engine drivers in Europe reported sick in order not to have to deliver their human cargo to a concentration camp or a death camp.

All the postwar French tourist propaganda to the contrary, we should remind ourselves that the Paris policemen who fired on German soldiers in August 1944 might well have been the same policemen herding Jewish women and children into the Vélodrome d'Hiver in July 1942 for transportation to Auschwitz. And while this took place, millions of other Parisians went about their daily business. A little more compassion and goodwill toward the victims would have been nearly without danger; no French policeman was jailed or executed for failing to report for duty on the day of Jewish deportations. We also know, incidentally, that all German SS men and policemen were free not to participate in the mass shooting of Jews and Gypsies in conquered Eastern Europe. Yet only a few of these men made use of this privilege, with some later confessing that they had felt ashamed of their "uncomradely" behavior.[1] Indeed, compassion and goodwill were two qualities in short supply during World War II, one of the greatest tragedies that humans ever brought upon themselves.

Times have changed, of course. Unlike in the early 1940s, today it is generally considered an insult in Europe or anywhere else to call someone a Nazi or a National Socialist. Nor does anyone like to be called a quisling or a collaborationist. Even fanatical anti-Semites strongly deny that they are anti-Semites. This is perhaps because at the end of the war, all the major political parties the Allies were putting in power had arisen from the wartime resistance: Communists, Socialists or Social Democrats, Christian Democrats or Christian Socialists, and various more conservative but still anti-Nazi groups, such as the Gaullists in France. Outright Fascist or National Socialist Parties were for quite a while not tolerated. It is true, however, that many Western-oriented countries, from Norway to Greece, kept the Communists in opposition from the very beginning. It is also true that in Eastern Europe, the Soviet-supported Communist Parties of Romania, Bulgaria, and Yugoslavia immediately shunted aside, or even persecuted, their former non-Communist resistance partners. But the great wartime leftist resistance coalitions persisted, at least for a while, in France, Italy, Czechoslovakia, and Hungary. Only in 1948 did these grand coalitions fall victim to the Cold War. In France and Italy, the Communists went into permanent and bitter opposition; in Czechoslovakia and Hungary, the non–Communist Party leaders either joined the ruling Communist Party, went to jail, or went into exile. There arose the famous Iron Curtain, which divided Europe and specifically Germany into two parts, a situation that changed definitely only around 1990, when the Soviet troops departed from Eastern Europe. Thereafter, all the countries of that region became more or less well-functioning, multiparty democracies.

Despite regional conflicts, such as the terrible Balkan wars of the 1990s, and the recent bewildering growth of nationalist, xenophobic, and anti–European Union agitation all across Europe, the danger of a new European conflagration seems remote. This is because even during the war but especially on the ruins of 1945, the idea of European cooperation gained millions of followers. Even some collaborators, especially in Western Europe, liked to prophesy a future unified Europe, although under Nazi German and not under British-American or Soviet leadership. As recent historiography has shown, many technocrats in the wartime collaborationist governments, especially at Vichy, consciously built the foundations of European economic cooperation. Meanwhile, resisters, especially of the Left, planned a new society based on various degrees of social and economic equality, central economic planning, the nationalization of key energy sources, industries, and banks, as well as a series of humanitarian reforms: all this for making life bearable not only for the privileged but for everyone. Today, despite many disappointments, these ideas and principles still predominate on much of the continent.

The road to today's European Union had been shown by such statesmen as the French Robert Schuman and Jean Monnet, the German Theodor Heuss and Konrad Adenauer, the British Clement Attlee and Ernest Bevin, the Italian Alcide de Gasperi, and the Belgian Paul-Henri Spaak. Rejecting flamboyant names and ideologies, these men patiently laid the foundation of such important, although often pedestrian-sounding, institutions as the Schuman Plan for Franco-German economic cooperation, the Coal and Steel Community, the Common Market, NATO, the European Parliament, the European Monetary Agreement, the Schengen Area Agreement, and the common currency called the euro. Some of these institutions are no longer needed; others do not work to full capacity; still others face great problems. Yet as a result of these and similar agreements, today's Europeans can travel from Ireland to Romania and from Sweden to the island of Malta without ever showing their passport; moreover, they are free to take up employment and settle wherever they wish. Qualified young Europeans may study at any European university, and they are offered generous European study and research fellowships. In all, being a citizen of the European Union today brings great privileges. Of course, citizens of the union must—or at least should—adjust to the needs and preferences of other cultures as well as to the whims of sometimes overzealous European bureaucrats.

Only those who once experienced life in pre–World War II Europe or in the 1950s and 1960s can truly appreciate the changes that have occurred. There is no more standing in line with a petition in hand for a passport, and in Eastern Europe for an additional exit visa, called a "window," without which the valid passport was worth nothing. Nor do today's Europeans need to ask for transit visas, which could be obtained only with a valid entry into the country of destination, even if the transit would take only an hour. And what effort and aggravation it took to obtain the foreign currency without which no airplane ticket could be had! Or how about the notorious "previsas," whose validity tended to expire before the passport was issued, so that the process would have to be started again? In brief, travel and life in today's Europe finally resemble travel and life in the United States or Canada or Brazil. And although all such progress is greatly due to the postwar political, economic, and military presence and influence of the United States in Europe, it is also to be attributed to the mostly young men and women of the wartime resistance movement—as well as perhaps to some individual collaborationists—who had dreamed of a new, unified, and better Europe.

NOTES

1. On the German policemen's right not to participate in the murders, see Christopher R. Browning, *Ordinary Men: Reserve Police Battalion 101 and the Final Solution in Poland* (New York: HarperCollins, 1992).

SUGGESTIONS FOR FURTHER STUDY

SECONDARY SOURCES ON OCCUPATION,
COLLABORATION, AND RESISTANCE IN EUROPE

General

Buruma, Ian. *Year Zero: A History of 1945.* New York: Penguin, 2013.

Cattaruzza, Marina, Stefan Dyroff, and Dieter Langewiesche, eds. *Territorial Revisionism and the Allies of Germany in the Second World War: Goals, Expectations, Practices.* New York: Berghahn Books, 2013.

Foot, M. R. D. *Resistance: European Resistance to Nazism.* New York: McGraw-Hill, 1977.

Gildea, Robert, Olivier Wievorka, and Annette Warring. *Surviving Hitler and Mussolini: Daily Life in Occupied Europe.* Oxford: Berg, 2006.

Haestrup, Jorgen. *Europe Ablaze: An Analysis of the History of the European Resistance Movements, 1939–45.* Odense, Denmark: Odense University Press, 1978.

Larsen, Stein U., and Jan P. Myklebust, eds. *Who Were the Fascists: Social Roots of European Fascism.* New York: Oxford University Press, 1985.

Littlejohn, David. *The Patriotic Traitors: The History of Collaboration in German Occupied Europe, 1940–45.* Garden City, NY: Doubleday, 1972.

Macksey, Kenneth. *The Partisans of Europe in the Second World War.* New York: Stein and Day, 1975.

Mazower, Mark. *Hitler's Empire: How the Nazis Ruled Europe.* New York: Penguin, 2008.

Michel, Henri. *The Shadow War: Resistance in Europe, 1939–1945.* Translated by Richard Barry. London: Andre Deutsch, 1972.

Naimark, Norman M. *Fires of Hatred: Ethnic Cleansing in Twentieth Century Europe.* Cambridge, MA: Harvard University Press, 2001.

Rings, Werner. *Life with the Enemy: Collaboration and Resistance in Hitler's Europe, 1939–1945.* Translated by Maxwell Brownjohn. Garden City, NY: Doubleday, 1982.

Rousso, Henry, ed. *La collaboration.* Paris: MA Éditions, 1987.

Seidler, Franz Wilhelm. *Die Kollaboration, 1939–1945*. Munich: Herbig, 1995.
Sémelin, Jacques. *Unarmed Against Hitler: Civilian Resistance in Europe, 1939–1943*. Translated by Suzan Husserl-Kapit. Westport, CT: Praeger, 1993.
Wilkinson, James F. *The Intellectual Resistance in Europe*. Cambridge, MA: Harvard University Press, 1981.

Regional Studies

Armstrong, John A. "Collaborationism in World War II: The Integral Nationalist Variant in Eastern Europe." *Journal of Modern History* 40 (1968): 396–410.
Judt, Tony, ed. *Resistance and Revolution in Mediterranean Europe, 1939–1948*. London: Routledge, 1989.
Moore, Bob, ed. *Resistance in Western Europe*. Oxford: Berg, 2000.
Nagy-Talavera, Nicholas M. *The Green Shirts and Others*. Stanford, CA: Stanford University Press, 1970.
Snyder, Timothy. *Bloodlands: Europe Between Hitler and Stalin*. New York: Basic Books, 2010.
Sugar, Peter F. *Native Fascism in the Successor States, 1918–1945*. Santa Barbara, CA: ABC-Clio, 1971.

Baltic Countries (Estonia, Latvia, and Lithuania)

Daumantas, Juozas L. *Fighters for Freedom*. New York: Manylands Books, 1975.
Lumans, Valdis. *Latvia in World War II*. New York: Fordham University Press, 2006.
O'Connor, Kevin. *The History of the Baltic States*. Westport, CT: Greenwood Press, 2001.
Vardys, V. Stanley. *Lithuania Under the Soviets: Portrait of a Nation, 1940–65*. New York: Praeger, 1965.

Belgium, the Netherlands, and Luxembourg

Conway, Martin. *Collaboration in Belgium: Leon Degrelle and the Rexist Movement*. New Haven, CT: Yale University Press, 1993.
de Jong, Louis. *The Netherlands and Nazi Germany*. Cambridge, MA: Harvard University Press, 1990.
Foray, Jennifer L. *Visions of Empire in the Nazi-Occupied Netherlands*. Cambridge: Cambridge University Press, 2012.
Hirschfeld, Gerhard. *Nazi Rule and Dutch Collaboration: The Netherlands Under German Occupation, 1940–1945*. Oxford: Oxford University Press, 1988.
Warmbrunn, Werner. *The Dutch Under German Occupation, 1940–1945*. Stanford, CA: Stanford University Press, 1953.
———. *The German Occupation of Belgium, 1940–1944*. New York: P. Lang, 1993.

Bulgaria

Miller, Marshall Lee. *Bulgaria During the Second World War*. Stanford, CA: Stanford University Press, 1975.

Todorov, Tzvetan. *The Fragility of Goodness: Why Bulgarian Jews Survived the Holocaust.* Princeton, NJ: Princeton University Press, 2001.

Channel Islands

Bunting, Madeleine. *The Model Occupation: The Channel Islands Under German Rule, 1940–1945.* New York: HarperCollins, 1996.

Czechoslovakia

Bryant, Chad. *Prague in Black: Nazi Rule and Czech Nationalism.* Cambridge, MA: Harvard University Press, 2007.

Jelinek, Yeshayahu. *The Parish Republic: Hlinka's Slovak People's Party, 1939–1945.* East European Monographs. Boulder, CO: distributed by Columbia University Press, 1976.

Luža, Radomir. *The Hitler Kiss: A Memoir of the Czech Resistance.* Baton Rouge: Louisiana State University Press, 2002.

Mastny, Vojtech. *The Czechs Under Nazi Rule: The Failure of National Resistance, 1939–1942.* New York: Columbia University Press, 1971.

Ward, James Mace. *Priest, Politician, Collaborator: Jozef Tiso and the Making of Fascist Slovakia.* Ithaca, NY: Cornell University Press, 2013.

France

Aubrac, Lucie. *Outwitting the Gestapo.* Translated by Konrad Bieber. Lincoln: University of Nebraska Press, 1992.

Azema, Jean-Pierre, et al. *Collaboration and Resistance: Images of Life in France, 1940–1944.* Translated by Lory Frankel. New York: Harry N. Abrams, 2000.

_____. *From Munich to the Liberation, 1938–1944.* Cambridge: Cambridge University Press, 1984.

Burrin, Philippe. *France Under the Germans: Collaboration and Compromise.* Translated by Janet Lloyd. New York: New Press, 1995.

Clinton, Alan. *Jean Moulin, 1899–1943: The French Resistance and the Republic.* New York: Palgrave, 2002.

Cone, Michele S. *Artists Under Vichy.* Princeton, NJ: Princeton University Press, 1992.

Corpet, Olivier, and Claire Paulhan, eds. *Collaboration and Resistance: French Literary Life Under the Nazi Occupation.* Translated by Jeffrey Mehlman. Brooklyn: Five Ties, 2010.

Dank, Milton. *The French Against the French: Collaboration and Resistance.* London: Cassell, 1974.

Gordon, Bertram. *Collaborationism in France During the Second World War.* Ithaca, NY: Cornell University Press, 1980.

Hirschfeld, Gerhard, and Patrick Marsh, eds. *Collaboration in France: Politics and Culture During the Nazi Occupation, 1940–44.* Oxford: Berg, 1989.

Hubert, Agnès. *Résistance: A Woman's Journal of Struggle and Defiance in Occupied France*. Translated by Barbara Mellor. New York: Bloomsbury, 2008.

Kedward, H. R. *Vichy France: Collaboration and Resistance, 1940–1944*. Oxford: Blackwell, 2000.

Kedward, H. R., and Nancy Wood. *The Liberation of France: Image and Event*. Oxford: Berg, 1995.

Marrus, Michael R., and Robert O. Paxton. *Vichy France and the Jews*. New York: Basic Books, 1981.

Mitchell, Allan. *Nazi Paris: The History of an Occupation, 1940–1944*. Oxford: Berghahn Books, 2010.

Paxton, Robert O. *Parades and Politics at Vichy: The French Officer Corps Under Marshal Pétain*. Princeton, NJ: Princeton University Press, 1966.

_____. *Vichy France: Old Guard and New Order, 1940–1944*. 2nd ed. New York: Columbia University Press, 1982.

Schoenbrun, David. *Soldiers of the Night: The Story of the French Resistance*. New York: New American Library, 1980.

Steernhell, Zeev. *Neither Right nor Left: Fascist Ideology in France*. Berkeley: University of California Press, 1986.

Sweets, John F. *Choices in Vichy France: The French Under Nazi Occupation*. New York: Oxford University Press, 1994.

Taylor, Lynne. *Between Resistance and Collaboration: Popular Protest in Northern France, 1940–45*. New York: St. Martin's Press, 1999.

Germany

Fest, Joachim. *Plotting Hitler's Death: German Resistance to Hitler, 1933–1945*. London: Weidenfeld and Nicolson, 1996.

Hoffmann, Peter. *German Resistance to Hitler*. Cambridge, MA: Harvard University Press, 1988.

_____. *Stauffenberg: A Family History, 1905–1944*. Cambridge: Cambridge University Press, 1995.

Large, David Clay, ed. *Contending with Hitler: Varieties of German Resistance in the Third Reich*. Cambridge: Cambridge University Press, 1991.

Nelson, Anne. *Red Orchestra: The Story of the Berlin Underground and the Circle of Friends Who Resisted Hitler*. New York: Random House, 2009.

Von Klemperer, Klemens. *German Resistance Against Hitler: The Search for Allies Abroad, 1938–1945*. Oxford: Clarendon Press, 1992.

Greece

Mazower, Mark. *Inside Hitler's Greece: The Experience of Occupation, 1941–44*. New Haven, CT: Yale University Press, 1993.

_____. *Salonika: City of Ghosts*. New York: HarperCollins, 2006.

Hungary

Deák, István. "Admiral and Regent Miklos Horthy: Some Thoughts on a Controversial Statesman." *Hungarian Quarterly* 37, no. 143 (1996): 78–89.

———. "A Fateful Compromise. The Debate over Collaboration and Resistance in Hungary." In *The Politics of Retribution in Europe: World War II and Aftermath,* edited by István Deák, Jan. T. Gross, and Tony Judt, 39–73. Princeton, NJ: Princeton University Press, 2000.

Fenyo, Mario. *Hitler, Horthy, and Hungary: German-Hungarian Relations, 1941–1944.* New Haven, CT: Yale University Press, 1972.

Ormos, Mária. *Hungary in the Age of the Two World Wars, 1914–1945.* New York: Columbia University Press, 2007.

Italy

Behan, Tom. *The Italian Resistance: Fascists, Guerrillas, and the Allies.* London: Pluto, 2009.

Delzell, Charles F. *Mussolini's Enemies: Italian Anti-Fascist Resistance.* Princeton, NJ: Princeton University Press, 1961.

Pavone, Claudio. *A Civil War: A History of Italian Resistance.* Translated by Peter Levy. New York: Verso, 2013.

Poland

Davies, Norman. *Rising '44: The Battle for Warsaw.* New York: Viking, 2004.

Garlinski, Józef. *Poland in the Second World War.* New York: Macmillan, 1985.

Gross, Jan T. *Neighbors: The Destruction of the Jewish Community in Jedwabne, Poland.* Princeton, NJ: Princeton University Press, 2000.

———. *Polish Society Under German Occupation: Generalgouvernement, 1939–1944.* Princeton, NJ: Princeton University Press, 1979.

———. *Revolution from Abroad: The Soviet Conquest of Poland's Western Ukraine and Western Belorussia.* Princeton, NJ: Princeton University Press, 2002.

Gutman, Israel. *Resistance: The Warsaw Ghetto Uprising.* Boston: Houghton Mifflin, 1994.

Gutman, Ysrael, and Shmuel Krakowski. *Unequal Victims: Poles and Jews During World War II.* New York: Holocaust Library, 1986.

Hanson, Joanna K. M. *The Civilian Population and the Warsaw Uprising of 1944.* Cambridge: Cambridge University Press, 1982.

Kochanski, Halik. *The Eagle Unbowed: Poland and the Poles in the Second World War.* Cambridge, MA: Harvard University Press, 2012.

Korbonski, Stefan. *The Jews and the Poles in World War II.* New York: Hippocrene, 1989.

Lukas, Richard C. *The Forgotten Holocaust: The Poles Under German Occupation, 1939–1944.* Lexington: University Press of Kentucky, 1997.

Pilecki, Witold. *The Auschwitz Volunteer: Beyond Bravery.* Translated by Jarek Garlinski. Los Angeles: Aquila Polonica, 2012.

Romania

Drogan, I. C. *Antonescu: Marshall and Ruler of Romania, 1940–1944.* Bucharest: Europa Nova, 1995.

Malaparte, Curzio. *Kaputt.* Santa Fe, NM: Marlboro Press, 1982.

Maldeck, R. G. *Athene Palace.* Portland, OR: Center for Romania Studies, 1998.

Scandinavia

Abrahamsen, Samuel. *Norway's Response to the Holocaust: Historical Perspective.* New York: Holocaust Library, 1991.

Hoidal, Oddvar K. *Quisling: A Study in Treason.* Oxford: Oxford University Press, 1989.

Petrow, Richard. *The Bitter Years: The Invasion and Occupation of Denmark and Norway, April 1940–May 1945.* New York: Morrow, 1979.

Reilly, Robin. *The Sixth Floor: Danish Resistance Movement and the RAF Raid on Gestapo Headquarters, March 1945.* London: Cassell, 1969.

Soviet Union, Russia, and Ukraine

Berkhoff, Karel C. *Harvest of Despair: Life and Death in Ukraine Under Nazi Rule.* Cambridge, MA: Harvard University Press, 2004.

Dallin, Alexander. *German Rule in Russia, 1941–1945.* New York: St. Martin's Press, 1957.

_____. *Odessa, 1941–1944: A Case Study of Soviet Territory Under Foreign Rule.* Iasi, Romania: Center for Romanian Studies, 1998.

Salisbury, Harrison. *The 900 Days: The Siege of Leningrad.* Cambridge, MA: Da Capo Press, 1969.

Stepyan, Kenneth. *Stalin's Guerrillas: Soviet Partisans in World War II.* Lawrence: University Press of Kansas, 2006.

Yugoslavia and Albania

Amery, Julian. *Sons of the Eagle: A Study in Guerrilla War.* New York: Macmillan, 1948.

Burgwyn, Julian. *Empire on the Adriatic: Mussolini's Conquest of Yugoslavia, 1941–1943.* New York: Enigma Books, 2005.

Djilas, Milovan. *Wartime: With Tito and the Partisans.* New York: Harcourt Brace Jovanovich, 1988.

Greble, Emily. *Sarajevo, 1941–1945: Muslims, Christians, and Jews in Hitler's Europe.* Ithaca, NY: Cornell University Press, 2011.

Martin, David, ed. *Patriot or Traitor: The Case of General Mihailovich.* Stanford, CA: Hoover Institution Press, 1978.

Milazzo, Matteo. *The Chetnik Movement and the Yugoslav Resistance.* Baltimore: Johns Hopkins University Press, 1975.

Roberts, Walter R. *Tito, Mihailovic and the Allies, 1941–1945.* Durham, NC: Duke University Press, 1987.

Steinberg, Joanathan. *All or Nothing: The Axis and the Holocaust, 1941–1943.* London: Routledge, 1990.

Tomasevich, Jozo. *War and Revolution in Yugoslavia: The Chetniks.* Stanford, CA: Stanford University Press, 1975.

SECONDARY SOURCES ON POSTWAR RETRIBUTION IN EUROPE

Courtois, Stéphane, et al., eds. *The Black Book of Communism: Crimes, Terror, Repression.* Translated by Jonathan Murphy and Mark Kramer. Cambridge, MA: Harvard University Press, 1999.

Deák, István. "Political Justice in Austria and Hungary After World War II." In *Retribution and Reparation in the Transitional Democracy,* edited by John Elster, 124–146. Cambridge: Cambridge University Press, 2006.

Deák, István, Jan T. Gross, and Tony Judt, eds. *The Politics of Retribution in Europe: World War II and Aftermath.* Princeton, NJ: Princeton University Press, 2000.

De Zayas, Alfred M. *Nemesis at Potsdam: The Anglo-Americans and the Expulsion of the Germans.* Rev. ed. London: Routledge and Kegan Paul, 1979.

_____. *A Terrible Revenge: The Ethnic Cleansing of the East European Germans, 1944–1950.* New York: St. Martin's Press, 1993.

Djilas, Milovan. *Memoir of a Revolutionary.* New York: Harcourt Brace Jovanovich, 1973.

Elster, Jon, ed. *Retribution and Reparation in the Transition to Democracy.* New York: Cambridge University Press, 2006.

Frommer, Benjamin. *National Cleansing Against Collaborators in Postwar Czechoslovakia.* Cambridge: Cambridge University Press, 2005.

Golsan, Richard J., ed. *Memory, the Holocaust, and French Justice: The Bousquet and Touvier Affairs.* Hanover, NH: University Press of New England, 1996.

Henke, Klaus-Dietmar, and Hans Woller, eds. *Politische Säuberung in Europa: Die Abrechnung mit Faschismus und Kollaboration nach dem Zweiten Weltkrieg.* Munich: Deutscher Taschenbuch Verlag, 1991.

Herf, Jeffrey. *Divided Memory: The Nazi Past in the Two Germanys.* Cambridge, MA: Harvard University Press, 1997.

Lagrue, Pierre. *The Legacy of Nazi Occupation: Patriotic Memory and National Recovery in Western Europe, 1945–1965.* Cambridge: Cambridge University Press, 1999.

Lottman, H. *The Purge: Justice and Revenge in Post-Liberation France.* New York: Morrow, 1986.

Naimark, Norman M. *Fires of Hatred: Ethnic Cleansing in Twentieth Century Europe.* Cambridge, MA: Harvard University Press, 2001.

_____. *The Russians in Germany: The History of the Soviet Zone in Germany, 1945–1959.* Cambridge, MA: Harvard University Press, 1999.

Novick, Peter. *The Resistance Versus Vichy: The Purge of Collaborators in Liberated France.* New York: Columbia University Press, 1968.

Palmer, Domenico. *Italian Fascists on Trial, 1943–1948*. Chapel Hill: University of North Carolina Press, 1991.

Rousso, Henry. *The Vichy Syndrome: History and Memory in France Since 1914*. Cambridge, MA: Harvard University Press, 1994.

Taylor, Telford. *The Anatomy of the Nuremberg Trials*. New York: Alfred A. Knopf, 1992.

Virgili, Fabrice. *Shorn Women: Gender and Punishment in Liberation France*. Translated by John Flower. Oxford: Berg, 2012.

FILMS

Fascism, Nazism

Amarcord. Directed by Federico Fellini. Italy, 1974.
Mephisto. Directed by István Szabó. Hungary, Germany, and Austria, 1981.
Olympia. Directed by Leni Riefenstahl. Germany, 1936.
The Tin Drum. Directed by Volker Schlondorff. Germany, 1979.
Triumph of the Will. Directed by Leni Riefenstahl. Germany, 1935.

The Holocaust

Au revoir les enfants. Directed by Louis Malle. France, 1987.
Divided We Fall. Directed by Jan Hoebejk. Czechoslovakia, 2001.
The Garden of the Finzi-Continis. Directed by Vittorio De Sica. Italy, 1971.
Gruber's Journey. Directed by Radu Gabria. Romania, 2008.
The Pianist. Directed by Roman Polanski. Multinational, 2002.
The Revolt of Job. Directed by Imre Gyöngyössy. Hungary, 1983.
The Round Up. Directed by Roselyne Bosch. France, 2010.
Schindler's List. Directed by Steven Spielberg. United States, 1994.
Shoah. Directed by Claude Lanzmann. France, 1985.
Shop on Main Street. Directed by Ján Kadár. Czechoslovakia, 1965.
Sunshine. Directed by István Szabó. Hungary, 2000.
The Wannsee Conference. Directed by Heinz Schirk. Germany, 1984.

Collaboration and Resistance

Czechoslovakia

Closely Watched Trains. Directed by Jiřy Menzel. Czechoslovakia, 1966.
Divided We Fall. Directed by Jan Hoebejk. Czechoslovakia, 2000.
Shop on Main Street. Directed by Ján Kadár. Slovakia, 1965.

France

Army of Crime. Directed by Robert Guédiguian. France, 2009.
Army of Shadows. Directed by Jean-Pierre Melville. France, 1969.
Battle of the Rails. Directed by René Clément. France, 1946.
Casablanca. Directed by Michael Curtiz. United States, 1942.

Lacombe, Lucien. Directed by Louis Malle. France, 1974.
The Last Metro. Directed by François Truffaut. France, 1980.
Lucie Aubrac. Directed by Claude Bern. France, 1997.
Mr. Klein. Directed by Joseph Losey. France, 1976.
The Sorrow and the Pity. Directed by Marcel Ophüls. Switzerland, 1970.
The Train. Directed by John Frankenheimer. France and Italy, 1964.

Germany
Bonhoeffer: Agent of Grace. Directed by Eric Till. Germany, 2000.
The Restless Conscience. Directed by Hava Beller. United States, 1994.
Sophie Scholl: The Final Days. Directed by Marc Rothemund. Germany, 2005.
Stauffenberg. Television film directed by Jo Baier. Germany and Austria, 2004.
Swing Kids. Directed by Thomas Carter. Germany, 1993.
Taking Sides. Director István Szabó. Multinational, 2001.
Valkyrie. Directed by Bryan Singer. Germany and the United States, 2008.
The White Rose. Directed by Michael Verhoeven. Germany, 1982.

Great Britain
Carve Her Name in Pride. Directed by Lewis Gilbert. Britain, 1958.
Charlotte Grey. Directed by Gillian Armstrong. Britain, 2001.
Island at War. Television series directed by Peter Lyndon. Britain, 2004.
Odette. Directed by Herbert Wilcox. Britain, 1950.

Greece
Captain Corelli's Mandolin. Directed by John Madden. Britain, 2001.

Italy
General Della Rovere. Directed by Roberto Rossellini. Italy, 1959.
Life Is Beautiful. Directed by Roberto Benigni. Italy, 1997.
Rome, Open City. Directed by Roberto Rossellini. Italy, 1945.
Seven Beauties. Directed by Lina Wertmuller. Italy, 1976.

Netherlands
The Silver Fleet. Directed by Vernon Sewell. United States, 1943.

Norway
Heroes of Telemark. Directed by Anthony Mann. United States, 1965.

Poland
A Generation (1954), *Kanal* (1956), and *Ashes and Diamonds* (1958). Trilogy directed by Andrzej Wajda. Poland.
Katyń. Directed by Andrzej Wajda. Poland, 2007.
To Be or Not to Be. Directed by Ernst Lubitsch. United States, 1942.

Soviet Union, Russia, and the Baltic Countries

Come and See. Directed by Elem Kimov. Soviet Union, 1985.
Days of Glory. Directed by Jacques Tourneur. United States, 1944.
Defiance. Directed by Edward Zwich. United States, 2008.
The North Star. Directed by Lewis Miles. United States, 1943.

Yugoslavia

Chetniks. Directed by Lewis King. United States, 1943.

Postwar Europe

Judgment at Nuremberg. Directed by Stanley Kramer. United States, 1961.
Man of Marble. Directed by Andrzej Wajda. Poland, 1977.
The Marriage of Maria Braun. Directed by Rainer W. Fassbinder. Germany, 1978.
The Reader. Directed by Stephen Daldry. Germany and the United States, 2008.
The Third Man. Directed by Carol Reed. Britain, 1949.

INDEX

ABOUT THE AUTHORS

ISTVÁN DEÁK, who is Seth Low Professor Emeritus at Columbia University, was born in Hungary and began his university studies there. He continued to study history in Budapest, Paris, Munich, and at Columbia University, where he obtained his PhD in 1964. His publications include *Weimar Germany's Left-Wing Intellectuals: A Political History of the "Weltbühne" and Its Circle* (1968); *The Lawful Revolution: Louis Kossuth and the Hungarians, 1848–1849* (1979), translated into German, Hungarian, and Romanian; *Beyond Nationalism: A Social and Political History of the Habsburg Officer Corps, 1848–1918* (1990), translated into German, Hungarian, and Italian; and *Essays on Hitler's Europe* (2001), translated into Hungarian. Deák also edited and wrote along with Jan T. Gross and Tony Judt *The Politics of Retribution in Europe: World War II and Its Aftermath* (2000). He has been a frequent contributor to the *New York Review of Books* and the *New Republic*. István Deák is an outside member of the Hungarian Academy of Sciences and has received several other honors.

NORMAN M. NAIMARK is the Robert and Florence McDonnell Professor of East European Studies at Stanford University and Sakurako and William Fisher Director of the Stanford Global Studies Division. He is also Senior Fellow at the Hoover Institution and the Freeman-Spogli Institute of International Studies. Naimark is author and editor of a number of books, among them *The Russians in Germany: A History of the Soviet Zone of Occupation, 1945–1949* (1995); *Fires of Hatred: Ethnic Cleansing in 20th Century Europe* (2001); and *Stalin's Genocides* (2011).